Modern Political Communication

For Fleur

Modern Political Communication

Mediated Politics in Uncertain Times

James Stanyer

polity

Copyright © James Stanyer 2007

The right of James Stanyer to be identified as Author of this Work has been asserted in accordance with the UK Copyright, Designs and Patents Act 1988.

First published in 2007 by Polity Press.

Polity Press
65 Bridge Street
Cambridge CB2 1UR, UK

Polity Press
350 Main Street
Malden, MA 02148, USA

ISBN-13: 978-07456-2797-7
ISBN-13: 978-07456-2798-4 (pb)

A catalogue record for this book is available from the British Library.

Typeset in 10.5 on 13 pt Swift
by Servis Filmsetting Ltd, Manchester
Printed and bound in India by Replika Press pvt Ltd

The publisher has used its best endeavours to ensure that the URLs for external websites referred to in this book are correct and active at the time of going to press. However, the publisher has no responsibility for the websites and can make no guarantee that a site will remain live or that the content is or will remain appropriate.

Every effort has been made to trace all copyright holders, but if any have been inadvertently overlooked the publishers will be pleased to include any necessary credits in any subsequent reprint or edition.

For further information on Polity, visit our website: www.polity.co.uk

Contents

Preface and Acknowledgements

The key challenge facing political communication scholarship in the twenty-first century is to comprehend and respond to the transformative powers of modernity; indeed, some of the most interesting and thought-provoking recent work in the field has documented the rapid transformation of political communication in advanced industrial democracies (see for instance, Bennett and Entman, 2001; Blumler and Gurevitch, 1995, 2000; Dahlgren and Gurevitch, 2005; Mancini and Swanson, 1996; Mazzoleni and Schulz, 1999; Swanson, 1997, 2004). Many authors have pointed to the fact that the political communication systems of advanced industrial democracies are experiencing similar changes (for a synoptic account see Swanson, 2004). The assertion is that the globalizing forces of modernity mean that once separate national political communication systems are undergoing analogous developments; despite different regulatory structures and 'cultural codes', distinct political communication systems now have much in common and the challenges they face are increasingly similar (Esser and Pfetsch, 2004; Swanson, 2004). The advanced industrial countries in which these political communication systems are embedded are being buffeted by a variety of global social, economic, political and technological forces. These global forces have, in turn, unleashed a complex chain of internal reactions and counter-reactions. The various elements of the once stable tripartite political communication systems in advanced industrial countries are increasingly in a state of flux (Blumler and Gurevitch, 2000).

While there is a consensus about the fluid nature of contemporary political communication systems, there has been little agreement about the consequences of change for democratic life. Indeed, opinion can be crudely divided between those in the field who are pessimistic about the consequences, and those who adopt a more optimistic tone. For the pessimists, the current developments are undermining the ability of citizens to make informed decisions; in short, political communicators are not providing what citizens need to participate fully in political life. Some critics point to media marketization and the rise of 'infotainment' and the 'dumbing down' of political infor-mation as the problem (Franklin, 1997; McChesney, 1999; Patterson, 1993). Others draw our attention to political professionalization, with the rise of news management and campaign professionals, as the main issue (Plasser with Plasser, 2002; Negrine and Lilleker, 2002; Sussman, 2005). Either way, the core concern of the pessimists is that political communication in late modernity is increasingly failing to serve citizens well, and in extremis might be undermining the fabric of democracy. It should be noted that concern is not limited to the academic world, and emerges at intervals in wider civil society. Political elites often try to pin the blame on the media, and media professionals point to politicians' obsession with controlling the media (see Schlesinger, 2006).

Those who take a more optimistic view have increasingly pointed to the benefits of such changes for citizens. Brants (1998), Brants and van Kempen (2002), McNair (2000) and Popkin (2006) have all challenged the notion that market-driven political communication automatically means poorer information for citizens; they highlight not only the new styles and increased volume of political coverage in the multi-channel environment, but also the greater scrutiny of political elites. Similarly, Norris (2000) has questioned the view, pervasive in the 'media malaise thesis', that the news media has a negative impact on audiences. Others have revealed the democratic potential of new communication technologies to enhance political participation (Bucy and Gregson, 2001; Coleman, 2002a; Gurak and Logie, 2003).

Juxtaposing these opposing interpretations serves as a reminder of the current tumult in the field. There have of course been attempts to synthesize new positions. There has also been an acknowledgement amongst the pessimists of some 'potentially redemptive' aspects of change (Blumler and Gurevitch, 2000). As Dahlgren observes, in a fast-evolving political communication system 'there is a need to be alert for progressive potentials' (2004: 14). Indeed, this rapprochement can be seen in a synthesis recently elucidated by Bennett and Entman (2001). In the preface to *Mediated Politics* they outline what they see as 'broad tensions' facing mature democracies. The first is between diversity and commonality, between more varied political views provided by the ever expanding channels of communication and the fragmentation of shared political experience that this brings. Second, and perhaps more normatively, there is a tension between the information necessary for citizens to participate effectively in democratic life and the infotain-ment-driven focus of increasingly commercially driven media. The third tension they see is between the need to treat people as citizens on the one hand and as consumer publics on the other. The notion of tensions is an apt way to think about the often contradictory nature of change. As Bennett and Entman remind us, it is important to focus on the opportunities that change brings, in addition to concerning ourselves with the negative consequences of modernity. The marketization does pose a challenge to citizen-oriented forms of political communication, but this is one trend amongst others that perhaps offer opportunities for certain citizens. The public sphere can be conceived of as being more accessible to oppositional voices than in the past; the internet, for example, has opened up widely documented opportunities for resource-poor political advocates to communicate (Coleman, 2002a). But, at the same time, online citizen involvement often remains dominated by the wealthy who have greater access to such technology (Chadwick, 2006; Gardner and Oswald, 2001). In other words, there has been a myriad of often contradictory consequences.

It is against this backdrop of upheaval in the field, and as a contribution to understanding developments in modern political communication systems, that this book has been written. The book follows recent notable attempts to comprehend the complex and often contradictory trends in contemporary political communication (see for example, Bennett and Entman, 2001; Blumler and Gurevitch, 2000; Esser and Pfetsch, 2004; Mancini and Swanson, 1996; Mazzoleni and Schulz, 1999; Swanson, 1997, 2004). It adopts the 'systemic perspective' pioneered by Blumler and Gurevitch (1995, 2000). Such a perspective has several advantages over traditional message-centred approaches that dominate the field. It has the benefit of allowing a relatively clear exposition of the often complex reactions and counter-reactions at work in evolving tripartite political communication systems. Unlike message-centred approaches, it does not see relations between political communicators and audiences solely in terms of the production and reception of content without any reference to the 'broader set of processes at work' (Blumler, 1990: 103). It is therefore not limited to questions of media effects or hegemony maintenance. The book is concerned with developments in relation to each of the main components of political communication systems. For example, it is concerned with wider questions about how political candidates, parties and governments respond to the changes in the media and electoral terrain they encounter; how the traditional news media adapt to alterations in patterns of media consumption; the reaction of an increasingly divided citizenry to the changing political media environment; and the complex and intricate process of interaction between each element of a system. The book is also mindful of the consequences of these developments and whether such evolving systems continue to serve *all* citizens well, for, as Peter Golding reminds us, this is the 'critical benchmark of enquiry in communications research' (1990, p. 100).

In examining these developments, it draws on a wide body of sources, many outside the field. These sources provide new insights into the changes being experienced by, and the challenges facing, advanced industrial democracies. Indeed, it is important for the field to take account of society-wide trends and what they mean for democratic political communications. Research on civic and political engagement, voter dealignment and campaign finance provided a crucial background context for this examination of democratic political communication systems.

The book argues that political communication systems in different advanced industrial democracies are witnessing similar developments, and that these have 'led to similar but by no means identical consequences' (Swanson, 2004: 46). This 'conventional view', as Swanson terms it, is supported by a growing number of case studies of trends in national political communication systems, and by the emergence of a body of comparative work (see Blumler and Gurevitch, 2001; Crigler and Jensen, 1991; Esser and Pfetsch, 2004; Kaid et al., 1991; Swanson and Mancini, 1996). From the outset, I wanted to adopt a more systematic examination that looked at analogous developments across a set number of countries, avoiding the random approach some studies adopt. I decided to focus on two democracies to provide a more satisfactory in-depth examination of developments rather than to embark on a multi-country study (see Peters, 1998). The United States of America and the United Kingdom of Great Britain were chosen because they represent two different advanced industrial democracies, with highly developed political communication systems, that have witnessed similar socio-economic and technological systemic trends. This choice also reflects my own knowledge and interests, and, as a single authored study, the practical realities of research – there is a wealth of easily accessible data sources on both countries. It should be noted though, that this book is not an overly formalistic comparative exercise (see Peters, 1998). I did not think it appropriate to adopt such a strict approach for a text aimed at a general as well as a specialist audience.

Material for the book came from a variety of primary and secondary online sources, including data provided by government bodies, private research centres, journal articles and research monographs; the websites of research centres and government bodies proved a particularly valuable source of data, especially on the viewing habits and political behaviour of citizens (see appendix for more details).[1] However, the difficulties of comparative research have been well documented (see Blumler et al., 1992; Esser and Psfetch, 2004; Livingstone, 2003; Peters, 1998; Swanson, 1992), and comparisons of different data sources can prove problematic, particularly data gathered separately in different countries, often along different lines. It is a problem not unique to this study; all multi-country studies face similar problems if they do not use specially gathered data (Livingstone, 2003; Norris, 2000). My focus in this book necessitated the use of a variety of data sources. For instance, data on viewing of political programmes by socio-economic status, in both countries, is gathered independently, and while the use of such data possibly lacks the scientific rigour some scholars crave, it serves to move beyond pure impression to produce a more informed picture of viewing of political programmes.

In sum, the book sets out to explore some common developments in political communication systems of two different mature or advanced industrial democracies. The aim is to identify and map these similar trends and emerging issues, and tease out what they mean for democratic political communications in these two nations. It should be noted that the book assumes a certain level of knowledge of both countries.

This book would not have been possible without the help of numerous people and institutions. I would like to thank the University of Leicester for granting me a semester's leave to start the project in 2004, and Loughborough University's Department of Social Sciences for allowing me the time to finish. I would also like to thank Oxford University Press and Taylor and Francis for granting me permission to reproduce parts of my work already published by them. A special thank you goes to John B. Thompson, without whom the project would not have got off the ground, to the team at Polity, especially Andrea Drugan, for being patient and understanding, and to Sarah Dancy. I would like to thank all the members of the Curry Club, colleagues in the Department of Social Sciences, former colleagues at the Centre for Mass Communication Research, all those who attended and made comments at various seminars and conferences, where different chapters of this book were presented, and the anonymous reviewers of the manuscript. I am also eager to personally thank Andrew Chadwick, John Corner, Simon Cross, David Deacon, Roger Dickinson, John Downey, Patrick Dunleavy, Bob Franklin, Peter Golding, Richard Heffernan, Oliver James, Raymond Kuhn, Jim McGuigan, Sabina Mihelj, Graham Murdock, Ralph Negrine, Henrik Örnebring, Heather Owen, Mike Pickering, John Richardson, Dominic Wring and Gillian Youngs for their comment, help and encouragement. Special mention should go to John Fogden, Peter and Di Stanyer, and especially to Fleur, to whom I owe a special debt of gratitude for her constant support throughout the time spent writing this book. Any errors are of course my own.

Introduction: Actors, Systems and Systemic Trends

THE political communication systems of mature representative democracies are constantly evolving, but there is a sense that in the last twenty years or so, many have undergone a fundamental change – a 'paradigmatic shift' as some have called it (Blumler and Gurevitch, 2000; Dahlgren, 2004). In simple terms, the global process of modernization, variously described by social theorists (see Beck, 2002; Castells, 2004; Giddens, 1991, 1999), has impacted on each of the components of national political communication systems, unleashing in its wake a series of reactions and counter-reactions. These once stable national systems, which characterized much of the twentieth century, are increasingly becoming ones that have been described variously as 'turbulent, less predictable, less structured' (Blumler and Kavanagh, 1999: 211) and 'chaotic' (McNair, 2003: 552). The relationships between political advocates, media professionals and their audiences have been transformed, as institutions and actors have sought to adapt to the new realities of political communication; such adjustments have in turn had implications for the wellbeing of democracy.

This book focuses on the impact of social, political, economic and technological change on the political communication systems of the United States and the United Kingdom. It examines how political advocates (candidates, parties and governments), media organizations and citizen audiences are adapting to these changes in political communication systems. It pays special attention to the evolving relationship of political communicators and their audiences, and to the changing attitudes of citizens towards the output of political communicators, and their willingness to engage politically. Of course, the book is mindful of the consequences of this changing dynamic for the health of democracy (see Jacobs and Skocpol, 2006). The aim of this Introduction is to contextualize the approach that has been adopted, introducing key concepts and outlining some of the external forces impacting on systems, before identifying what are the key developments and their consequences.

Democratic national political communication systems

Before examining the changing relations between political communicators and their audiences in more detail, it is worth revisiting the structural context. Those familiar with the concept of Blumler and Gurevitch's 'political communication system' might want to skip to the next section.

Despite its functionalist connotations, the notion of a political communication system is a useful heuristic device for conceptualizing the different institutions and actors engaged in political communication and their interrelationships. It is beneficial, its originators suggest, because it sheds light on 'the interdependence' of these institutions, 'the reciprocal nature of their relationship with each other and with the audience', and exposes the 'communication norms, roles, genres, formats, traditions and practices that tend to persist over time' (Blumler and Gurevitch, 1995: 100). In addition, one could add, as an approach it does not privilege any particular component of the system. This section is not intended to depict in detail the whole of the framework, as outlined in Blumler and Gurevitch's seminal essay 'Linkages Between the Mass Media and Politics' (in ibid., but originally published in 1977), but to provide a highlight of the key features.

The 'ideal type' political communication system consists of three sets of actors: political and media institutions, and citizen audiences embedded in a national socio-political environment. The 'two sets of institutions – political and media institutions – are involved in the course of message preparation in much "horizontal" interaction with each other' (ibid.: 12). At the same time these institutions are 'separately and jointly engaged in disseminating and processing information and ideas to and from the mass citizenry' – 'vertical' interaction (ibid.). They are dependent on the media for political information, but also contribute to the political communication system through participation in party- and media-initiated events. Interactions occur within a national socio-political environment, one with a political culture that has developed norms and values that govern behaviour and relations of actors within the system. Actions by each part of this tripartite communication system impact upon the other parts and each is adaptive, continually adjusting to changes in the wider environment and to the actions of the others. So the political communication system outlined originally by Blumler and

Gurevitch in the 1970s is dominated by a finite number of political actors and media institutions, interacting with each other within the confines of the liberal democratic nation-state, with citizens playing their role as receivers of political information and determiners of electoral outcome.

Accounting for change

However, such communication systems, as Blumler and Gurevitch remind us in their later work, are dynamic (1995; 2000). They note that systems are ever evolving and that, while the pace of change may vary, they are affected by external and internal 'sources of instability' (1995). In other words, change within political communication systems stems from external stimuli, and from internal reaction and counter-reaction of its institutions and actors. Blumler and Gurevitch argue that there are at least four main sources of instability built into a political communication system, two internal and two external. The external sources include the emergence of new communication technology, changes to 'the structure and culture of the surrounding social and political system' and changes to the laws governing media and the behaviour of political parties and candidates (ibid.: 204–5). The first internal source is the process of mutual adaptation, which sees political advocates and media professionals continually adapting to the other side's ploys. The second internal source is the changing relationship of political advocates and the media with their audiences. In sum, as Blumler and Gurevitch note:

> [C]hanges in political communication systems can be accounted for by the disposition of the three main sets of actors – politicians, journalists and audience members – to respond adaptively to the continually evolving perceptions and behaviours of each other within a continually changing environment, the dynamics of which are technological, sociological and political. (Ibid.: 205–6)

What I would like to do is expand a bit more on the process of 'mutual adaptation' outlined by Blumler and Gurevitch. The notion of actors 'mutually adapting' to the activities of each other, while insightful, slightly overlooks the strategic nature of action within the political communication system. For this I want to draw on Colin Hay's reappraisal of Bob Jessop's work, which provides a useful way to think about the strategic nature of activity. Actors in any system are strategic in that they are 'intentional'; their action is motivated by the aim of achieving a particular objective or outcome (Hay, 2002). This is important because media and political institutions are not only adaptive, but also goal-oriented. Office-seekers operate with particular aims, achieving elected office, for instance. The media, too, operate with particular aims, such as audience maximization. They act purposively in an 'attempt to realise their intentions and preferences' (ibid.: 151). It is not just media and political institutions: all three actors in the political communication system engage in goal-oriented political activity, and their mutual adaptation needs to be understood in this context too.

In addition, not only are actors in the political communication system 'intentional', but they also seek to 'monitor' their activity and the environment they are in. The three main sets of actors continually review and analyse their environment, responding to problems. Reflexivity can be seen as the ability of actors within a system to learn and apply their knowledge to overcome problems as they arise (ibid.). As Giddens notes, in contemporary societies there is 'the susceptibility of most aspects of social activity . . . to chronic revision in the light of new information' (1991: 20). It is in the light of the monitoring process that actors 'modify, revise or reject their chosen means to realise their intentions' (Hay, 2002: 151). As Hay observes, actors are strategic as well as reflexive 'devising and revising means to realise their intentions' (ibid.: 152).

Political communicators as strategic reflexive agents are engaged in a dynamic series of interrelations, which are played out in a 'strategic context' (ibid.). The strategic context could be seen as the competitive environments in which party and media actors operate. The context in which conduct unfolds is crucial in shaping that strategic action. The environment, Hay argues, is 'strategically selective'; that is, it 'favours certain strategies over others as a means to realise a given set of intentions' (ibid.: 149). This is not to say that it determines such activity. The 'context itself presents an unevenly contoured terrain which favours certain strategies over others' (ibid.).

In sum, change can be seen as the outcome of actors responding to the 'continually evolving perceptions and behaviours of each other' against the background of a system being buffeted by external forces. However, they respond thus for a reason, namely to secure a particular goal – such as electoral success, or economic success. It should be noted that this needs to be seen in the context of competitive environments. The actors are reflexive, engaged in the monitoring of their own activities – the activities of their rivals and their audience. The process of reflexivity is seen as allowing the effective achievement of a particular goal in a fast-changing socio-political environment.

Political communication systems in second modernity

Having discussed political communication systems and the way in which such systems evolve, I want to return to examining the 'systemic trends' impacting upon the political communication systems of the

US and the UK. The very societies in which political communication systems are embedded are undergoing transformation. The mature industrial economies of the West have seen a radical change in patterns of employment. In Castells' (2000) words, there has been a shift from an industrial to an informational or new economy. This shift has been characterized by the decline of manufacturing and other traditional 'blue-collar' jobs and the rise of the service sector (Glassman, 1997). The relatively healthy job security, pay and conditions of the first modernity are replaced by the growing uncertainty, unemployment and work casualization of the second modernity, resulting in widespread increases in levels of citizen anxiety (W. L. Bennett, 1998).

This transformation, together with a wholesale undoing of the post-war welfare revolution, has widened existing divisions in both countries. Income differentials are growing (Brandoleni and Smeeding, 2006; Castells, 2000; Jacobs et al., 2004). In the UK, income inequality over recent years has increased on average by 1.8 per cent per annum, and in the US by 0.79 per cent (Castells, 2000: 79). The US now has the largest income inequality compared to other advanced industrial democracies (Boggs, 2000; Jacobs et al., 2004; Lister, 1993). The wage gap between whites and other racial groups has grown; minorities disproportionately occupy lower-paid jobs and the income gains of minority groups are slowing (Jacobs et al., 2004). Migrants and members of ethnic minority groups are more likely to be unemployed and form part of the working poor, with low pay and little security (Castells, 2000). Such groups are economically deprived, or are structurally marginalized for other reasons, and represent a truly disadvantaged underclass (Wilson, 1987; cited in Castells, 2000).

A new geography of deprivation is also emerging. New marginalized communities have developed, often in areas of economic deprivation, amongst immigrant communities and the unemployed. In both countries there are areas of long-term economic deprivation and high levels of unemployment – so-called rustbelt cities; and areas with high immigrant populations in low-wage, unskilled jobs, or long-term unemployed – so-called gateway cities. The number of Hispanic immigrants living in the inner-city barrios of southern California has increased dramatically in recent years (Le Texier, 2004; Segura et al., 2001) and similar observations have been made about the growth of new immigrant populations in inner-city boroughs in the major metropolitan areas of the UK (Munck, 2005). These areas of deprivation stand in distinction to the increasingly affluent suburbs and regions.

The collective identities that accompanied the industrial age are slowly disappearing, replaced by 'personalized' identities of the second modernity (W. L. Bennett, 1998: 741, 755). As Mancini and

Swanson observe: 'old aggregate anchors of identity and allegiance in traditional social structures, are [being] replaced by overlapping and constantly shifting identifications' (1996: 8).

Ulrich Beck, reflecting on the wider processes of social change, sees the transformation in terms of a move from a simple first modernity to a reflexive second modernity (2002; 2003). The first modernity, one 'based on a nation-state society, on given collective identities such as classes, families, ethnicities', is being transformed into a second modernity, one characterized by individualization, globalization, risk and uncertainty (2002: 206). To this list could be added the growth of new communication technologies, which have greatly affected political communication systems: with the arrival of new delivery systems of cable and direct satellite broadcasting in the 1980s and, more recently, digital technology and the internet, there has been a pluralization of communication space. The era of spectrum scarcity and state regulation has been replaced by deregulated spectrum plenty.[1]

The 'geography of political communication is in flux' (Dahlgren, 2004: 14), as once isolated national political communication systems find themselves increasingly globally interconnected and integrated. In both countries, political communication systems become ever more porous, with information and ideas flowing freely across borders. The US and UK media economies are increasingly integrated into the global market economy, a trend that can be seen more and more in the patterns of media ownership in both countries (see McChesney, 1999).

These forces impact upon each of the actors in the respective British and American political communication systems, triggering a series of reactions and counter-reactions. One of the key focuses in Blumler and Gurevitch's own work and that of others (see also Swanson, 1997) has been in mapping one such chain reaction, namely that between political advocates and journalists.

The modern publicity process

The process of mutual adaptation between political advocates and media professionals, as they strive to achieve a particular aim of controlling 'popular perceptions of key political events and issues through the major mass media', is captured by the notion of the 'modern publicity process' (Blumler, 1990: 103). Political advocates compete to ensure that their message receives the greatest exposure, and that their agenda dominates the media output. However, the methods employed by political advocates to reach their target audiences inevitably clash, with not only the professional culture of journalists, but also the market imperatives of the new media environment. Blumler and Gurevitch observe that 'politicians are on the outlook for more effective ways of ensuring the delivery . . . of their message. Journalists are ever on guard against their feared conversion into mere propaganda mouthpieces' (1995: 205). Such an approach by political advocates has led to a documented backlash, or a journalistic fight-back (Blumler, 1997; Blumler and Gurevitch, 1995; Swanson, 1997). Journalists are increasingly on their guard against attempts by political candidates and spin doctors to manipulate copy and bully them. There has been a noticeable decline in deference amongst journalists towards the main political parties and politicians and a growth in the news media of 'disdaining coverage' (Semetko, et al., 1991). A visible contempt of politics and the emergence of 'metacoverage', where media management becomes the story, have been well documented as journalistic responses to the demands of politicians (Esser et al., 2001).

Such reactions have given rise to a 'disdaining dynamic' (Swanson, 1997) in political communication: political advocates have little option but continually to innovate and utilize new techniques to control the news agenda. Journalists then respond to the manipulation in ever more strident ways. Parties and candidates have to find new ways of reaching the public and this, in turn, prompts a further response from journalists. What has emerged is an 'unending spiral of manipulation and resistance' (ibid.: 1270).

The political communicator–audience nexus

The other key unfolding dynamic in both political communication systems, and one on which this book focuses, is the changing relationship between political communicators and citizen audiences. It could be argued that this evolving relationship has attracted less attention in the field, outside the context of media effects studies, compared to that focused on relations between political advocates and media professionals. That said, there are some illuminating insights by a few authors in the field into how this relationship may be evolving (see, for instance, Blumler and Gurevitch, 2000) and also in other disciplines such as political marketing (see, for example, Newman, 1999; Plasser et al., 1999; Wring, 2003 and 2004). This relationship needs to be placed in the wider context of changing political communication systems and be investigated in detail.

From certainty to uncertainty

It is impossible to describe the relations that characterized political communication systems of the first modernity without engaging in a certain level of generality, but they could be described, in simple terms, as stable, with a greater degree of certainty. One term used to describe a citizen's relation to political parties is loyalty. Much of the post-war period was characterized by a high degree of class–party voter alignment (Crewe and Thomson, 1999; Dalton, 2002). In the 1950s and 1960s, Michigan electoral studies in the US, and studies in the UK by Butler and Stokes, pointed to the alignment between social background, group membership and political identity (Norris, 1997). Political identity was a pre-given, shaped by group membership and social background. Class background or religious affiliation acted as a reference point in day-to-day political life, determining partisan alignment. Audiences also tended to be habitual media consumers, buying the same newspapers, for instance, often in line with their political affiliation (Schudson, 1978; Tunstall, 1996). The arrival of mass communication technologies, such as radio in the 1920s and television in the 1950s, transformed political communication, acting as a 'general interest intermediary' (Sunstein, 2001) and providing a shared window on events for citizens and an audience of millions for advertisers (see also Katz, 1996). Audiences for the electronic mass media had a limited choice of channels and could be relied on to watch at certain times. They were members of a national political community, and the media's role was to cater for their informational needs. The audience's connection to the political communication system was largely through this monological mass media. Citizen audiences were spectators – albeit as partisan-aligned witnesses – of the activities of political and media elites unfolding on a media stage. Relations today could be generally described as uncertain and unpredictable. The process of de-industrialization and the rise of the service economy has seen the decline of traditional, relatively stable class structures, and the identities based upon them, and their replacement by more fluid forms of association and identity.

There is widespread evidence of the demise of collective political identities. Since the 1970s, the US and the UK have witnessed the emergence of a generational pattern of dealignment (Dalton, 2000; Norris, 1997). The link between political identity and class and group membership is breaking down (Crewe and Thomson, 1999; Dalton, 2002; Franklin 2002). There has been a rise of the so-called 'floating voter', those not loyal to any particular party or engaging in split-ticket voting (Wattenberg, 1996). Many of the new breed of floating voters are young, generally well educated and not reliant on parties for political cues. Indeed, Dalton notes that while 30 per cent of young people in the US (under the age of 30) were strongly partisan in 1952, that figure had fallen by 1992 to 21 per cent (2000: 31). The decline of class/party affiliations has been mirrored by a fall in membership of labour unions: union membership in both countries is at an all-time low (Bryson and Gomez, 2002; Castells, 2000). The process of dealignment has been aided by key events, which in turn have led to the erosion of trust in politicians and political institutions (Orren, 1997).

Bennett, echoing Beck, argues that 'the energy people once devoted to grand political projects . . . is now increasingly directed toward personal projects of managing and expressing complex identities' (W. L. Bennett, 1998: 755). Political identity has changed from being assumed to being a positive commitment (Bauman, in Beck and Beck-Gernsheim, 2002). The emergence of a new generation of educated non-partisans has seen the flowering of a great diversity of political identities that are often associated with self-realization, lifestyle choice and post-material and ethical considerations (Inglehart, 1997a). The process of individualization has led to a sub-politicization of society (Beck, 1997; 2002; 2003). As Beck notes (1997), politics exists in new places, areas which were once considered outside politics, such as gay rights, the environment and human rights politics. Sub-politics has brought with it new forms of political action and expression. Political action is no longer confined largely to voting and collective action; now, direct action, consumer boycotts, email letter chains, online petitions, the wearing of t-shirts or wristbands are all part of the political communication repertoires of citizens of both democracies. Politicians increasingly need to find new ways of addressing these audiences and their concerns.

Audience fragmentation

In the new digital media environment, audiences are fragmented, and the mediated experiences have changed (Schulz, 2001). Audiences are subjected to an information and entertainment blizzard, a bricolage of messages and images from a variety of outlets. Political messages are spread across a greater number of outlets and channels (Blumler and Gurevitch, 2000). While mass communication reduced audience selectivity, the end of spectrum scarcity enables selective exposure, and more choice – and the public are increasingly exercising that choice, resulting in a 'breakdown of broadly shared political and social experience' (W. L. Bennett, 1998: 741; see also Sunstein, 2001).

Reconceptualizing relations with citizen audiences

Such 'systemic trends' have radically altered the relationship that political advocates and media institutions have with their audiences, on both sides of the Atlantic. It should be noted that to say that two systems are witnessing similar developments is not to say that they are becoming the same (see Hallin and Mancini, 2004); the differences between the US and the UK remain. However, although systems have evolved in distinct ways and have undergone different historical experiences, the components have adapted in similar ways to the challenges brought by global modernity.

In both countries, audience considerations are no longer of secondary importance for political communicators, but are central. Political advocates and media organizations are actively adapting to the challenges that these systemic trends bring. Office-seekers and incumbents, intent on winning elections, have responded to less predictable patterns of support in a number of ways, the most high profile of which has been the use of campaign professionals and market research techniques (Johnson, 2001; Newman, 1999; Webb, 2000). Such actors and techniques are now seen by politicians as being indispensable. In their wake, the approach and language of campaigning have changed: voters are seen as consumers who belong to different demographic segments, whose opinions need to be discovered and support maintained (Bartle and Griffiths, 2002; Denver et al., 2002; Stonecash, 2003). These actors and techniques have in turn been incorporated into government communications. Governments have increasingly sought to maintain public support throughout their term in office, engaging in a permanent campaign (Cook, 2002; Nimmo, 1999; Sparrow and Turner, 2001) and an increasing amount of resources are spent on public opinion research (Gould, 1998a; Tenpas, 2000; 2003). In turn, this has placed pressure on parties and candidates to be more effective fundraisers, to be able to afford the services of the professionals and to meet the cost of communication (Clawson, et al., 1998; West, 2000). At the same time, political elites have never been more vulnerable to mediated visibility (Sabato et al., 2000; Thompson, 2000). The control of media content and the privileged position that leading politicians once enjoyed have been largely lost; they are less able to control the flow of potentially damaging information and imagery in a multi-channel environment (Hayden, 2002; McNair, 2000; 2006; Williams and Delli Carpini, 2000).

Media news organizations, along with their audiences, have undergone a similar change. Faced with less predictable patterns of news consumption and greater pressures to be profitable, news organizations have engaged in a drastic reconceptualization of the citizen-centric model of news (Hallin, 2000). There has been a large-scale adoption of a market-oriented approach to news (Beam, 2001; Stepp, 2000). Audiences are seen as consumers with a series of interests that need to be addressed if their attention is to be maintained and profitability is to be achieved (Attaway-Fink, 2004). The notion of the consumer has become all-pervasive and a 'market logic' now permeates nearly all traditional news organizations and news rooms (Franklin, 1997; McManus, 1994; Underwood, 1998).

This needs to be set against the background of the liberalization of the media sphere. The once-regulated media markets in advanced industrial democracies have been subjected to deregulatory measures (Curran and Seaton, 2003; McChesney, 1999). There has been privatization of state-owned telecommunications monopolies and a dramatic increase of new entrants into the media marketplaces of both countries (Golding and Murdock, 2000; Murdock, 2000). Successive governments in both countries have adopted a laissez-faire approach to media regulation, intervening less in markets. The result is that the main news organizations have come under tremendous pressure from competition (Kurtz, 2002). In the UK, licence-funded broadcasting is under increasing financial pressure as commercial competition grows (Franklin, 1997). In policy circles, the public service model, once the dominant blueprint, is in retreat in the face of neo-liberal notions of consumer sovereignty and the benefits of competition. In the US, the process of marketization is intensifying (Delli Carpini and Williams, 2001; McChesney, 1999).

These factors militate against 'worthy but dull' political coverage. Conventional politics is treated more and more on news-value terms, having to compete with other events for attention (Blumler and Gurevitch, 1995). There has been a reduction in current affairs programming (Nahra, 2001; Hewlet, 2005), and a marginalization of the coverage of elections (Brookings Institution, 1997; Deacon et al., 2005). Increasingly, the coverage of conventional politics occupies a niche space (Hallin, 2006). The boundaries between serious political reporting and entertainment have become ever more blurred (Blumler, 1999; Hallin, 2000; Kerbel, 1999; Williams and Delli Carpini, 2000; Zaller, 1999), and there has been a growing focus on the personal lives of politicians, while journalists increasingly 'share the media stage' with a host of non-journalists (Holmes, 2000; Sabato et al., 2000).

In sum, political advocates and media institutions can no longer rely on citizen audiences for support or attention. If these strategic actors want to realize their intentions and achieve their goals, support and loyalty need to be continually cultivated and maintained (Bennett, 2003a). The traditional political communicators have to find new ways of fostering loyalty and support, through a combination of market research, personalized appeals and/or populist emotional pull.

Audience adaptation

Citizen audiences, in turn, are adapting to the new media and political environment. It is an environment that provides them with greater communication choice, and one that increasingly brings distant places and events live into their living-rooms. Citizens can now seek out the media that cater for their own particular views and tastes and partisans are increasingly drawn to those channels which reinforce their opinions (Davis and Owen, 1998). There is, moreover, a growing disillusionment with conventional politics, especially amongst certain sections of society (Dionne, 1992; Diplock, 2001; Doppelt and Shearer, 1999). Audiences are split between an engaged majority who are interested in and consume coverage of conventional politics and a politically disengaged disinterested minority who avoid such coverage (McKinney et al., 2005; Norris, 2000; 2001a). This disengaged minority tends to consist of the poorly educated, those on a low income, the welfare-dependent, young and those from an ethnic minority background. The engaged majority tends to be educated, relatively wealthy, middle-aged and white (Delli Carpini, 2000; Henn et al., 2002; Jacobs et al., 2004; Macedo et al., 2005; Whiteley, 2003). This is the same majority who also increasingly seek to exercise their voice using new technologies and protest repertoires (Bucy and Gregson, 2001; Norris, 2002b; Pattie et al. 2003b; Schlozman et al. 2004; Ward et al., 2003).

The consequences for democracy

The consequences of these developments need to be assessed in relation to the health of democratic political communication systems (see Golding, 1990). Some have pointed to the positive implications of such changes (McNair, 2000; Popkin, 2006), but such upbeat assessments need to be tempered by awareness of the potentially damaging implications. As mentioned, the decline of welfarism has widened existing divisions in both the US and the UK between the wealthy and the poor; areas of economic deprivation, amongst immigrant communities and the unemployed, contrast with the wealthy suburbs. The relatively wealthy and politically motivated citizens actively consume output and exercise their voice, while the economically deprived and often apathetic and marginalized tend not to (Macedo et al., 2005; Whiteley, 2003). As Blumler and Gurevitch (2000) acknowledge, there are also divisions along other lines as audiences fragment. Patterns of participation and engagement also vary increasingly between young citizens and their older counterparts (Bromley and Curtice, 2002; Wattenberg, 2002). Furthermore, these and other divisions are also reflected in the audience considerations of competing strategic political and media institutions, seeking the attention and support of some actors and ignoring others. These political communicators pursue those who vote, those with disposable income and those who will help them achieve their aims; while these groups become the target of ever more intense investigation and personalized messages, others are ignored (Gandy, 2001). As this book will show, national political communication systems have the tendency to become exclusive, serving some citizens better than others, a situation which may well be exacerbated by the activities of strategic political communicators.

Structure of the book

This book explores key developments within the political communication systems of the US and the UK, as described in this chapter. In line with previous studies, it focuses on the 'triad of actor types (advocates, mediators and audiences), situated in an socio-political environmental field, to specify possible influences on their mutual relations, and to identify overall patterns that may be resulting from their interactions' (Blumler and Gurevitch, 2000: 169). It is interested in how audience considerations are shaping the activities of political parties/candidates and traditional media outlets. It also looks at audiences' engagement with, and participation in, the political communication process. The book's chapters are grouped into three sections. Part I is concerned with the actions of political parties, candidates and governments. Part II looks at the developments in relation to media professionals and organizations. Part III examines changes in the relationship between citizen audiences and mediated political communication. The focus of the book's chapters is as follows.

The first chapter looks at the changing nature of campaign communication. Over the last 30 years or so, citizens have become subjected to more targeted communication during actual campaigns; contestants concentrate their communication efforts on the few voters who are able to change an electoral outcome. The vast majority of citizens are rendered spectators on the mediated electoral process. This chapter also highlights how expenditure on campaigns has increased dramatically, limiting effective participation to those able to raise millions of dollars/pounds, and creating further exclusivity. Only the parties and candidates that can raise huge funds to sustain their communication efforts, which increasingly seek to activate key groups of voters, will achieve victory.

Chapter 2 examines the rise of a promotional logic in government. It explores how consecutive administrations in both countries, once elected, have sought to maintain the support of voters by seeking to get their message across more effectively. Such attempts have seen the structural reforms of government, the widespread use of campaign professionals and campaign techniques. However, as the chapter shows, the greater feats of impression-management have not eliminated risks or maintained successive administrations' popularity, but have themselves become the story, with acts of media-management widely documented in the media.

Chapter 3 explores the increasingly intimate nature of relations between the public and politicians. Leading political actors have not only become recognizable performers but also intimate strangers, their private lives widely known by millions of citizens. Over the twentieth century, in the US and the UK, intimate aspects of leading politicians' lives have been rendered ever more visible, through the media, to a non-present audience of citizens. Increasingly, the chapter argues, mediated politics has come to be centred on the issue of character.

In chapter 4 the focus moves to the changing relationship between the established news media and its audience. It argues that the relationship has undergone a fundamental change over the last 50 years, as a result of a combination of factors. It tracks the transformation in the way that news organizations see their role vis-à-vis their audience, and the impact this has had on political reporting. In the new media environment the news media's democratic duties are under intense pressure; the coverage of conventional politics, especially election campaigns, is increasingly becoming a niche product and has all but been abandoned by some outlets.

Chapter 5 continues to look at the impact of the liberalization of media environments, this time in relation to the emergence of populist politics. The chapter examines the connection between the commercially driven populist political media and its audience in the US and the UK. It looks at this in relation to talk radio in the US and the national press in the UK. It argues that, against an increasingly uncertain socio-political environment, right-wing populism is becoming an increasing feature of political communication in both countries. The consequence is the exacerbation of already existing political divisions and tensions within society.

In chapter 6, the focus shifts to the citizen's engagement with mediated political communication. It examines the evidence of citizen disengagement from coverage of conventional politics. The chapter argues that both countries are witnessing the emergence of 'communicative engagement gaps' between an interested citizenry who regularly access political information from a variety of sources and a less politically engaged citizenry who are, at most, episodic spectators on national political life, but are increasingly likely to tune out, avoiding output completely. This divide, the chapter suggests, is along socio-economic, race and age lines.

Chapter 7 continues to explore the issue of communicative engagement in relation to how citizens exercise their political voice. It argues that citizens can articulate their views on political matters via a greatly expanded series of protest repertoires and media outlets, and through new technologies. Further, the public now inhabit a political environment where they are continually encouraged to vocalize their views by various organizational actors. This chapter explores the emergence of this self-expressive culture. It maps the ways in which the public seek to express their views, the growth of opportunities for attitude-expression and the attempts to mobilize opinion by various organizational actors. It also raises important questions about various levels of participation between different socio-economic groupings in both countries.

Finally, the Conclusion brings together the key themes of the book.

PART I

EXCLUSION, INTIMACY AND THE DRIVE FOR POPULAR SUPPORT

Data-Driven Electioneering and the Costs of Exclusive Campaign Communication

Both the UK and the US are saturated with elections: they occur at regular intervals for a variety of different offices and posts. In the US, there are federal elections for Congress and for the presidency; there are also state elections for representatives in state legislatures and for governor, as well as municipal, mayoral and judicial elections. One estimate is that there are some one million election races in a four-year cycle (Johnson, 2001). In Britain, in addition to the general election for the Westminster parliament, there are elections for national assemblies in Wales, Scotland and Northern Ireland, elections for the European parliament, local elections for councils and mayoral elections in certain municipalities.

All elections are accompanied by a campaign. The campaign is a finite period of intense candidate communication, after which citizens have the opportunity to decide who should represent them. However, especially in first-order national elections, campaign communication is increasingly exclusive. Contestants concentrate their efforts more and more on a few voters who are able to change the outcome of an election (Denver et al., 2002; Gandy, 2001; Sanders et al., 2005).

Such targeted campaign communication is reliant on expensive market research, which has to be paid for, and employs a growing number of campaign professionals. Campaign communication, in short, is increasingly capital-intensive, costing millions of dollars or pounds. Only the contestants who manage to raise huge funds can sustain their communication efforts. This chapter explores the growing exclusive nature of contemporary campaign communication in the US and the UK and its consequences.

The rise of the floating voter

The rise of exclusive campaign communication needs to be seen in the context of the transformation of the electorate that has taken place in the last 50 years. While there are differences in the extent to which trends have developed, it has been acknowledged on both sides of the Atlantic that voters are less attached to political parties than at any time previously (Crewe and Thomson, 1999; Dalton et al., 2000). This can be seen in two respects. First, voters are less likely to be members of political parties. In the US, membership of the two main political parties has dropped (Wattenberg, 2000). In Britain over the period 1980–98, party membership fell by 50 per cent; in the late 1990s, only 1.9 per cent of the electorate were members of political parties (see Mair and van Biezen, 2001).[1] Contestants are now less able to call on party members than in the past.

Secondly, and perhaps more importantly for political candidates and parties, there has been a decline in voter loyalty and a rise in the number of 'floating' voters or 'independents' – part of a wider documented process of 'mass de-identification with common institutions, symbols and authorities' (Bennett, 2003a: 140). The electorate no longer loyally support one political party throughout their adult life on the basis of class or religious background. As Dalton et al. note, 'fewer voters now come to elections with standing partisan predispositions' (2000: 60). Citizens' political identity is less likely to be expressed in party terms than at any previous generation. Young people, especially, are less likely than older generations to identify themselves as supporters of a party (Buckingham, 2000).

In Britain, the number of people strongly identifying with a political party has fallen from 45 per cent in 1964 to 9 per cent in 2005 (Sanders et al., 2005; see also Bromley and Curtice, 2002; Crewe and Thomson, 1999; Whiteley et al., 2001). In the US, there has been a clear erosion in the relation between class and voting patterns in presidential elections, although the change is less evident in congressional elections (Dalton, 2002). The number of voters identifying with one of the main two political parties in congressional elections has fallen from a high of 80 per cent in the 1950s to a low of 70 per cent in the 1990s (Petrocik, 1995). Wattenberg observes that around 75 per cent of the electorate identified themselves as either Democrats or Republicans during the period 1952–64, a figure which fell to 64 per cent by 1972 and continued at this level into the 1990s – 'party identification has declined in its importance as a shaper of thought and determiner of opinion' (1996: 30). The US has witnessed the rise of so-called split-ticket voting – voting for different parties' candidates in different ballots. Wattenberg notes that 'ticket-splitting [in the 1990s] has assumed massive proportions compared to the rate just two decades ago' (ibid.: 23).

These 'floating' voters or independents are motivated by factors other than loyalty. Research points to a complex mix of motivations (Petrocik, 1997; Sanders et al., 2005). For instance, the electorate may vote according to a candidate's or party's stance on certain issues (Budge and Farlie, 1983; Dalton, 2002). These include social, post-material, environmental and lifestyle issues. They might vote according to feelings of economic wellbeing. In addition, they might vote according to a contestant's record, credibility, his/her personality and image, or whether the candidate is in line with their aspirations (for a synoptic account, see Kendall and Paine, 1995; King, 2002). Bennett (2003a) observes that citizens take a more 'consumerist stance': in relation to political parties, they make demands: they want better public services, transport, health care, etc., and expect politicians to respond.

Market research and the electorate

To tailor their campaign messages to the various concerns of the swing voter, contestants spend a great deal of time and resources in finding out what those concerns are. In both countries, since the 1970s, there has been an increased use of market research in the campaign process (Newman, 1999; Wring, 2005). This way of approaching elections sees the electorate as consumers, with a series of preferences, aspirations, identities and lifestyles. It involves the identification of 'swing' voters, their values, views, concerns, and fears, and the development of messages which resonate with these voters. The successful contestant is the one that can address these.

Discovering voter concerns

Marketing specialists and techniques have become an established feature of campaigning (Johnson, 2001; Scammell, 1995). Although market research was pioneered by President Franklin D. Roosevelt, Norris (2000) notes that it was not firmly established as part of campaigns until the 1980s. Ronald Reagan was the first presidential contestant systematically to employ marketing techniques to aid his campaign in swing states; Denton and Woodward (1998) note that Reagan's bid for the presidency drew on marketing research conducted by US pollster Richard Wirthlin's company, Decision Making Information (DMI). The company conducted major tracking studies in nine swing states, costing some $1.5 million in total. A key part of the research was a psychographic study of the electorate which helped the Reagan team understand some of the motives of certain sections of the electorate. Today it would be unthinkable for those seeking major elected office not to employ a team of campaign professionals. Indeed, campaign professionals played a high-profile role in the election campaigns of Presidents Clinton and George W. Bush. Actors like David Gergen, Dick Morris, James Carville and Karl Rove have become household names (see chapter 3). Nearly all candidates for federal or state office now continually poll voter opinions in the run-up to and during election campaigns.

In Britain, the Conservative Party was the first systematically to employ market research techniques (Scammell, 1995). From the late 1980s, both the main political parties employed market research analysis and the services of US pollsters such as Richard Wirthlin and Stanley Greenberg, who used many of the techniques pioneered in the US (Sussman, 2005; Wring and Horrocks, 2001). Tony Blair, for example, retained the services of Philip Gould for nearly his entire period in office, and he and his party have used former Clinton pollsters Stanley Greenberg and, in 2005, Mark Penn (see also chapter 2). The main two political parties now routinely employ such practices. Philip Gould has been central to the Labour Party's use of such techniques (Wring, 2004). In 1997 he conducted some 300 focus groups prior to the election campaign and a further 70 during the campaign itself (Butler and Kavanagh, 1997). The same techniques were used in the 2001 campaign when Gould and his associates conducted three polls a week and focus groups six nights a week (Butler and Kavanagh, 2001). The views of these groups of voters who were considering switching to Labour were instrumental in determining party strategy (Wring, 2003). ICM pollster Nick Sparrow conducted focus groups five nights a week for the Conservatives during the 2001 campaign, together with regular surveys of voters in a selection of the 180 target seats (Butler and Kavanagh, 2001). As Gould notes: 'the most important thing a party must do in a campaign is listen to what the voters are saying, it means knowing what they are thinking and feeling and respecting it' (Gould, 1998a: 297). In Britain, before the 2005 campaign, the US firm Penn, Schoen and Burland allegedly conducted some 25,000 telephone interviews with swing voters to establish which messages to emphasize and how to counter the Conservatives. The party's campaign slogan – 'Forward not Back' – generated by Mark Penn, was also tested on these voters to see whether it resonated with them (Charter and Simon, 2006).

Swing voter attitudes

Market research reveals several things about swing voter attitudes. First, what they see as the most important issues. Traditionally, these have been so-called bread-and-butter issues, such as the economy, employment, health care, and law and order. However, the issues uppermost in the voters' minds may reflect other factors. Increasingly, voters are concerned about the environment, lifestyle issues and moral issues (for example, gay marriage, abortion, stem-cell research). With the War on Terror and the Iraq war, security is now an important issue. Research can also determine so-called 'wedge issues' – issues on which voters might be divided but that they feel strongly about – and may mobilize them. Bush's team found that for many Christian voters, and potential supporters, in battleground states, moral issues were important. In the UK, during the 2005 election campaign, the Conservatives found that immigration was the issue that mobilized many of their supporters.

Secondly, market research reveals how voters view the contestants' stance on the issues, and their competencies. Contestants will be seen as 'stronger' on certain issues than on others. This perception has traditionally been a reflection of history. Strengths of centre-left political parties and candidates tend to be issues such as health care, welfare, jobs and pensions, whereas for the centre-right they are law and order, defence and immigration (Budge and Farlie, 1983: Petrocik, 1997).

However, things are increasingly less clear-cut, for several reasons. Ideological boundaries between left and right are less unambiguous than they once were. In addition, the stance on certain issues of importance to voters, such as the environment, is impossible to place on a left/right spectrum (Clarke, 2002). In the US, in the 2004 presidential campaign, the Democrat candidate John Kerry did not adopt a classic left-wing agenda or George W. Bush a classic conservative one. Indeed, Kerry advocated conservative fiscal policies with a liberal lifestyle agenda, while George W. Bush called for an increase in certain industry subsides, welfare entitlements and a conservative moral agenda. In Britain, New Labour has adopted a traditional right-wing approach to law and order and immigration, with high spending on public services. Their main opponents, the Conservatives, have all but abandoned one of their main policy pledges to introduce tax cuts once elected, and committed themselves to greater public spending and an environmental agenda.

A contestant's perceived strength on an issue is less about a left or right party label, but more about the perceptions in the voters' minds about a candidate's stance on the issues (Bara and Budge, 2001;

Petrocik, 1997). Increasingly, the campaign teams, through research, seek to establish the issues on which they and their rivals have an advantage and those on which they and their rivals are at a disadvantage. These become the themes of the contestants' manifestos and of the campaign communication efforts. In 2005 in the UK, the Labour campaign focused on the party's strengths: health care spending, the economy and education; the Conservatives focused on crime, tax, immigration, clean hospitals and school discipline – issues on which the government had a perceived weakness amongst voters (Electoral Commission, 2006a). In 2000, amongst US voters, Gore's campaign was seen as strong on health care, education and social security and Bush's on defence, jobs and taxes and the family (Pew Research Center, 2000b). In the 2004 campaign, market research by the Republicans revealed that Bush had a major advantage over Kerry on security issues. On other issues of concern to the voters, such as the economy (jobs and taxes), Kerry was seen to be stronger. In such an environment, candidates' competencies or perceived abilities become important.

Finally, market research reveals how voters view the contestants' personalities and their competencies. It is used to discover the strengths and weaknesses of the candidates/party leaders and their opponents. In the 2000 presidential race, Bush received more favourable character evaluations than Gore; he was seen as more likely to get things done, make good judgements in a crisis and take tough decisions (Pew Research Center, 2000b). In the 2004 race, both candidates' competence in managing the war in Iraq and the War on Terror were seen as a key issue amongst voters, and both campaign teams attempted to scare key voter groups over their rival's ability to manage these issues. Kerry warned voters that Bush might reintroduce the draft, while the Bush campaign suggested that a vote for Kerry would hasten a further terrorist nuclear attack on the US. In the UK, in the run-up to the 1997 general election campaign, focus groups for both of the main political parties revealed the strength of Tony Blair compared to John Major (Butler and Kavanagh, 2001). The information was pivotal in informing the negative personal advertising campaigns of both parties.

Monitoring voter response

All campaign teams monitor the response of swing voters to see whether their communication effort is successful. In the US the presidential candidates have instated feedback loops. Norris (2000) notes that the 1992 presidential election saw the development of rolling tracking polls to monitor public reaction to the campaign on a day-by-day basis. In

Britain, the two main parties tracked the opinions of voters in target seats through the 2001 and 2005 campaigns to see if their campaign messages were having the desired effect (Electoral Commission, 2006a). Tracking polls measure the effect that everything is having on voter preferences, from name recognition and an opponent's image to the impact of various types of campaign communication (Stonecash, 2003).

Segmentation

Cluster analysis segments voters into groups, according to their preferences, aspirations, identities and lifestyles. The campaign teams use database information to build up a detailed picture of the voters in campaign battlegrounds. Information on attitudes towards a particular party or candidate, based on voting history or intentions, is cross-referenced with information from consumer databases, which may reflect a series of criteria such as socio-economic status, taste and lifestyle (Johnson, 2001; Sussman, 2005). With the cross-referencing of this information, 'common denominator characteristics' can be identified and profiles of different groups or neighbourhoods constructed (Gandy, 2001; Seawright, 2005). Gandy notes that computer-assisted packages classify US neighbourhoods into around 60 different types of geo-demographic cluster. For instance, one such cluster in the 1996 presidential campaign consisted of white suburban females with children, so-called 'soccer moms', who were identified by campaign teams as a key group of swing voters that Clinton and Dole needed to target (Andersen, 2000).

Although pioneered much earlier, the segmenting of electoral markets became well practised in US campaigns from the 1980s onwards, and in Britain more 'rigorous and far-reaching' after the 1992 general election campaign (Denver et al., 2002: 159; Norris, 2000). In the 2001 general election campaign, for example, Labour Party campaign managers segmented voters into one of four categories according to their response to a phone questionnaire. Denver et al. noted that Labour campaign managers were able to identify specific postcode areas in constituencies that may be amenable to certain campaign messages. So, for example, in areas where there was a significant proportion of so-called 'aspirants' (couples aged 25–40 with children, in low-skill white-collar or skilled manual jobs), 'the campaigners were advised to focus on mortgages, education and transport' (2002: 166). In this same campaign, one of the key segments identified by the Conservatives consisted of the so-called 'pebble-dash people'. These are the white-collar workers and professionals, married, aged 35–50, who live in semi-detached, often pebble-dashed suburban homes. The majority of this group of 2.5 million floating voters in 178 constituencies voted Conservative in 1992 before switching to Labour in 1997.

Increasingly, sophisticated computer software packages enable campaign teams to interrogate multiple databases and cross-reference findings to speed up the segmentation process. The 'voter vault' is one such piece of database interrogation software used by both President Bush's campaign in 2004 and the Conservatives in 2005. Building on previous innovations, this software allowed the cross-referencing of data on voting histories, voting intentions and views on selected issues, with information on the social profile of every postcode/ zipcode (Seawright, 2005). The voter vault software then grouped voters in each battleground seat/state in one of nine categories, ranging from opponents to supporters (ibid.). The Labour Party used similar software, 'Labour Contact', while in the US the Democrats used 'DataMart' to search a database of some 158 million records.

Targeted communication

Once the views of different segments of the electorate have been ascertained by campaign teams, they then begin targeting them with specific messages. The rationale behind this process is that 'different backgrounds, interests, and perhaps even cognitive styles, require different sorts of persuasive appeals' (Gandy, 2001: 145). Campaign teams further focus their communication efforts on a series of battleground states or constituencies which are key to winning elections. Instead of spending resources on mobilizing all voters, messages are targeted on activating key voters in a chosen marginal jurisdiction or constituency. These areas are bombarded with the carefully pre-tested political messages designed to resonate with the voters (Bennett and Manheim, 2001). Such a focus not only allows the targeting of party messages more effectively but also permits scarce resources to be carefully focused in order to provide the best return – 'more bangs for the proverbial buck' (see Johnson, 2001).

While there is some evidence that John F. Kennedy's 1960 presidential campaign targeted its message, the practice has become much sharper over the intervening years. In the 2000 presidential race, both Al Gore and George W. Bush focused nearly all their campaign activity on swing states such as Tennessee and Florida. In 2004, Bush and Kerry focused their campaigning on six large swing states: Florida, Minnesota, Iowa, Ohio, Pennsylvania and Wisconsin. In Britain, during the 1997, 2001 and 2005 campaigns, the three main parties largely focused their communication efforts on swing constituencies. For instance, the Conservatives officially targeted 180 seats in 2001 and 164 in 2005

(Denver et al. 2002; Seawright, 2005). Labour employed a similar target-ing strategy during the 1997, 2001 and 2005 campaigns, focusing resources on seats they had gained – so-called 'priority seats' (Denver et al., 2002). In 2005, Labour's campaign communication focused on the 100 marginal seats it needed to hold in order to stay in office (Electoral Commission, 2006a). The Liberal Democrats focused campaigning on 35 seats, an increase of 10 on 2001 (Electoral Commission, 2006a)

With the key battlegrounds identified and the profiles of different neighbourhoods in these battlegrounds constructed, the campaign teams then decide how to target each cluster with pre-tested political messages. In addition to the mass media, campaign teams increasingly utilize a variety of direct media, which can be easily aimed at specific audiences.

Direct media

Direct media enable the delivery of many individualized messages. Direct mail, telephone or email can be used to recruit volunteers, mobi-lize supporters, ask for funding and persuade undecided voters. The messages can vary from personalized messages asking for support from the candidates or celebrities, to calls from party workers. Candidates often use personalized automated phone messages or videos/DVDs with personal messages. In the US, from the late 1960s onwards, the postal service began to be widely used to deliver campaign literature (Johnson, 2001; Sussman, 2005). In the 1972 presidential race, direct mail was a key component of both McGovern's and Nixon's campaign communica-tion (Denton and Woodward, 1998). The telephone became an impor-tant communication tool in the campaigns of the 1980s (Johnson, 2001), and candidates now routinely hire phone banks to reach thousands of voters. For example, during the 2004 presidential campaign, 55 per cent of voters surveyed said they were contacted by phone (Pew Research Center, 2004d). Virtually all Senate candidates and 90 per cent of House of Representative candidates use direct media, and in most races it plays a dominant role in disseminating candidate messages (Johnson, 2001), During the 2006 mid-term election campaign, for example, 71 per cent of registered voters surveyed reported receiving candidate mail and 64 per cent a phone call (Pew Internet, 2006).

In Britain, targeted mail-shots started to be systematically used by political parties from the 1983 general election onwards and tele-canvassing from the mid-1980s (Wring and Horrocks, 2001). By the 2001 general election campaign, these had become firmly entrenched means of campaign communication (Pattie and Johnston, 2003; Whiteley and Seyd, 2003). At the start of the 2005 campaign, the Conservatives made some 300,000 phone calls and posted around

800,000 pieces of mail to voters in target seats (Seawright, 2005). The director of the Conservative campaign, Lynton Crosby, sent a personalized phone message to Conservative voters in target seats, asking them to 'take a stand' and get involved in the campaign (Seawright, 2005: 953). Labour, in the run-up to the 2005 campaign, sent 370,000 pieces of mail to voters in key marginal constituencies (Savigny, 2005). They used a call centre in Tyneside throughout the campaign, capable of targeting 100,000 voters a month (ibid.). Undecided voters were also the recipients of automated phone messages from leading actors in the party, urging them to vote Labour (Electoral Commission, 2006a). One significant item of mail dispatched by the Labour campaign team in 2005 were DVDs. Building on the success of the 2001 campaign, when the party distributed a message from the Prime Minister on video to undecided voters in marginal seats, they sent out DVDs to the same group of swing voters (Electoral Commission, 2006a).

Email presents another means of targeting voters. In the 2004 US presidential campaign, the main candidates used large email databases to single out certain voter groups. Howard Dean successfully raised millions of dollars on the back of an email campaign (S. Davis, 2005). The Kerry and Bush campaigns used email to solicit campaign donations. According to one estimate, Kerry raised $82 million through online donations and Bush some $64 million, up from $50 million in 2000 (ibid.). Of those voters surveyed in 2004 by the Pew Research Center, 14 per cent reported being contacted by email; 14 per cent also reported being contacted this way in 2006 (Pew Research Center, 2004d; Pew Internet, 2006). In Britain, email is becoming more widely used in election campaigns. In the period leading up to the 2005 campaign, the main parties experimented by distributing a small number of e-newsletters to party members (Jackson, 2004). During the 2005 campaign, all three main parties sent messages to those who had signed-up to receive emails – mainly supporters and party members. One estimate suggested that 100,000 had registered to receive Labour Party emails (Grant, 2005). The Conservatives claimed to have sent around 200,000 emails a month and the Liberal Democrats to have doubled the size of their email database of 3,000 voters since the 2001 general election (Dudley, 2005). In 2005, email was used as a rebuttal tool to equip supporters and members with key facts with which to attack or respond to events, to raise donations and to get supporters to volunteer.

Mass media advertising

Advertising through the media represents one of the main ways in which contestants can get their message across. However, advertisements are increasingly carefully focused on key areas necessary to secure victory. In the US, congressional election advertising expenditure is focused on key wards that contestants need to secure; in presidential campaigns, advertising expenditure is focused on local television markets in swing states. In the 2000 presidential campaign, spending on TV spots was focused on major swing states. Of 261,000 adverts aired between 1 June and 7 November 2000, 48 per cent (125,000) were concentrated on some five battleground states. For the Republicans, 22,000 adverts were aired in Florida, 13,000 in Ohio, 12,000 in Pennsylvania, 10,500 in Michigan and 8,000 in California. Gore and the Democrats aired 14,000 adverts in Pennsylvania, 13,000 in Ohio, 12,000 in Michigan, 12,000 in Florida and 8,500 in Wisconsin (Campaign Media Analysis Group Report, 2001). The messages were tailored to the identified concerns of specific audiences in these local television markets (Andersen, 2000).

In Britain, parties with more than 50 MPs standing for election are entitled to a television Party Election Broadcast, with the main parties given a set number of broadcasts of fixed lengths of 160, 220 or 280 seconds. However, political parties are able to purchase other forms of advertising to target key groups of voters. Campaign teams of all the main parties focus advertising on marginal constituencies. The most common form of bought advertising is the billboard and the main parties rent prominent advertising hoardings in marginal constituencies. The parties also seek to target marginal constituencies via adverts in the regional press. According to one party strategist, regional newspapers are more localized and personal compared to the national media and more effective at getting 'local messages across' (Electoral Commission, 2006a). The targeted voters are subject to a blizzard of negative adverts focused on the opponent's record and personality (Ansolabehere and Iyengar, 1995; Sancho, 2001), the logic being that, with only a short time or limited space to make an impact, attacking an opponent is more effective in persuading undecided voters (Ansolabehere and Iyengar, 1995).

Setting the news agenda

Setting the news media agenda is perhaps the least direct means of reaching the target voters, but is nevertheless important. Campaign teams approach the election with a view to steering the media agenda towards issues in their manifesto, reinforcing their other messages. Each day of the campaign is planned around a series of events, with key announcements designed to capture media coverage. The planning grid is now a common feature of campaigns, detailing the main theme that is intended to be communicated on a daily basis by the candidate or, in Britain, by the main parties. Each day of the campaign is designed with a series of opportunities to grab media attention and further illustrate aspects of a contestant's policy: a press conference, a speech by the contestant, TV interview, photo opportunity, and speech on the campaign trail. One area that campaign teams have exploited for some time is the party leaders'/presidential contestants' tour around the country, visiting prearranged venues with an entourage of journalists in tow, to be greeted by a crowd of cheering supporters (Crouse, 1972; Deacon et al., 2001, 2005; Kerbel, 1999).

While trying to steer the agenda towards issues that favour them, the contestants simultaneously criticize their opponents' policies, their record and ability to deliver, and their personalities. The news is often also a good outlet for 'dog-whistle messages' – messages that, rather like a dog whistle, can only be heard and responded to by certain identified groups. Dog-whistle messages were used by both US campaign teams in 2004. In order to mobilize the four million Christian voters who did not vote in 2000 and who were crucial to the outcome in swing states, Bush announced that he was opposed to gay marriage and would seek to outlaw it via a constitutional amendment. He used several speeches and interviews to condemn partial-birth abortions and Kerry's stance on the issue. Kerry, seeking to activate gay and lesbian voters in the same states, emphasized his position against workplace discrimination (Cloud, 2004).

In 2005, the UK Conservative Party's campaign team sent out a series of controversial messages designed to resonate with key groups of voters in marginal seats. With the slogan 'Are you thinking what we are thinking?' the campaign sought to generate fear about government policies on health, immigration, the growth of stealth taxation and its soft stance on the EU and crime (Deacon et al., 2005; Seawright, 2005). The 'dog whistle' generates fear amongst certain groups that policies of the opposing candidate or party will have a negative effect on them, and that they need to turn out to vote to prevent this from happening.

Popular media

Activity is further focused on TV programmes that are watched by target voters; these are usually non-news programmes that are high ratings grabbers. Popular television shows and magazines, for instance, afford politicians an opportunity to raise their profile with an audience beyond those who watch traditional political output. The sofa of an evening talk-show gives the contestants an opportunity to connect with one audience; being a guest on a day-time show enables them to project an image to another. In 1992, Bill Clinton appeared on a variety of talk shows, 'answering personal questions on MTV; matching his wits with talk show host Phil Donahue; impersonating Elvis

Presley and Marlon Brando for interviewers Larry King and Charlie Rose; playing saxophone on the Arsenio Hall show' (Schroeder, 2004: 269). The appearances were designed to enable key groups of women voters to connect with Clinton. Blair, some years later, followed a similar strategy. In 2005, his team launched 'Operation Matrix', which promoted Blair to a variety of important audiences (Wring, 2005). Shows such as ITV's *Saturday Night Take-Away*, *Richard and Judy* on Channel Four and *The Wright Stuff* on Channel Five were picked because they provided Blair with access to identified potential supporters such as 'school-gate mums', and 'hard working families' (ibid.).

The rising cost of campaign communication

Money has always been an element of campaigning in both countries; however, the rising cost of campaigning in recent years means it is increasingly dominated by wealthy organizations and individuals (Johnson, 2001; Sussman, 2005). In the US in 2004, George W. Bush was estimated to have spent $345 million, $159 million more than in 2000 (Center for Responsive Politics). His challenger, John Kerry, spent £310 million, $190 million more than the previous challenger Al Gore, and a massive $244 million more than President Clinton spent on his re-election campaign in 1996 (ibid.; Kettle, 2000b). Even allowing for inflation, this represents a significant increase in real terms. It is not just presidential candidates. In 2004, candidates contesting seats in Congress spent, according to one estimate, a combined $1.156 billion on campaigning, an increase of $425 million on the $765 million spent ten years earlier (Federal Election Commission, 2005b). The pattern seems set to continue: in 2006, candidates for congressional seats in the mid-term elections spent an estimated $800 million by September that year (Center for Responsive Politics).

Candidates in the US are not the sole spenders on campaign communication. The Republican and Democrat National Committees spend large amounts of money. In 2004, the Democrat National Committee (DNC) spent $120 million 'independently advocating the election or defeat of presidential candidates' and the Republican National Committee (RNC) spent $18.2 million (Federal Election Commission, 2005a). The RNC spent a further $46 million on 'generic media adverts' for Bush, while the DNC spent $24 million on 'generic media adverts' for Kerry. In addition, both also spent around $16 million each on campaign coordination (ibid.).

Millions of dollars are also spent by advocacy groups[2] not necessarily 'officially' associated with either candidate. In 2004, independent spending by such groups totalled $192.4 million; this figure represents a major increase in spending compared to $14.7 million in 2000 and $10.6 million in 1996 (Davies, 1999; Federal Election Commission, 2005a).

If expenditure by candidates, these groups and the parties are combined, the totals are much higher. During the 2000 presidential election campaign, candidates, parties and special interest groups spent about $1 billion between them, overshadowing the $600 million spent in 1996 (Kettle, 2000a). In 2004 that overall figure had risen to between $1.2 and $1.5 billion (Center for Responsive Politics).

In Britain, in comparison, the amount spent on election campaigns by political parties is small. Political parties are provided with free television spots, and local constituency spending is severely limited. Nevertheless, spending by political parties has risen. In 2005, £41.2 million was spent in total, an increase of £14.5 million on 2001 (Electoral Commission, 2002; 2006b): Labour spent £18 million, an increase of £7 million from 2001; the Conservatives spent £18 million, an increase of £5 million. Despite attempts to stop a return to the large spending of the late 1990s, when Labour spent £27 million, and the Conservatives £28 million during the 1997 campaign, the amounts spent seem to be rising once more (Butler and Kavanagh, 1997; Electoral Commission, 2002, 2006b; Scammell, 1995). These figures do not include money spent by other organizations. As in the US, money can also be spent by third parties. Since 2001, third parties that register with the Electoral Commission can spend up to £998,000, and spending by those that do not register is limited to £25,000. In 2005, a total of £1.7 million was spent, an increase from the £1.2 million spent in 2001. The trade unions have been the biggest spenders: the health union, UNISON, spent £774,000 in 2001 and £682,000 in 2005 on billboard and newspaper adverts promoting increased funding for the NHS; the shop-workers union, USDAW, spent £84,279 in 2001 on posters and the office-workers union, MSF, spent £4,726 on leaflets. Other periodic spenders include Charter 88, which spent £136,000 in 2001, the Democracy Movement, which spent £103,000 on an advertising campaign in 2001, and the Conservative Rural Action Group, which spent £550,000 in 2005 (Electoral Commission, 2002, 2006b).

Market research

Candidates spend a significant proportion of the resources they raise on campaign teams and market research. In the US, an estimated 20 per cent of a candidate's budget goes on staff (Sussman, 2005). The Republicans and Democrats spend large amounts of money on polling and on consultants for their presidential candidates. The Republican

Table 1.1 Breakdown of campaign spending by the main British political parties during the 2001 and the 2005 general election campaigns; % of total spent

Items of expenditure/year	Conservatives 2001	Conservatives 2005	Labour 2001	Labour 2005	Lib Dems 2001	Lib Dems 2005
Advertising	34%	46%	46%	29%	14%	37%
Direct mail/party literature	10%	25%	13%	15%	4%	29%
Market research	14%	7%	8%	9%	5%	4%
Party election broadcasts	4%	2%	3%	3%	4%	3%
Media/press conferences	3%	3%	7%	2%	17%	2%
Manifesto	8%	1%	5%	2%	7%	3%
Other (rallies, transport, etc.)	27%	16%	18%	40%	49%	22%

Source: Compiled from Electoral Commission, 2002, 2006b. All figures rounded.

National Committee spent $16 million on polling for Reagan, and $1.8 million on polling for Bush Snr (Tenpas, 2000). The DNC spent $4 million on polling for Carter, and between 1993 and 1999 it spent $12.5 million on outside consultants for Clinton in addition to his personal spending (ibid.). During his tenure, Clinton spent $2.7 million on some 100 polls with Dick Morris. For the first year of the Bush Jnr presidency, the RNC had spent $1 million on polls (Fritz et al., 2004).

In Britain, as can be seen in table 1.1, 7 per cent of the 2005 Conservative campaign budget, 9 per cent of Labour's and 4 per cent of the Liberal Democrat's was spent on market research and canvassing, which, with the exception of the Conservatives, this represents an increase in spending on 2001. A significant proportion also goes on campaign specialists, with big name consultancies commanding high prices. For example, in 2005 Labour was estimated to have paid Mark Penn around £530,000 for his services during the campaign and the Conservatives paid £400,000 for the assistance of Lynton Crosby (Charter and Simon, 2006; Wring, 2005).

Direct media

Direct mail is another draw on finances. In the first two months of 2005, before the campaign had started, Labour spent some £222,000 on direct mail and the Conservatives around £800,000. Throughout the campaign the Conservatives spent 25 per cent of their budget on materials sent directly to the electors, Labour spent 15 per cent and the Liberal Democrats 29 per cent (Electoral Commission, 2006b). Table 1.1 shows that these figures represent a significant increase on the 2001 general election campaign.

Table 1.2 Spending on campaign television advertising during 2004	
Campaigners	**Expenditure ($ millions)**
G. W. Bush + John Kerry	$255.8
Candidates for the Senate	$67.0
Candidates for the House	· $32.0
Democrat-leaning 527s[a]	$66.5
Republican-leaning 527s	$10.9

[a] 527s are 'independent' campaigning groups – named after the section of the US tax code which created them – and cannot expressly support or oppose a particular candidate (Justice and Ruttenberg, 2004).

Source: Compiled from Campaign Media Analysis Group Report, 2004. Figures for 1 April – 30 September.

Advertising

In the US, candidates spend a large proportion of campaign funds on purchasing television air time, estimated to be anything from 60 to 85 per cent of total budget (Campaign Media Analysis Group Report, 2004; Johnson, 2001), the cost of which escalates around campaign times as the networks raise their prices. In total, about $188 million was spent on 261,000 airings of adverts by the four main candidates in the 2000 presidential campaign (Campaign Media Analysis Group Report, 2001). In the 2004 presidential campaign, as can be seen in table 1.2, the two front runners spent $255.8 million airing 262 adverts 420,700 times. Table 1.2 also shows that candidates for congressional office spent a combined figure of $99 million on television adverts. If spending on television adverts in races for state offices is included, the figure rises sharply. In 2000, candidates campaigning for federal and state offices spent an estimated $600 million on political adverts. This is a sixfold increase (in inflation-adjusted dollars) from 1972 (Taylor, 2000); other estimates put the figure higher at $771 million (Campaign Media Analysis Group Report, 2001). Sussman (2005) notes that the amount spent in inflation-adjusted dollars between 1980 and 2000 rose by 400 per cent. In 2002, candidates in all races spent a similar combined figure of $1 billion on television advertising (ibid.).

In Britain, although television and radio adverts are free to air, their production costs are not covered, and advertising in newspapers and on billboards also has to be paid for. Advertising accounts for the largest part of the overall budget. In 2005, Party Election Broadcast production costs accounted for 2 per cent of the Conservative's budget, 3 per cent of Labour's and 3 per cent of the Liberal Democrat's – a slight fall on 2001 (see table 1.1). However, the amount spent on advertising rose. In 2005, paying for advertising accounted for 46 per cent of the Conservative's budget and 37 per cent of the Liberal Democrat's, which represents a rise from 2001, although the amount Labour spent on advertising in 2005 was less than in 2001.[3]

Money talks?

In order to communicate, candidates and parties increasingly need to fundraise. In the US, the ability to raise money increasingly affects the capability of candidates to communicate their message, whether they are running in presidential, congressional or state elections (Gierzynski, 2000) and research has shown that success is partially related to campaign expenditure (Herrnson, 2000). While it may not guarantee success, money is a 'necessary ingredient' to win (Gierzynski, 2000). Other factors being equal, those candidates who spend more tend to be more successful (Clawson et al., 1998; Gierzynski, 2000). Money is often critical in the early stages of a campaign, especially for unknown challengers (Denton and Woodward, 1998). In 1996, 92 per cent of House races and 88 per cent of Senate races were won by the candidates who spent the most money (Johnson, 2001: 175). In 2000, the highest spenders lost in only 29 out of hundreds of Congressional contests (Sussman, 2005). There is a growing number of wealthy candidates running for office and using their own money to fund their campaigns. Steve Forbes spent an estimated $437 million of his own money on the 1996 primaries and Ross Perot spent $8.2 million in 1992 (Johnson, 2001). Those candidates with the biggest 'war chests' can sustain a campaign, hire the necessary expertise and pay for the cost of communicating (ibid.).

In Britain, the majority of campaign spending is by the two main political parties. In 2001, 36 parties spent a total of £26.7 million; nearly 90 per cent of this sum was spent by the two main parties – £23.7 million. If we add the Liberal Democrat's £1.36 million, that figure rises to 94 per cent of spending. The other 33 parties spent some £1.6 million (Electoral Commission, 2002). In 2005, 78 parties spent £41.2 million; around 87 per cent of this sum was spent by the two main parties – £36 million. Despite the caps on spending, national and minor parties cannot match the spending of the main parties. They are unable to afford the campaign teams, market research, direct mail and advertising budgets of the main parties.

It is not surprising that fundraising has become a full-time activity for candidates and major political parties. President Clinton spent much of his time in the White House fundraising to pay for his re-election campaign (West, 2000). Similarly, in Britain, the main political parties are involved in continuous fundraising activity between campaigns. The need to raise money has in turn generated a series of scandals in both countries (see chapter 2).

Attempts to curb the role of 'big' money

There have been numerous attempts to regulate campaign finance in both the UK and the US. In Britain, there have been strict spending constraints on individual constituencies for some time, meaning that campaigning can only be financed centrally by the parties. In addition, campaign spending was further curtailed in 2001 by the Parties, Referendums and Elections Act, which capped spending by each party, subject to periodic review – although spending outside campaign periods is not restricted. However, there have been calls for tighter regulation of fundraising too, in light of revelations that a few wealthy donors have made millions of pounds of undeclared 'soft loans'[4] to the main political parties. These disclosures have prompted real concerns about the influence party donors might seek to exercise.

In the US there have been attempts since 1904 to limit the amount of money that individuals may donate indirectly to political action committees and incentives to exercise voluntary adherence by candidates to spending limits by offering presidential candidates matching federal funding (Gierzynski, 2000). The McCain-Feingold campaign finance law, the Bipartisan Campaign Reform Act, in 2002 was an attempt to remove so-called 'soft money'[5] from campaigns, limiting the amount individuals and organizations could donate to parties and campaigns.

Despite the new restraints, both parties in the US have increased the amount of money they have raised. Instead of removing money, the fundraising activities of candidates targeted a wider constituency than before. Candidates and parties have been forced to think of new techniques to raise funds, including 'internet solicitations, door-to-door canvassing and holding special low dollar fundraising events designed to attract new donors' (Justice, 2004). In 2004, the DNC raised $299 million and the RNC $330 million – a substantial increase on 2000 (ibid.).

The McCain-Feingold laws have not addressed this issue. Corporations and wealthy individuals can continue to support candidates indirectly to the tune of millions of dollars; the top ten donors in 2004 donated $115 million to various so-called 527s – the biggest donor was an individual financier, George Soros, who gave $26 million (Political Money Line, 2004). There is no limit on the amount an organization or individual can donate to 527 'independent' campaigning groups. While these groups are forbidden from saying, for instance, 'Vote for candidate X or Y', they are free to campaign for or against any candidate. They can spend as much money as they are able on advertising that, for instance, attacks a candidate's character or defends it. In 2004, the first presidential campaign since the introduction of the

McCain-Feingold laws, 527s were active, campaigning on both sides. Of the top ten best resourced 527s in 2004, seven were Democrat-leaning and three Republican (Political Money Line, 2004). Kaid and Dimitrova (2005) observed that there were a large number of political adverts by 527s in the 2004 presidential campaign. In total, Democrat-supporting 527s spent $66.5 million on TV adverts and Republican 527s spent $10.9 million (see table 1.2).

There remains much doubt about how independent 527s really are, given the effective coordination of their political messages with the candidates' campaigns. Groups such as 'Swift Boat Veterans for Truth' had ties with Mr Bush's lawyer, Benjamin Ginsberg, who acknowledged having worked with the group (Justice and Rutenberg, 2004). Stanley Greenberg, closely associated with the Kerry campaign and 527 Democracy Corp and the director of Moveon.org, also helped run Kerry's website (ibid.)

The included and the excluded voter

With the process of partisan dealignment, the function of campaigning has altered in both countries. Schier (2000) argues that the purpose of campaigning dramatically changed between what he terms the 'partisan era' (1876–92) and the present. The function of campaigns in the partisan era was to mobilize loyal supporters. Campaigns had broad targets, and parties employed mass mobilization techniques. However, in the present era, the purpose of campaigning, in Schier's words, is to 'activate' key voter groups. While the aim of campaigning in the partisan era was to have mass appeal, in the contemporary era the goal is to be exclusive, and to have a limited appeal. Activation is a 'finely targeted, exclusive method contemporary parties employ to cultivate popular support' (ibid.: 3). Schier is not the only one to make such observations. Wattenberg (2000) notes that the era of party mass mobilization has come to an end, to be replaced by a more targeted form of campaigning (see also Gandy, 2001). Gronbeck and Wiese observe that there has been a 'de-massification' of campaign processes (2005: 529). Although these authors are US-focused, a similar point could be made about UK politics. The aim of campaigning during the period of strong class–party voter alignment in British politics was to mobilize mass support. The process of partisan dealignment transformed the activities of political parties. The purpose of campaign communication became to activate floating voters in marginal constituencies (Denver et al., 2004).

Building on the arguments of Schier and others, it is reasonable to argue that there has been a key change in the nature of campaign communication. The function of campaigns, and hence campaign communication, for a significant period during the twentieth century, has been to mobilize supporters. The intended goal of 'local-active' communication techniques such as rallies, door-to-door canvassing and pamphleteering, as well as party election broadcasts and adverts on radio and television, was to mobilize supporters (see also Norris, 2000). Indeed, the mass media enabled mass appeals by contestants to stable groups of supporters without the need for face-to-face contact. In short, in the era of partisan alignment, campaign communication was designed to be inclusive.

In the contemporary electoral environment, campaign communication is designed to be exclusive. Activation of key groups and constituencies represents a much better return on campaign expenditure than general mobilization. This has several unintended consequences. The UK and the US have both seen a rise in voter turnout gaps (see chapter 6); activation strategies perpetuate such gaps. Resources are focused on discovering the opinions of 'pebble-dash people' or 'soccer moms' – those key demographics who regularly vote. As Gandy (2001) observes, those who are seen as unlikely to vote – the socially excluded and marginalized – are likely to be ignored by campaign teams. The result is that 'the excluded tend to draw the correct conclusions that they do not count politically' and may withdraw further (Bennett, 2003a: 144; see also chapter 6).

Resources are also targeted almost exclusively on key battleground jurisdictions. In terms of spending as a percentage of their total estimated spending, six battleground states in 2000 accounted for the majority of Gore's and Bush's budget – 64 per cent in the case of Bush and 65 per cent in the case of Gore's campaign (Campaign Media Analysis Group Report, 2001).[6] As mentioned earlier, in 2000 spending on advertising focused on a handful of swing states. In 2004, Bush and Kerry spent nearly $200 million on TV adverts in the top five marginal states (Campaign Media Analysis Group Report, 2004). Chosen audiences in these areas were subject to a blizzard of specifically targeted information from the contestants. For example, the US the city of Toledo, Ohio, was deluged with 15,000 adverts for the two presidential candidates in the six-month run-up to the November 2004 poll. The overwhelming focus of the campaign in swing states in turn leads to campaign news coverage focusing on the race in these battlegrounds.

Conversely, seats or states that are not marginal become mere spectators of the campaign – they are not targeted directly. As Bennett observes, 'those who are unlikely to shift the outcome of the election will hear few messages aimed at them' (2003a: 144). Data show that outside the battleground states in 2004, 35 and 39 per cent respectively claimed not to have seen a Kerry or a Bush spot, compared to only 13 per cent and 16 per cent respectively in the battleground states (Pew Research Center, 2004a). Similarly, data on campaign contact by the parties during the 2004 presidential campaign revealed that 76 per cent of voters were contacted in swing states, compared to 55 per cent in safe Republican states and 59 per cent in safe Democrat states (Pew Research Center, 2004d). In Britain, spending on campaign communication has been concentrated in some 100–160 marginal seats, while in the other nearly 500 constituencies, especially safe seats, it is non-existent. In both the 2001 and 2005 general election campaigns, the marginality of the constituency was one of the key criteria determining the placement of billboard adverts by all the main parties (Electoral Commission, 2006a). It was also a factor guiding the spending on newspaper adverts, which were placed in newspapers serving regions where there were marginal seats which the parties stood a good chance of winning (ibid.). Voters in marginal constituencies are more likely to receive campaign mail or a telephone call than those in a safe seat (Butler and Kavanagh, 2001). In 2005, they were five times more likely to have received a telephone call or doorstep contact than those in a safe seat. Spending on more elaborate forms of direct mail, such as DVDs, was almost exclusively focused on marginal constituencies (Electoral Commission, 2006a). Millions of dollars and pounds are spent in each contest on communicating with, in effect, a minority in swing seats; indeed most of the resources in the 2005 British general election campaign were targeted on around 800,000 voters (Electoral Commission, 2005e).

This has the effect of perpetuating the distortions in voter turnout. Intensive campaigning increases the chances of going to the polls (Denver et al., 2004; Macedo et al., 2005). In both countries, in national campaigns, turnout was higher in battleground states and constituencies where campaign communication was intensive. In the US, in the 2004 presidential campaign, turnout in five key battleground states (Iowa, Minnesota, Ohio, Pennsylvania and Wisconsin) averaged 72 per cent, with a high of 79 per cent in Minnesota (US Census Bureau, 2005). This compares to an average turnout of 56 per cent in five states where there was little campaign activity (Hawaii, Georgia, West Virginia, Texas and Nevada) – turnout in Hawaii was 51 per cent, some 28 per cent below Minnesota (US Census Bureau, 2005).

In Britain in 2001 and 2005, turnout was some 9 per cent higher in marginal seats than in ultra-safe ones (Curtice, 2005; Whiteley et al., 2001). The lowest turnouts have been found amongst the traditional supporters of the Labour Party, in safe Labour seats. The ten seats with the lowest turnout in 2001 and 2005 were all safe urban Labour seats, with a predominance of people on low incomes, the lowest being Liverpool Riverside, where there was a turnout of 34.1 per cent (Curtice and Steed, 2002). Supporters in safe seats are not seen as crucial to electoral success, and campaign resources are not going to be allocated to mobilizing their support. 'The gap between the turnout in safe Labour seats and that in the rest of the country has grown at every election' (Curtice, 2005).

Campaign communication is exclusive in a second sense. National elections, despite attempts at reform, are increasingly becoming a costly spectacle dominated by a few wealthy political communicators, who spend ever larger amounts of money to secure victory. Minor parties and candidates not able to compete in the fundraising stakes are at a disadvantage. This is not to argue that those who outspend their rivals are automatically successful, but candidates unable to raise such resources are at a distinct disadvantage against rivals who can employ larger campaign teams and determine their exposure through buying air time or billboard space (Davies, 1999).

For large swathes of the electorate, therefore, there is relatively little reciprocity between the representatives and the represented at the one period where, it could be argued, it is essential. Few of the wealthy candidates or parties address them or listen to their views, nor is there any incentive other than civic duty for them to get engaged and turn out to vote. It is only a relative minority, who happen to live in a swing state or marginal constituency, who find that their role is more than that of onlooker. The audience not in the swing states, and not targeted, may, and often do, exclude themselves from the process.

Conclusion

This chapter has shown that data-driven campaigning and targeted communication increasingly dominate election campaigning. This approach to campaigning is seen as necessary by office-seekers in order to achieve their goals in an age of decreasing voter loyalty. It is, though, hugely expensive, with contestants spending millions of dollars or pounds. The instrumental nature of this approach means the concentration of resources is on relatively few citizens. Campaign communication is increasingly focused on key groups of voters and marginal seats/swing states that will determine the outcome of an election. The aim of targeted messages is to activate specific groups of voters, not to mobilize all citizens to participate. This process of segmentation and targeting leads to the exclusion of sections of the electorate, reinforcing existing turnout gaps. For the majority of citizens, the election campaign is a media spectacle; they are observers of events, on the sidelines unless they are in a battleground state or key constituency and the object of strategic communication. Many will vote out of civic duty, but it is hardly surprising that an increasing number of them are losing interest in media output, unaware what contestants stand for, and unprepared to vote for a particular candidate or party (see chapter 6). In democracies where elections are only about winning, and contestants have little incentive to engage all the electorate, the outcome can only be growing electoral marginalization.

CHAPTER
02

Governing and the Push for Effective Promotion

THE post-war era has witnessed a fundamental shift in the nature and purpose of government communication (Cook, 1998; Tulloch, 1993). An obsession with promotion increasingly shapes all government communication efforts in the US and the UK. Many of the techniques pioneered in the public relations and public opinion industries, and practised during election campaigns, have become the mainstay of government communication, the belief being that such promotional techniques are essential for administrations to get their message across and maintain public support.[1] This conviction is married with an unrelenting drive to find ever more effective ways of message promotion and new means of maintaining public support.

This chapter looks at the rise and dominance of a 'promotional logic' in government circles. Focusing on the White House in the US, and Number 10 Downing Street in the UK, it highlights the changing attitudes of political elites to communication in the post-war era. The chapter examines a series of key executive initiated changes in government communication, such as the emergence of widespread news management, greater coordination of message dissemination, the use of campaign professionals, the adoption and adaptation of campaigning techniques and the institutionalization of public opinion research. I argue that these changes are part of an identifiable and continuing trend. On entering office, successive administrations have sought to improve communications in various ways, adapting older media management techniques and introducing new ones in order to maintain public support. The effort to find more effective ways of reaching the public continues throughout an administration's term of office. Governments are always seeking new ways to respond to the challenges they face, finding novel means to control negative publicity and connect with citizens. However, the outcome of this promotional logic has not been what executives necessarily crave: over time they still become unpopular, and increasingly the very effort of 'handling the media' and managing public opinion itself becomes the news story, creating an image of governments as deceitful, calculating and obsessed with their own popularity. Finally, the chapter draws on the example of the invasion and occupation of Iraq to illustrate some of its arguments.

The all-encompassing promotional rationale

In simple terms, over the post-war period government communication has gone from a largely reactive operation, catering for the needs of a growing Washington or Westminster news media, to a proactive operation, designed to ensure 'effective' promotion of administrations and policy across a wide variety of outlets. But more than this, managing mediated communication has come to be seen as key to creating and maintaining support (Barnett and Gaber, 2001; Han, 2001). The rationale is that the more effectively an administration can 'sell' policy, justify its decisions, defend its actions and acclaim its achievements in the media, the more likely it is to be able to maintain the support of key sectors of the public and ultimately increase its chance of re-election. The supposition is that promotional techniques delivered success during the campaign and can similarly repeat that in government. Before examining the changes in more detail, it is worth reflecting on the basis of this rationale.

The need continually to nurture support this way can be seen as a reaction to several factors. First is the changing electoral reality that governments face. Political actors are no longer able to rely on party loyalties of old, with support being increasingly contingent on performance. Whereas once the incumbent executives could put the campaign for re-election on the back burner, at least until nearer the next election, now they cannot afford to do so. The received wisdom is that the official campaign period is often too short a time period in which to regain lost support (see Nimmo, 1999). Administrations, once elected, have to maintain the support of a more dealigned electorate throughout their term in office (Bennett, 2003a). Even where re-election is not an option, issues of 'legacy' and party pressure mean that they cannot afford to neglect public support.

Second, it can be seen as a response to the ubiquity and visibility of public opinion measures. The support which administrations crave has never been more visible. The number of opinion polls, commissioned and regularly published, on the popularity of governments has grown dramatically in the post-war era. There was only one job approval poll conducted during the first 100 days of the Truman administration in 1945. In the first 100 days of the Clinton presidency there were 37 (Bowman, 2000). In Britain, the picture is similar. Tony Blair and his government's popularity are tracked with greater regularity than the governments of 40 years ago. The widespread visibility of changing government popularity in almost daily tracking polls creates an environment where public responses are instantly measured and publicized and need to be responded to. Failure to maintain approval or support can soon become the story, and a government can easily be seen as out of touch.

The process of promotion is now continuous throughout the life cycle of any administration; as Bennett notes, to keep the executive's message in the public mind, promotion 'must never stop' (2003: 143) (see also Needham, 2005; Nimmo, 1999). Administrations in both countries are gripped by a promotional mindset, which has its roots in campaign practices (see chapter 1). In the White House, according to one observer, there is now a preoccupation with how to sell initiatives (Cook, 1998). The same obsession can be seen in Downing Street (Heffernan, 2004; Seymour-Ure, 2003). For instance, since the late 1990s, Downing Street has set about changing the central ethos of government communication, namely, that communication should be about informing the public and not selling the latest government initiative (Heffernan and Stanyer, 1998).

Government actors not only need to promote the content of what they do; they also need to be aware of the importance of the impressions they create in the media and the minds of the audience of voters (Thompson, 1995). The belief is that the media impression is as important, if not more important, than the reality of the daily business of government. In an age of electoral volatility, the premise is that governing is also about creating and maintaining a favourable public impression, one of competence and probity. As Blair's polling guru, Philip Gould, observed in a leaked memo, 'unless you handle the media well, you cannot govern competently' (cited in Rose, 2001: 6).

It has been suggested by some that the origins of this promotional group-think in government can be found in the Eisenhower presidency of the 1950s (Nimmo, 1999; Schudson, 1978); others point to Kennedy in the 1960s, or later to the Nixon administration (Cook, 1998; Denton and Woodward, 1998; Han, 2001). By the time of the Reagan presidency this promotional rationale can be seen as firmly established in the White House, consisting of seven news management principles: plan ahead; stay on the offensive; control the flow of information; limit reporters' access to Reagan; talk about the issues the White House wants to talk about; speak in one voice; and repeat the same message many times (Han, 2001: 181). The Reagan administration's perspective has been widely adopted by subsequent presidents. In Britain, while some observed such promotional tendencies in the

Wilson government of the 1960s, the consensus is that such a culture developed slightly later with the Thatcher government, but reached its apex with the Blair government (Palmer, 2000; Scammell, 1995; Seymour-Ure, 2003; Tulloch, 1998). Like the Reagan White House, Blair's media chief, Alastair Campbell, introduced his own guiding principles, the three Rs – rhetoric, repetition and rebuttal (Wheeler, 2004). This is not to suggest that regime is an unimportant factor. The White House Office of Communication was less important to Carter than it was to Nixon, but was subsequently returned to strategic prominence with Reagan in 1981 (Cook, 1998). Prime Minister John Major was less interested in promotion than Blair has been. Indeed, it was the deemed lack of effective control of government presentation under Major's press secretary, Gus O'Donnell, which acted as a spur for Campbell and the New Labour administration (Jones, 1995). That said, it would now be unthinkable for an executive not to employ such techniques.

However, it is not just about 'going public', to quote Kernel (1997)', but also about responding to problems encountered and finding more effective ways to reach the public through the media. Improving government communication, enabling administrations to 'define, justify, legitimate, persuade and inspire' more effectively, so as to maintain support, has been one of the main focuses on successive administrations in Britain and the US (Denton and Woodward, 1998: 184). Both elected and appointed professionals strive to find ever more effective ways to promote government actors and their policy initiatives. They continually try to discover new ways of securing favourable media coverage for incumbents and their initiatives. The spread of this reflexive promotional logic can be seen not only in the strategies introduced by successive executives but also in their constant improvement. The next section outlines the reflexive nature of government promotional activity.

Hitting the ground running

The promotion of key policies has moved from being an afterthought to being an integral part of legislative activity. Once elected, governments now engage in the tireless selling of their core policy objectives (Cook, 1998; Heffernan, 2004). The national news media remain amongst the main targets for much of this promotional activity. New administrations try to make the most of their honeymoon period, seizing control of the news media agenda with a raft of announcements and pledges. Clinton's health care reform package in the early 1990s and, more recently, George W. Bush's massive tax cuts package received substantial early promotion (Han, 2001). Tony Blair spent the early part of his tenure continually laying out New Labour's aspirations in government (Franklin, 2001; Heffernan and Stanyer, 1998).

Making and controlling the news

In order to get their legislative agenda into the news and dominate the national news agenda, all administrations now standardly use a variety of public relations techniques (Cook, 1998; Palmer, 2000). Information subsidies[2] are widely deployed to maximize the exposure that policy receives. In the initial stages there is a lot of hype about what the new administration is going to do, the established media-briefing channels are utilized and journalists are relentlessly courted by spin doctors and administration personnel (see also Grossman and Kumar, 1981). Intentions are further announced in a round of carefully coordinated public speeches by leading administration actors, with the content of these speeches routinely trailed in advance to all news outlets. Presidents, prime ministers and leading government actors no longer stand aloof from the public in a way they once did (Ponder, 1999; Seymour-Ure, 2003). They are now central to the promotional dynamic, the public face of the regime, there to propagate a message and regularly 'going public' at every opportunity (Kernell, 1997). Their speeches are followed by a series of interviews and photo opportunities to illustrate matters for television news. These techniques, and a variety of other public relations techniques, are routinely applied by every branch of government (Cook, 1998; Maltese, 2003; Jones, 1995, 1999; Heffernan and Stanyer, 1998). In addition, public relations efforts are targeted on specific outlets, with rivalry between outlets exploited (Jones, 1995, 1999; Kumar, 2001a). Administrations ration the goodies, so to speak, giving certain media outlets exclusive information to ensure favourable coverage (Blumler and Gurevitch, 1995). They control the flow of key spokespeople to enable a clear message to be disseminated. The local and regional media are offered exclusives, especially in key policy areas. In 1993, for instance, President Clinton held 25 special sessions with reporters from the provincial media and held regular satellite interviews with the regional media. Downing Street has used similar tactics, arranging special briefings for the regional and Sunday press and more recently for foreign correspondents (see Jones, 1997, 1999).

The publicity process continues after legislation has been passed, reinforcing in the voters' minds that they are benefiting from the policy. Follow-up promotional strategies have been introduced and are now routinely used (Palmer, 2000). For example, the Bush team sent out flyers to various states stating that 91 million people had received a tax cut of $1,126 and 109 million a cut of $1,544 since Bush entered office (Fritz et al., 2004). The Blair government has been quick to extol its achievements and boast about its record levels of public spending.

Explaining the big picture

Such promotion, however, has been made more complex by the transformation of the news media environment (McNair, 2006). Strategies that once worked for predecessors often fail to gain the required publicity or any publicity at all. This 24-hour news media environment poses real and significant challenges to message dissemination which administrations have sought to overcome in a variety of ways.

One strategy, developed during campaigns and widely adopted in government, is to simplify the message. A simple message is more likely to be heard amongst the background noise. As early as the 1970s, in the US, the Nixon administration implemented a 'line of the day' to minimize confusion. By the 1980s the strategy was widely used by the Reagan administration. Cook (1998) describes a daily scenario where senior staff in the Reagan White House would decide on the 'line of the day', the line being the message they wanted to communicate. After Clinton was elected, his communication team set about distilling his agenda into a straightforward story for public consumption (Needham, 2005). A similar strategy has been adopted by the Bush team, termed 'message of the day' (Fritz et al., 2004). In the Britain, on taking office in 1997, Blair's communication team instructed departmental press offices to stress the so-called 'big picture' in each government initiative (Heffernan and Stanyer, 1998). As former British government minister, communication supremo Peter Mandelson, observed, 'you need to explain what you are doing and keep describing the big picture' (cited in Rose, 2001: 220). In one widely reported leaked memo, Philip Gould urged Blair to concentrate on making fewer, but more substantial, announcements rather than overwhelming the public with a daily raft of measures (Hall and Watt, 2001: 2; see also Needham 2005). Alastair Campbell instituted the 'line for the following day's news agenda' in 2001, the aim being to get a single authoritative message across to the media (Heffernan, 2004: 21).

Promotional task forces

Government communication strategists are always looking for more effective means of promotion. A simple 'line of the day' to gathered ranks of journalists may not in itself be enough to publicize successfully a particular initiative or hold public support, especially where government faces opposition. One of the newer strategies has been to assemble a team of actors, a 'communication cluster' or 'staff unit', to concentrate on promoting particular initiatives (Kumar, 2001a; Maltese, 2000). The aim of this promotional task force is to achieve particular publicity goals. Although short-lived, the Clinton administration, for instance, recreated their campaign 'war room' when in office. The war room pushed the administration's big initiatives on health, the economy and the North American Free Trade Agreement at the beginning of the President's first term. The administration 'commandeered a large room [in] the Old Executive Office building, set up two horseshoe-shaped table arrangements, and crammed in twenty or more staff' (B. H. Patterson, 2000: 159). A hive of activity, 'at one desk cabinet members and other surrogates are scheduled for television and radio appearances around the country; at another, rapid responses are being shot out to counter opponents' charges' (ibid.).

The White House Iraq Group (WHIG), an equivalent of Clinton's war room, was formed by Bush in 2002, to promote the need to remove Saddam Hussein by force. WHIG included all the top administration actors, together with presidential advisers and a strategic communications unit (Fritz et al., 2004), and set about systematically selling the case for regime change in Iraq. Key to this campaign was the need to construct an image of Iraq to reinforce the impression of its danger. In Britain, Tony Blair assembled a similar task force of close advisers, including Alastair Campbell (Miller, 2004; Stothard, 2003), which met regularly to decide on strategy to make the case for war. In Britain, use of the promotional task force has been most in evidence in the run-up to election campaigns. Communication operations in this period have often been organized by a specially assembled committee (Scammell, 1995).

Improving planning and coordination

One of the key identified problems of the expanding public relations apparatus has been one of lack of coordination between the different actors (Jones, 1995, 1997; Maltese, 2003). Indeed, successive governments have been critical of the disharmony of their own communication machinery. Without coordination, the potential for contradictory messages and generating the impression of confusion is high, especially given the growing number of departments and press officers. Achieving better coordination has now become of central importance for newly elected governments (Kumar, 2001b; Maltese, 2000; Palmer, 2000). However, in the contemporary media environment, effective promotion requires ever more sophisticated acts of orchestration, which governments have not found easy.

In both countries in the post-war period, but especially since the 1990s, successive governments have sought more efficient ways of coordinating the different parts of the public relations apparatus (Wheeler, 2004; Maltese, 2000). Increasingly, the task of coordinating the promotion of government initiatives is given to an actor or group of actors, who are usually close to the Prime Minister or President (Heffernan, 2004; Maltese, 2003). In addition, there are regular, high-level coordinating meetings with senior members of the administration. Such meetings, generally held weekly, are a feature of the White House and Westminster communications operations, when media coverage of the key message being promoted by the government is discussed (Cook, 1998; Jones, 1997; Kumar, 2001a). In the White House, there are regular meetings between the Communication Director, the Chief of Staff, the press secretary, the President's scheduler and other relevant staff, in order to assess the administration's priorities and the strategies in place to achieve them, and to amend existing schedules (Kumar, 2001a; B. H. Patterson, 2000). For instance, every Monday during the Clinton presidency, there was an amplification conference informing the different departments of what was going to happen (B. H. Patterson, 2000). The Bush team continued this practice. Fritz et al. (2004) observe that the Bush administration has borrowed from the Clinton White House, establishing a 24-hour media centre to coordinate promotion.

In Britain prior to the Thatcher government in 1979, such attempts effectively to coordinate the presentation of policy across a range of departments were at best sporadic; certainly, Downing Street did not try to coordinate the news operation as it does today (Heffernan, 2004; Seymour-Ure, 2003). Over time, Downing Street has sought to ensure effective coordination of the communication operations of the different departments of state by centralizing control over their media operations (Barnett and Gaber, 2001). The coordination of presentation under Blair's government was placed in the hands of a Strategic Communication Unit (SCU). Composed of six full-time members of staff – a mixture of civil servants and political appointees – the aim of the unit was to help coordinate the communications effort across departments, 'pulling together and sharing with departments the government's key policy themes and messages' in a more effective way than previously (Select Committee on Public Administration, 1998, para 19).

The promotion of policy/legislation is planned in advance, taking account of the smallest detail, with the publicity objectives being factored into the legislative timetable. The weekly news grid, or message calendar, used so effectively in election campaigns (see chapter 1), has been utilized by administrations; in both countries, administrations now work with elaborate planning grids which map out promotional initiatives months in advance. As well as being used to plot all policy announcements and see what other events they might be up against, the message calendar is also used to synchronize government announcements, making sure that there are no clashes between departments or with events outside government that might over-shadow announcements, such as a major sporting occasion (Franklin, 2003).

In Britain, the message calendar has been combined with the instal-lation of a communication intranet to link press officers in different departments, alert them to the planned policy launches and prevent any confusion in message delivery. To this end, the Knowledge Network project can provide government departments with 'the line' to take on a whole range of issues. The SCU approves plans for all launches and announcements by government departments: it is designed to ensure effective coordination of announcements.

The drive for more effective coordination in Britain has extended to government ministers in an attempt to coordinate ministerial contact with the media in an unprecedented way. Blair's 1997 revamped version of Question of Procedures to Ministers noted:

> All major interviews and media appearances, both print and broadcast, should be agreed with the No. 10 Press Office before any commitments are entered into. The policy content of all major speeches, press releases and new policy initiatives should be cleared in time with the No. 10 Private Office; the timing and form of announcements should be cleared with the No. 10 Press Office. (Mountfield, 1997: 7)

In the US, various administrations have sought to control media access to White House staff. For instance, on taking office in 1993, the Clinton team issued a memo stating that all requests for interviews needed to be cleared by the communication office and required advanced notification (B. H. Patterson, 2000). James Baker had issued similar guidelines to the staff of the Reagan White House ten years earlier (Han, 2001).

Keeping in touch

Although contemporary administrations are not the first to use polling evidence, the importance of polling to incumbents has increased, with research being used to determine how government promotional gambits play with the public and, in certain instances, to determine the very initiatives which government should promote. Market research becomes increasingly central to message promotion and image management, with the techniques outlined in chapter 1 regularly used by administrations in both countries.

Franklin D. Roosevelt was the first US President to make use of opin-ion polls in the 1930s, but it was not until the Nixon administration in the late 1960s that polling information was more commonly used. Every administration since Nixon has regularly utilized polling data, with memos widely circulated and regular meetings held to discuss findings (Bowman, 2000; Heith, 2004; Tenpas, 2000). Also, the frequency with which public opinion research was conducted has increased over time. Clinton's obsession with market research has been well documented, but President Reagan showed an equal obsession (Bowman, 2000; Kurtz, 1998; Newman, 1999). Reagan met with the pollster Richard Wirthlin 25 times in the first 29 months of his presidency (Bowman, 2000). Clinton met with pollsters weekly throughout the first year of his presidency and commissioned monthly tracking surveys (Bowman, 2000; B. H. Patterson, 2000). This research was designed to help Clinton make more effective decisions at key moments. For example, during the budget stalemate between the President and Congress, which closed down government in November 1995, Dick Morris conducted polls on a daily basis to determine the course of action the President should take (B. H. Patterson, 2000). The outcome was successful for Clinton (Newman, 1999). Polling evidence also led to the Clinton administration abandoning policy initiatives. In 1997, the White House planned to 'tackle HIV by promoting needle exchanges for drug addicts'. However, polling conducted before the launch of the policy revealed it could negatively affect Clinton's popularity and the launch was cancelled (Charter and Simon, 2006: 29). George W. Bush 'promised to govern upon principles and not polls and focus groups' (cited in Stonecash, 2003). However, by 2002 he was adjusting his policy agenda in light of evidence from polls and focus groups, a practice he has continued, most recently adapting aspects of the administration's policy on Iraq in response to public opinion research (Fritz et al., 2004).

In Britain until very recently, use of public opinion research by governments for electoral purposes has been intermittent, with some administrations more inclined to utilize research than others. In the 1950s, Conservative Central Office, on behalf of the government, employed NOP to conduct polls 'to determine the impact of policy and propaganda' in the run-up to the 1959 election (Taylor, 1997: 210; see also Scammell, 1995). While Harold Wilson, Edward Heath and Jim Callaghan made limited use of market research, Margaret Thatcher was making regular use of polls and focus groups in the run-up to the 1983 and 1987 general elections. These explored her image on so-called caring issues such as health, education and employment. Indeed, one focus group prior to 1987 revealed that her combative virtues were seen as vices (Cockerell, 1988: 307). However, the Major government conducted no polling for the four years following their 1992 election victory and then only used tracking polls in the last six months before the 1997 campaign (Butler and Kavanagh, 1997; Sparrow and Turner, 2001). This picture changed with Tony Blair's election as Prime Minister. Blair followed President Clinton's lead, continuing to employ Philip Gould to provide tracking polls for Labour throughout its first two terms in government and not just in the run-up to elections. Gould's company tracked issues such as 'handling of the economy, public services, pensions, living standards, taxes, leadership, economic competence, trust, and sense of direction' (Butler and Kavanagh, 2001: 33). Opinion research is further intensified in the run-up to elections. For example, prior to the 2001 campaign, Gould's company carried out two focus groups a week (ibid.). The findings of the tracking polls and focus groups were regularly reported back to Blair and to the cabinet in special presentations.

In certain instances, market research has been used to determine the very initiatives which government should promote. Newman (1999) observes that Clinton used polls and focus groups not only for feedback but also to chart the direction of policy. Polling and focus groups were used to find out public fears and priorities and design attention-grabbing policies around these issues. The Clinton administration sought to ensure that their policy agenda was in tune with the public's, applying the so called '50 per cent rule', endorsing anything that more than 50 per cent of the electorate supported (ibid.).

The Clinton White House held regular strategy meetings at which the opinion poll and focus group findings would be dissected by the President and his team. These meetings would highlight concerns that eventually found their way into policy announcements, which would be sold in the media. Apparently Clinton was involved, if Morris is to be believed, in framing polling questions, although the President never publicly acknowledged this, preferring to appear to be in touch with the public extemporaneously (Liebovich, 2001). A host of so-called family-friendly initiatives found their way into the legislative and media agenda as a result of market research that revealed the concerns of American parents. Parental concerns about violence on television led to numerous attacks on Hollywood and the introduction of V-chips in televisions to allow parents to control what children watch. There were also initiatives on school discipline, children's reading deficiencies, teenage smoking and 'deadbeat dads' (Needham, 2005).

In Britain, Tony Blair went some way to adopting this approach. Focus group concerns about anti-social behaviour led to a raft of measures, including Anti-Social Behaviour Orders (ASBOs), on-the-spot fines for yobs, parenting orders and limits on alcohol promotions to curb binge drinking. These initiatives were then promoted to give the impression that government was responding to the needs and concerns of the voter. Perhaps the height of such marketed response were the national 'listening' initiatives. The Blair government launched the 'Big Conversation' in November 2003 as a pre-election manifesto consultation exercise. It was advertised as a listening exercise in which the public could open a dialogue with the government – in effect a giant focus group. Big Conversation meetings were organized around the country, attended by different government ministers, and supplemented by online exchanges. The concerns expressed in these meetings, and online, became widely promoted government policy, such as a ban on smoking in public places, measures to control anti-social behaviour and binge drinking, and measures to stop criminals profiting from writing books. In May 2006, the Blair government repeated the initiative, calling it 'Let's Talk'.

UK governments are as increasingly eager as those in the US to capitalise on groundswells in public opinion. For example, the Blair government pounced on the *Sun*'s 'get tough on asylum' campaign (see chapter 5), seeing an opportunity to show that the Labour government was in tune with the concerns of the voters and the key electoral audience of *Sun* readers. The Director of Communications arranged an interview for the *Sun* with the Home Secretary, where he promised 'tough measures to crack down on asylum cheats'. As one government spin doctor observed, 'the impression given was that the government had acted on the *Sun*'s concerns' – and those of its readers – on a hot button issue (White, 2004).

In sum, on taking office, administrations have introduced a variety of techniques aimed at improving the effectiveness of government communication and have sought to ensure that they remain in touch with the views of a volatile electorate. However, as the next section will show, governing presents its own set of pitfalls.

The unpredictable nature of governing, and worsening media relations

Executives might be more able to promote initiatives and track public opinion but they are unable completely to control the environment in which they operate. When they do occur, mistakes, policy failures, rivalries and scandals are exposed in the 24-hour news media and commented upon by a growing army of pundits and critics. Media representations of these events may well have the potential to undermine the popularity of an administration during its term in office.

Current administrations, like their predecessors, are not immune from crises of one kind or another. In the UK, Tunstall notes, 'waiting for a British political crisis can be like waiting for a London Bus; there is a long wait, before three arrive close together' (1996: 301). This, Tunstall observes, had been the experience of Prime Minister Harold Macmillan in 1963, Harold Wilson in 1967–8 and John Major in 1993–4. In 2005–6, the Blair government had to react to a string of mini-crises: paedophiles in schools, cash for peerages allegations, a failure to deport foreign criminals, ongoing squabbles between the Prime Minister and his Chancellor Gordon Brown – as well as constant rumblings about when Blair would resign and, last but not least, Iraq.

The so-called 'sixth-year curse' affected George W. Bush, just as it impacted on his predecessors, Nixon, Reagan and Clinton (Shogan, 2006). Ongoing revelations about Iraq, the bungled nomination of Harriet Myers to the Supreme Court, the Plame affair (see below), the Jack Abramhoff lobbying scandal and the aftermath of Hurricane Katrina, just like Watergate, Iran-Contra and Monica Lewinsky, all undermined the Bush regimes' ability to get their message out effectively. For example, 24-hour coverage of the aftermath of Katrina saw a rash of lurid headlines, and an impression of a government unwilling, or unable, to react (McNair, 2006). Of course, administrations respond and continue to utilize the strategies used during the honeymoon period, but often such strategies are not enough to prevent government achievements being drowned out by a continuous stream of negative news.

There are particular sources of unplanned negative publicity that all administrations face. They vary in scale and severity: some have the potential, in certain extreme situations, to bring about the end of an administration – for example Watergate and Nixon – but all have the ability to distract media attention from the messages that governments want to communicate, and can undermine support. Despite media management strategies, such events are no less likely to happen today than at any time previously. In fact, their impact is often greater because of the presence of the media. It is worth highlighting some of the risks that all administrations face in terms of their degree to erode support.

Gaffes, outbursts and performances that backfire

The least potentially damaging forms of unplanned occurrences are gaffes, outbursts and performances that backfire (Thompson, 1995). Their coverage in the media may cause mild or even severe embarrassment and divert media attention away from the message of the day, but are rarely terminal in their consequences, unless the politician makes them frequently. In Britain, the Deputy Prime Minister John Prescott is particularly gaffe-prone – for example, punching a demonstrator on the 2001 campaign trail, and forgetting to pay tax on one of his official residencies. President Gerald Ford was also particularly gaffe-prone, with his mishaps regularly featured in the news bulletins (West and Orman, 2003). More recently, George W. Bush has often appeared tongue-tied in front of the cameras, providing much fodder for the news media. With websites and books devoted to his blunders, there are too many examples to cite here, but one that is illustrative concerns a visit to China in November 2005. After answering reporters' questions, Bush left his first press conference of the trip from the wrong side of the stage. Finding himself unable to open a set of locked double doors, despite tugging vigorously at the handles, he had to stand and smile at the world's media until an aide escorted him to the proper exit.

The exploits of such political actors often find their way into satire/comedy shows that remind the audience of the particular politician's track record. Unguarded comments made when microphones are still recording have caused severe embarrassment. Ronald Reagan's comments about bombing Russia, or John Major's description of some of his cabinet colleagues as bastards, stand out. Stage-managed events that do not go according to plan are particularly newsworthy. In 2001, Tony Blair was on the receiving end of a slow hand clap, when he chose to use his speech to the Women's Institute conference to address a television audience and not the one in the hall. The bursting of his publicity bubble received widespread attention in the media, while the speech's message was lost.

Unauthorized leaks

Perhaps of greater consequence for administrations is the unauthorized release of information into the public domain. Leaks are not a new phenomenon but, despite a raft of legislation in both countries, they continue to emerge. In the US, there have been numerous high-profile unauthorized leaks of classified documents to the media. One well-known example concerned the Pentagon Papers. These were a highly confidential 47-volume report about the progress of the Vietnam War, which was leaked to the *New York Times* in 1971 by Dan Ellsberg and Anthony Russo, officials in the Defense Department. The *New York Times* published extracts from the Papers, as did the *Washington Post*, until the Nixon White House managed to get a restraining order placed on them (for a detailed account, see Rudenstine, 1998). In the UK, there have been similar high-profile cases where leaks have severely embarrassed the government (Tant, 1995). In the 1980s civil servants Clive Ponting and Sarah Tisdall both disclosed sensitive information – Ponting on the Falklands War, and Tisdall on the movement of nuclear cruise missiles. In the Tisdall case, the

Thatcher government took legal action against the *Guardian* newspaper for publishing the information.

In an age of electronic mail and the internet, leaking of confidential material has never been easier. In Britain since 2005, there have been high-profile leaks on the government's identity card initiative, and on proposed social security and immigration policy. In fact, government leaks have become so frequent that the Blair government was thinking about creating a permanent post to investigate leaks and take the necessary action (Hencke, 2006). In the US, President Bush called in the FBI to try to halt leaks of classified information to the media (Nelson, 2002). Despite these measures, and a raft of secrecy legislation in both countries, information continues to leak. Since the invasion of Iraq there have been numerous leaks of classified documents and confidential memos on the build-up to the war, which have revealed the pessimistic prognoses of the security services on the situation in Iraq. These have caused major embarrassment for the governments in both countries. In the US, extracts from the National Intelligence Estimate – a report based on information from 16 intelligence agencies – were leaked on several occasions, greatly discomforting the Bush administration. In September 2004, leaked extracts revealed private concerns about the deteriorating security situation in Iraq. In 2006, extracts leaked to the *New York Times* suggested that Iraq had become 'a *cause celèbre* for jihadist groups'. In the UK, pessimistic security reports have also been frequently leaked, as well as sensitive documents about the legality of the Iraq war. These have regularly caused the Blair government much discomfort. For example, in 2006, a transcript of a conversation between Bush and Blair, when they discussed Iraq in detail and when Blair allegedly persuaded Bush not to bomb the Al-Jazeera news channel offices in Baghdad, was leaked to the *Daily Mirror*. Embarrassing or potentially damaging – either way, unauthorized leaks divert media attention away from the message that governments want to promote, and focus attention on government 'behind-the-scenes' activity.

Personality clashes

Turf wars between actors in an administration sometimes become public, with rival actors keen to attack each other in the media. An example from Britain concerns the power struggle between the Prime Minister and his Chancellor Gordon Brown, which has intermittently burst into public view during New Labour's time in office, with the rivals' supporters briefing against each other (Heffernan, 2004). Turf wars and spats between administration actors can generate the impression of a divided administration and undermine support.

Official investigations

Official investigations into the activities of an administration – like leaks – can also serve to focus media attention away from the message that government wishes to promote. In the US, Schudson notes, the Watergate scandal 'generated the governmental machinery for official investigation and pursuit of scandal . . . the special prosecutor's office [which would pursue Clinton with such vigour] existed in response to Watergate' (2004: 1234, 1231). Congress introduced the Ethics in Government Act in 1978, which led to the establishment of a special prosecutor – with the intention of preventing another Watergate. Tunstall observes that in 'the last two decades there has been about one new investigation launched per year' including Kenneth Starr's investigation into the Whitewater real estate affair, which produced the Starr Report (2002: 234). Another high-profile official investigation concerned the leaking of CIA agent Valerie Plame's name to a journalist – a federal offence. The Plame investigation ended in the indictment of White House personnel, most notably the Vice-President's Chief of Staff – Lewis 'Scooter' Libby – and led a key strategist in the Bush White House, Karl Rove, having to give testimony five times to the committee of inquiry – each occasion being front page news. In addition, there are a number of congressional, Senate and House committees that can conduct investigations which, if not damaging, may well prove a distraction for the White House. For example, on the Iraq War, a Congressional Committee of Inquiry and a Senate Committee on Intelligence produced a series of findings on pre-war intelligence that were widely reported and were embarrassing for the Bush administration.

In the UK, although there is nothing exactly like the Special Prosecutor's Office, in the wake of several corruption scandals a Committee on Standards in Public Life was set up to investigate alleged wrong-doings by politicians, including government ministers. Subsequently, under its Parliamentary Commissioner, the Committee has conducted a range of inquires, some of which have served as a source of negative publicity and became a source of embarrassment for the Blair government. In 2002 government minister Keith Vaz was found guilty of providing misleading information to the House of Commons about his financial interests, a story which gained wide exposure. There are also select, standing and special parliamentary committees that are able to scrutinize various aspects of government activity. The findings of several parliamentary committees on government communication, for instance, have been widely reported and posted on the internet, reinforcing the impression of the Blair government's obsession with spin (see for example, the Select Committee on Administration, Sixth Report, 1998).

In addition, governments are 'pressured' to establish committees of inquiry. For example, in the early 1990s, in the aftermath of the collapse of the trial of several businessmen charged with illegal sale of weapons to Iraq, the Scott Inquiry was set up by the Major government to investigate how much ministers knew about the unlawful sale of arms by British firms. The committee's findings were front-page news, revealing that the Major government knew more than they acknowledged about weapons sales, and proved very damaging (Negrine, 1996; Tumber, 2004). In 2004, the Butler Inquiry was set-up by the Blair government to investigate the failings of the pre-Iraq war intelligence. The findings of this Inquiry, and those of the earlier Hutton Inquiry, served to keep a potentially damaging issue in the public eye. Although not an official inquiry, an investigation was launched by police in 2006 into allegations that the government and main political parties had given honours in return for donations, in breach of the Honours (Prevention of Abuses) Act. The inquiry received widespread media attention, especially when Tony Blair and high-profile figures close to him, such as cabinet ministers and his chief fundraiser, Lord Levy, were questioned.

Often, of course, information is leaked from these investigations before the final reports are made public. For example, in the US, leaks from within the Office of the Special Council during what became the Lewinsky Affair received widespread attention in the media. Leaks from the Senate Governmental Affairs Committee provided detailed information about the campaign fundraising abuses at the White House in 1996, which saw donors being able to buy access to the President and even a stop-over in the 'Lincoln Bedroom', depending on the size of the donation to the President's campaign for re-election. These leaks made it hard for the Clinton White House to get on the front foot and push its agenda.

Scandals and scandal syndrome

Revelations generated by a committee of inquiry, official reports or journalistic investigations may sow the seeds of a full-blown financial, sexual or power abuse scandal which could bring down an administration, as Watergate brought down the Nixon administration (Thompson, 2000). Full-blown scandals typically unfold over a long period of time, with the initial disclosures and denials being followed by further allegations and further denials, all widely reported in the media, along with expressions of disapproval and often scathing personal criticism (ibid.). As a major scandal unfolds, the different actors involved are engaged in a titanic struggle to secure a confession or ensure silence. Ultimately though, it is the 'smoking gun' – the incriminating evidence – and subsequent legal proceedings, with an admission of guilt or the determining of innocence, which often decide final closure and dissipation (ibid.).

While this focus on standards of those in public life has led to the exposure of corrupt practices, which a more deferential news media may have ignored, there has also been the rise of what can be termed 'scandal syndrome' (ibid.). Whereas once only a major scandal was a newsworthy event, now every indiscretion by politicians, every breach of a code, however small, is reported as a scandal (see chapter 3). Many of these revelations are given the 'gate' suffix to add a thin veil of credibility, following 'Watergate', but most bear no resemblance to the painstaking investigation of that particular piece of presidential corruption (see Kuhn, 2002; Schudson, 2004). For example, during President Clinton's tenure, there was a series of stories about presidential impropriety given 'gate' status: 'troopergate', 'filegate' and 'donorgate'.

Scandal syndrome can be seen clearly in the example of the reporting of breaches of the ministerial code of conduct introduced by the Conservatives in the UK and enhanced by the Blair government in 1997. Jones notes:

> [O]ne of the key requirements was the importance of ministers understanding that it was *the impression which their conduct created which mattered as much as the facts*. Ministers were told to avoid accepting 'any gift of hospitality which might, or might reasonably appear to compromise their judgement or place them under an improper obligation' and to 'avoid any danger of an actual or apparent conflict of interest' between their ministerial position and their financial affairs. They were required to work within 'the letter and the spirit of the code'. (1999: 264; my emphasis)

For the opponents of the government in the press and elsewhere, every transgression or apparent transgression by government ministers of the high standards could be highlighted as evidence of misconduct, with every denial or protestation only serving to reinforce the stories' newsworthiness. While many of the transgressions actual or apparent where revealed in the Sunday press, the press pack and the broadcasters were quick to follow. There has been a catalogue of revelations in the UK since 1997. What follows are some of the highlights.

In 1998 millionaire government minister Geoffrey Robinson was found to be a beneficiary of numerous offshore trusts, which was at odds with the government's stated aim of clamping down on tax avoidance (Jones, 1999). Also in 1998 was so-called 'Mandygate', when it was revealed that Geoffrey Robinson had provided government minister Peter Mandelson with a soft loan of £373,000 to help purchase a £500,000 house in London's Notting Hill. The insinuation was that the loan would colour any findings from an ongoing investigation in

Robinson's business dealings being conducted by Mandelson's department. In 2002, press and broadcast headlines were dominated by the revelation that steel magnate and Labour Party donor Lakshmi Mittal had had his bid to buy a Romanian steel plant endorsed by Tony Blair. There was a rash of allegations concerning favours for other party donors: Paul Drayson, Richard Desmond and Duncan Bannatyne. In 2006, the Deputy Prime Minister John Prescott was accused of breaking the ministerial code when revelations surfaced in the media that he had accepted gifts from an American businessman hoping to open a casino in the UK. In sum, it is not only major scandals that can prove damaging, but also the constant revelations of various committees and journalistic investigations over a longer period of time.

Worsening relations

All governments on taking office experience an initial honeymoon period in media relations, generally marked by cooperation. As Grossman and Kumar observe in a US context, but equally applicable to the UK, 'news organizations communicate the White House line and channel the ideas and image of the President to their audiences. White House officials cooperate with reporters' objectives' (1981: 274). Over time – often quite a short time – goals begin to diverge. Regularly, after the initial honeymoon period, incumbents find the news media only too willing to report such potentially damaging events as outlined above – especially the partisan media, which add their own spin to coverage. The left-leaning *Daily Mirror* in the UK has joined the right-wing press in vociferously attacking the Blair government. In the US, talk radio was the site of some of the most hostile criticism of Bill Clinton (see chapter 5). The shared view of which stories are newsworthy dissolves in this second phase. While administrations are more interested in communicating their achievements, the news media tend to be more focused on other events. Executives despair at their inability to set the media agenda. Failure to control the agenda often leads to suspicions of journalists and their motives, doubts that can grow throughout the period in office. In the second term of the Blair administration, Downing Street began to see the journalists as a 'distorting prism', with their own agenda not complementary to that of the government. Similar sentiments could be expressed by presidential teams in the face of overtly hostile Washington press coverage (Tenpas, 2000).

There is a view, especially amongst those who have been in office a while, that the media not only distort government messages but are also out to bring the government down. For governments of the 'left' the threat is usually seen as forces of conservatism; for those of the 'right' the menace is the liberal/left-wing media establishment. In the

UK, Harold Wilson was particularly sensitive to news media criticism and compiled a list of alleged misdeeds of critical correspondents (Rose, 2001). Margaret Thatcher believed, as did Wilson and Jim Callaghan, that television news coverage was feeding her unpopularity (Cockerell, 1988). Prime ministerial paranoia has been shared by US presidents. Nixon saw himself as the victim of the anti-conservative bias of a liberal media establishment, while Clinton, several decades later, saw himself as the target of a right-wing media conspiracy. Attempts at more intensive news management build up well-documented resentment amongst journalists further exacerbating the problem (Jones, 1999; Kurtz, 1998). Once the honeymoon period ends, diverging journalist/government news interests mean journalists do not necessarily see it as their role always to reflect the administration's agenda. All too often relations break down (Kuhn, 2002; Kurtz, 1998). Paranoia and failure to control the media agenda leads to a final phase of detachment, where relations are characterized by mutual antagonism (Grossman and Kumar, 1981). During this phase, relations reach an all-time low. However, as the next section will show, administrations find new ways to get their message across.

Rebutting and bypassing the news

Administrations are always seeking new ways to deal with the challenges posed by the news media and new means of reaching audiences. Traditionally, the strategy for dealing with bad news has been publicly to denounce journalists as biased, partisan and bent on bringing down the administration, to introduce reporting restrictions or, in certain circumstances, to try to gag the media through the courts. However, this line of attack has the tendency itself to become the news, and can seem heavy-handed and prove counter-productive. Administrations now increasingly turn to rebuttal. Rebuttal – limiting the impact of negative reports – has moved from an after-thought to a central part of an administration's media management operation. The wisdom is that governments need continually to respond to potentially damaging events and persistently to fend off critics and attack opponents. The response to potentially harmful reports needs to be quick, 'closing them down' before they develop into damaging stories. Administrations often find themselves refuting accusations, denying rumours or off-the-cuff comments by ministers or aides. Incumbents, forced to respond to a damaging event such as a major scandal, will employ such a strategy in order to close down negative news and minimize harm. Of course, such rebuttal will include a fair amount of threats, bullying and arm-twisting of journalists.

In the US, President Reagan's team developed a strategy to deal with misconceptions about him and his policies generated in the news media: all factual errors were challenged by the team, and offending journalists were issued with a fact sheet (Han, 2001). The Clinton White House had a dual rebuttal operation. The first was the so-called 'scandal squad' based in the Counsel's Office. Any journalists who asked about the Whitewater land deal, the Paula Jones case, Lewinsky or White House fundraising were automatically referred to the Counsel's Office. In addition, a 'political response team' was developed to respond to or neutralize negative issues before they developed into damaging stories (Kumar, 2001a). In Britain, the Blair government created a media-monitoring unit to scrutinize the news media on a 24-hour basis, providing warnings to departments of breaking negative news, and allowing them time to respond. Alastair Campbell instructed press officers: 'If a story is going wrong, or if a policy should be defended, we must respond quickly, confidently and robustly' (*The Times*, 2 October 1997; cited in Heffernan and Stanyer, 1998).

Live and direct

While responding to negative news, administrations still need to get their message across. As journalistic relations worsen, information subsidies on their own are no longer effective enough to break through the media gates and reach the public (Cook, 1998). Once the honeymoon ends, administrations continually search for new ways to get their message across. The White House is always looking 'for opportunities to reach out to the grass roots, over the heads of Washington or New York media' (B. H. Patterson, 2000: 148). Briefing the news media continues, but administrations also increasingly seek to promote their message direct to the public through other outlets.

Going over journalists' heads is not exactly a new process: Franklin D. Roosevelt was quick to harness radio to reach the electorate, bypassing the anti-New Deal press, with his fireside chats and regular radio broadcasts. In the US in the 1950s, the President's press secretary saw this opportunity in the growing presence of television to bypass the press and talk directly to the public (Grossman and Kumar, 1981). Kennedy saw the advantages of harnessing television to reach the public with his message (Tebbel and Watts, 1985). For Nixon, it was a need to bypass what he saw as the liberal media. Of recent presidents, Clinton, in particular, has been keen to use 'alternative outlets' to get his administration's message across (Diamond and Silverman, 1997; Han, 2001; Kurtz, 1998).

There is a range of non-news outlets to which all US presidents have access. There are key televised events, such as the State of the Union

Address, which are broadcast live nationally and provide an opportunity for the President to communicate key policy issues. George W. Bush made a dozen 'state of the union'-like addresses over the 20-month period between September 2001 and May 2003 (Domke, 2004). In Britain, the Prime Minister can use slots such as his party conference speech and other formal occasions for a similar purpose. There are also opportunities for the executive to use guaranteed slots in the media schedules, and some of these have been used regularly. In the US, Reagan inaugurated a weekly radio address from the Oval Office, a trend continued by his successors. Reagan, Clinton and Bush senior and junior have regularly used the weekly presidential address on national public radio to get key messages across.

In Britain, successive prime ministers have sought new ways to reach the public, bypassing a news media perceived by governments as increasingly hostile. For instance, Margaret Thatcher's adviser, Gordon Reece, was always searching for 'less confrontational outlets to showcase the Prime Minister' (Cockerell, 1988: 288). During his tenure as the government's Director of Strategy and Communication, Alastair Campbell revealed a similar drive. He introduced a series of changes which made visible behind the scenes media briefing activities in an unprecedented way: their aim, to circumvent the distorting prism of the press and allow government ministers to communicate to the public directly. In 2002, Downing Street decided to introduce regular formal televised briefings, in which the Prime Minister, or government ministers, along with experts and advisers, could be questioned on the record by a wide range of journalists, including correspondents of foreign news outlets, and not just political reporters.

Further, Tony Blair, Bill Clinton and George W. Bush all utilized the internet to get their messages directly to the public. In the US, Clinton launched the White House website, which included back copies of presidential speeches, press briefings and a virtual tour of the White House. In addition, there are also presidential webcasts (B. H. Patterson, 2000). In Britain, Downing Street launched its website in early 2000. It had a start-up budget of £133,000 and a staff of three. The site included a news section, outlining the main government initiatives, a chat room where visitors can post messages, photos of inside Downing Street and stored video recordings of Prime Minister's Question Time in the House of Commons. There has also been an additional weekly webcast by Tony Blair, spelling out government policy, accessible from the site.

From chat show sofa to soap operas

Although, with the growth of media outlets, the above channels provide a means of direct access, such addresses fail to command the large audiences they once did (Wattenberg, 2004). The majority of the public will at most see the edited highlights of such speeches. Administrations are always looking for new outlets through which to bypass the news-value criteria of the national news media, and communicate to different sections of the population.

Drawing on lessons from campaigning, administrations increasingly target specialist and popular media outlets. There are political magazine TV programmes such as *Meet the Press* in the US, or *AM* on Sundays in Britain. Talk shows provide another well-used outlet (see chapter 5). Output from these shows is regularly picked up and screened on other outlets (Jones, 1995). More imaginative promotional techniques have also been regularly used. For instance, Clinton's team, as part of the effort to sell his health care reform plans in the early 1990s, targeted talk radio. In all, 200 hosts were briefed, and 50 invited to air their shows from the White House front lawn, where they could access key staff to talk about health care (Diamond and Silverman, 1997).

Perhaps one of the more innovative ways to sell government policies and initiatives to specific audiences has been through soap operas. Various administrations have tried to persuade the writers of soap operas to include government-initiated issues in the plot lines. In 1997, the US Congress approved a $2 billion anti-drugs television advertising campaign. The Clinton government tried to strike a deal with the television networks whereby they would provide a free advertising slot for every slot paid for by the government. However, the networks were not keen, because of the dot.com advertising boom, and the deal fell through. In response, the government offered the networks an alternative: the proposed money would be unchanged if they were to rewrite parts of popular television series, such as *ER* and *Beverly Hills 90210*, to include the government anti-drugs message. The networks accepted the deal, which, had they rejected, would probably have cost them $25 million in lost advertising revenue. One government official explained the editorial process as thus: 'they ran the scripts past us and we gave comments' (Sullivan, 2000: 11).

In Britain, the Blair government approached the main producers of television and radio soaps to encourage the insertion of storylines related to the latest government policies and to explain how new government initiatives would effect certain characters. A change in government policy often finds its way into a storyline. For instance, government policy on absent fathers and child maintenance payments found its way into a storyline on *East Enders*. The government's new hard-line strategy on benefit fraud featured in *Coronation Street*. Similarly, the government was keen to ensure that its initiatives for the over-75s, such as free television licenses and the winter fuel allowance, were reflected in the lives of some of the main soaps' more elderly characters – such as Joe Grundy from *The Archers*, Dot Cotton from *East Enders* and Vera Duckworth from *Coronation Street*. A government spokesperson observed: '[I]t's a perfectly good storyline for them. We're not expecting Joe Grundy to say "Thanks to the Wonderful Tony Blair I've got more money." They could write it in a way that informs the listeners, who might be in a position like Joe Grundy' (McSmith, 2000: 4).

The rise of 'process coverage'

Paradoxically, one outcome of the obsession with finding more effective means of promotion has been that promotional strategies have become the story. Whereas once, McNair observes, 'the persuasive-manipulative techniques to which citizens were subjected, remained hidden from all but the journalistic and political elites themselves' now 'coverage of political process is an important part of an expanded public sphere' (2000: 50). Attempts by politicians and spin doctors to manage the media and the strategies they use have become a newsworthy issue. 'Spin' has entered the English language and, like 'spin doctor', has become a word formula used in a variety of contexts to mean anything from presentation to lying.

Esser et al. (2001) have documented the transformation of the news coverage of politics from a focus on issues to a focus on media manipulation. They argue that the 1988 US presidential election marks a watershed in news coverage, with the emergence of what they term 'metacoverage' – 'the self-referential reflections on the nature of the interplay between political public relations and political journalism' (2001: 17; see also Gitlin, 1991). The particular type of metacoverage relevant here is what Esser et al. term 'process news'. This is news about 'backstage manoeuvres of campaign operatives to guide or influence journalists' (2001: 19). Esser et al.'s research reveals that US newspapers covered more than 1,341 spin doctor activities during the 1996 campaign and the British press covered 874 in 1997 (ibid.: 33). In the US 47 per cent and the UK 42 per cent of all spin doctor stories referred to their interaction with journalists (ibid.: 34). 'Process coverage' is not confined to the election periods but is also characteristic of much coverage of politics; news about 'backstage manoeuvres of campaign operatives to guide or influence journalists' is substituted for news about the backstage moves of government spin doctors to shape news media output. Political news coverage of government has been dominated by stories about spin and spin doctors, as chapter 3 shows (see also Kuhn, 2002).

Selling the removal of Saddam and support for the invasion of Iraq

This brief case study aims to illustrate some of the key issues outlined in the chapter so far. It examines the efforts of the Bush and Blair administrations to build public support for the invasion of Iraq. It also shows that, despite their sophisticated media management apparatus, both administrations have had major difficulties maintaining public backing in light of almost continuous 'bad' news. In 2002–3, both administrations used a variety of the promotional techniques to try and persuade the public of the need to invade Iraq. Ten months or so before the conflict, the Bush team developed its public relations offensive in liaison with Downing Street (Domke, 2004; Miller, 2004). The aim of the White House and Downing Street offensive was to reinforce the impression that Saddam posed an imminent threat to world security. In the US, the Bush team built the case for war through a series of carefully planned speeches by the President and administration actors, in rounds of follow-up interviews and through behind-the-scenes press briefings (Domke, 2004; Fritz et al., 2004). During these events, the Bush administration selectively disclosed intelligence agency findings to justify the need to invade Iraq. This intelligence, the administration argued, showed, first, that Saddam possessed weapons of mass destruction and was a threat to world security; and, secondly, that the regime had links to terrorist groups, such as Al-Qaeda, and that it intended to transfer weapons capability to such groups. A further argument was that Saddam was a brutal dictator and Iraq needed to be liberated from tyranny (Fritz et al., 2004; Rampton and Stauber, 2003; Rutherford, 2004). For example, Bush went directly to the public in a series of televised presidential speeches between 2002 and 2003. In these speeches, he warned that Saddam was developing nuclear weapons, had attempted to purchase uranium and had chemical and biological weapons such as anthrax (Rampton and Stauber, 2003). These messages were reinforced in a myriad of television interviews with leading White House actors. In addition, the Defense Secretary, the Secretary of State and the Vice-President, in a series of speeches and interviews, made the case for Iraq's Al-Qaeda connection (Fritz et al., 2004; Rampton and Stauber, 2003).

In Britain, Tony Blair and his government engaged in a similar public relations offensive to try to persuade the public of the need to rid Iraq of weapons of mass destruction by force, rather than give the UN inspectors any more time to find them. As in the US, a key element in this campaign of persuasion was intelligence information, which was used to reinforce the argument that Saddam's weapons of mass destruction represented a 'clear and present danger' to Britain – including the now infamous claim that they could be launched in 45 minutes. Blair set up a cross-departmental committee, chaired by Alastair Campbell, to decide on the best way to promote intelligence on Iraq (Miller, 2004). The information was published in two dossiers and posted on the web to make the case for an invasion all the more compelling. Blair argued that Saddam had concealed his weapons of mass destruction and the UN weapons inspectors could not find them, so the only option was to remove them by force. The US and UK promotional offensives were meticulously coordinated. The 'line of the day' was carefully decided through a daily 'conference call' between Campbell and the White House communications team (Miller, 2004). The stance to take was then relayed on to the government information officers via email (ibid.).

The Prime Minister and ministers took their arguments to the country, engaging in a round of television and radio interviews. Blair, in cooperation with ITN, also participated in a special edition of the evening news, where he made the case for armed intervention to a group of voters sceptical of the need for force. In an effort to get his argument across to a wider audience, news interviews were combined with the targeting of non-news and current affairs outlets. For instance, at the beginning of March 2003, Blair appeared on an hour-long show on MTV to discuss Iraq with a group of young people from Europe and the Middle East.

However, the evidence of the pre-war promotional offensive did not go unchallenged (Stanyer, 2004; McNair, 2006). Opponents of the invasion, inside and outside government, were given a wide airing in the media. In the UK, Downing Street was confronted not only by antagonists on their backbenches but also by a well-organised and media-aware 'stop the war' coalition, which planned a series of high-profile demonstrations. The demonstration in London in February 2003 attracted an estimated million protestors. The anti-war campaign was boosted when so-called intelligence material in the second government dossier was found to have been plagiarized from a PhD thesis. In the US, an anti-war movement mobilized against the invasion, and there were numerous rallies, marches and 'die-ins' (see Sinderbrand, 2003). The pressure group MoveOn.org generated a petition against the war, and joined together with other anti-war groups under the banner 'Win Without War' (Rutherford, 2004). The group placed a series of adverts in the press and on television, including a reworking of the 1964 Daisy Girl campaign advert, which was widely covered on news outlets (Rutherford, 2004).

Almost before the 'fog of war' had cleared, there were a series of revelations about the pre-war intelligence and the promotion of the case for an invasion. The main accusation on both sides of the Atlantic was that both administrations had embellished intelligence material, 'sexed it up' to make the case for removing Saddam more convincing. The leak of information to the media from inside both administrations started to shed light on the behind-the-scenes promotional strategy. For example, in the UK on 29 May 2003, a report by BBC Radio Four's *Today* programme's defence correspondent, Andrew Gilligan, carried an allegation that Downing Street had embroidered intelligence in a dossier about Saddam's weapons of mass destruction, released in September 2002, to make the need for invasion more compelling, inserting, against the wishes of the intelligence services, the claim that Saddam had the ability to launch weapons of mass destruction in 45 minutes. The row that erupted between the government and the BBC following these allegations led to the naming and the suicide of the source, a civil servant and former weapons inspector in Iraq, Dr Kelly (Stanyer, 2004).

The criticism of both administrations was further fuelled by failure to find weapons of mass destruction or weapons programmes, or to find any connections to Al-Qaeda, as well as by question-marks over the legality of the invasion under international law. These failures led to a series of investigations. In the US, there have been various committees of inquiry. For example, a Senate Committee on Intelligence report, released in 2006, concluded that there was no evidence to support one of the main White House arguments that Saddam Hussein had links to Al-Qaeda. In the UK, the Prime Minister agreed to the setting-up of a judicial inquiry into the events surrounding Dr Kelly's death. Overseen by Lord Hutton, the inquiry started in August 2003. It heard 25 days of evidence from more than 30 sources, including the Prime Minster, Alastair Campbell, the Defence Minister, Dr Kelly's widow, the Chairman and Director-General of the BBC, civil servants and journalists. Although television cameras were not allowed in court, the witness testimony and documentary evidence was made public on the Inquiry website. On the day of Alastair Campbell's appearance, the site received 16,778 hits and 300,000 page views (Stanyer, 2004). This was followed by the Butler Inquiry into the pre-war intelligence on Iraq. The inquiries attracted a vast amount of media coverage and further stinging criticism of the actions of both governments. Attempts by Bush and Blair to get on the front foot in the aftermath of the invasion and maintain public support have also been undermined by a string of incidents in Iraq itself, such as the release of photographs of prisoner abuse, allegations of war crimes by coalition forces and the rising death toll of coalition troops. The impact on public support can be clearly seen in opinion polls conducted in the US and the UK.

A series of polls in the US and the UK asked members of the public if their government's decision to invade Iraq was right. Tables 2.1 and 2.2 show that both governments were successful in persuading the public of the need to invade Iraq in 2003, with a majority thinking the governments had made the right decision. However, both administrations have subsequently been singularly unsuccessful in maintaining

Table 2.1 Do you think the US made the right decision or the wrong decision in using military force against Iraq?

	Right Decision	Wrong Decision	Unsure
March 2003	74%	21%	5%
March 2004	55%	39%	6%
February 2005	47%	47%	6%
March 2006	45%	49%	6%

Source: Compiled from Princeton Survey Research Associates for Pew Research Center data retrieved

Table 2.2 Do you think the US and Britain were right or wrong to take military action against Iraq?

	Right	Wrong
March 2003	59%	35%
February 2004	49%	42%
April 2005	31%	54%
February 2006[a]	24%	64%

[a] Populus question was: 'Thinking about the build-up to the war in Iraq and everything that has happened since, was taking military action the right thing to do, or the wrong thing to do?'

Source: Compiled from YouGov and Populus data retrieved from UKpollingreport. 'Don't knows' excluded.

Table 2.3 Do you think the US should keep military troops in Iraq until the situation has stabilized, or do you think the US should bring its troops home as soon as possible?

	Keep troops	Bring home	Unsure
October 2004	57%	36%	7%
June 2005	50%	46%	4%
March 2006	44%	50%	6%

Source: Compiled from Princeton Survey Research Associates for Pew Research Center data retrieved from Pollingreport.com.

support for a major part of their foreign policy. The tables show public support for military action has steadily declined in both countries, despite both governments attempts to go on a PR-offensive. What is more, public opinion has turned against their policy of 'staying to finish the job'.

Tables 2.3 and 2.4 show that a majority of the American and British public in 2004 favoured troops staying in Iraq until the objectives had been achieved in line with Bush's and Blair's policy, but by 2006, a majority favoured a withdrawal of troops regardless of whether it had become a stable democracy. The results of the 2006 US mid-term

Table 2.4 Do you think that British troops should stay in Iraq for as long as it takes to make sure that Iraq is a stable democracy or do you think that British troops should be withdrawn from Iraq as soon as possible?

	Stay	Withdraw
October 2004	49%	42%
February 2005	24%	66%
February 2006	38%	62%

Source: Compiled from Populus data retrieved from UKpollingreport. 'Don't knows' excluded.

elections, which saw the Democrats take control of both houses of Congress in a backlash against Iraq, reinforces this evidence.

This case study shows that both governments were able to build a case for an invasion, persuading a majority of the public in each country, but that they have subsequently been unable to maintain backing in the face of an uncontrollable flow of damaging revelations on Iraq. Indeed, the backstage manoeuvres of administration personnel, and their manipulation of evidence and news media output, has become one of the most prominent news themes for the whole period (2003–6). Attempts by both administrations to justify their decisions, defend their actions and acclaim their achievements in Iraq have been dismissed as spin by a news media jaded, if not cynical, of their motivations and strategies, with attempts at rebuttal covered as more evidence of regime spin. In the face of continuous leaks, criticism from within his own party, a hostile press pack, low poll ratings and electoral meltdown, President Bush seems to have had few alternatives left but to change tack. He has responded by signalling a shift in management style if not policy direction. In a live television event on the day after the 2006 mid-term elections, he 'symbolically replaced' his Defense Secretary Donald Rumsfeld with Robert Gates – a so-called 'policy realist'. In the UK, the Blair government has also been keen to indicate a shift in direction, with government ministers talking publicly of timetables for withdrawal. However, all this said, it seems unlikely that Iraq will bring an end to the dominance of the 'promotional logic' in government; new administrations will employ similar strategies. The continuation of this logic can perhaps be seen as evidence of just how pervasive this group-think has become.

Conclusion

This chapter has shown that consecutive administrations, once elected, have increasingly seen effective promotion as key to maintaining and building public support, the received wisdom being, 'if you can maintain public support for a course of action, the chances of being re-elected are so much higher'. Indeed, successive administrations have tried to make communication more effective in a variety of ways when old have methods failed.

The re-election imperative, set against an increasingly uncertain and visible public opinion environment, drives administrations continually to innovate and find new ways of reaching the electorate. We have seen how administrations have adjusted to declining public support and hostile news coverage by communicating more directly with the public and by keeping in touch with voter opinion through market research. However, such adaptation takes place in a communication and political environment that is growing in complexity and providing ever more challenges for incumbents.

The invasion and occupation of Iraq has exposed some of the limits of this promotional logic: it cannot make an unpopular war popular. Iraq is not just the exception though, as Han observes in her study of eight post-war presidents, nearly all of whom were restricted to some extent in 'their capacity to control both the image and the message of the their administrations' (2001: 247). A similar observation could be made of UK prime ministers – the longer they are in office, the less popular they become. Despite this, promotional group-think persists, driven in part by a strategic community and political leaders desperate to maintain public support once elected – Iraq and other failures have not brought this approach to governing to an end. However, one noticeable consequence is that promotional strategy and those who promote policy have themselves become the story – an issue that will be explored further in the next chapter.

CHAPTER
03

Personalized Politics and the Erosion of Privacy

Leading politicians, along with sports, film and television stars, have become a familiar part of the public's daily media consumption. Their lives and personalities, competencies and abilities, are the subject of widespread discussion and speculation. Presidents, prime ministers and ministers have joined the growing class of celebrities. They are regular media performers and as such become well known and are immediately recognizable to the public. Their visibility in a media-saturated environment, and their consequent familiarity, is a key feature of contemporary political communication systems. However, it is not just leading political actors who have been rendered visible, but also a growing band of advisers and family members connected to them.

The arrival of the electronic media in particular has provided the public with a regular flow of images of these main political actors, as well as information. Leading politicians in the US and Britain have not only become recognizable performers but also 'intimate' strangers: over the twentieth century, their private lives have slowly come to be considered the acceptable subject of journalistic revelation and self-disclosure. The private lives of leading politicians have never been so visible to citizen audiences.

This chapter documents these trends on both sides of the Atlantic. It explores the rise of the recognizable and intimate political celebrity (Schickel, 2000), arguing that these trends are being driven by a twin process of self-disclosure and media exposure.

The rise of the recognizable politician

The media have transformed the visibility of leading political actors. In the pre-media age, visibility of leaders was linked 'to the sharing of a common locale' with the public. It was limited to those physically present at a meeting or rally (Thompson, 1995: 125). The emergence of the media, first print and then electronic, transformed the sense of 'public' in late modern democracies (ibid.). Gamson notes, for instance, that a consequence of the inclusion of photographs in the press in the late nineteenth century was a 'dissemination of the face' (in Turner, 2004: 10). Through the photograph, political actors, for the first time, were visible 'independent of their capacity to be seen . . . directly by a plurality of co-present individuals' (Thompson, 1995: 126). The link between visibility and physical presence had been broken.

It is, though, the arrival of the electronic media that fundamentally transformed the visibility of leading political actors. Through radio and television, political actors could be seen and heard by members of the public even though they weren't actually physically present. Thompson (1995) observes that television in particular creates a new form of 'publicness' that is similar to traditional co-presence. Indeed, Schickel, in his study of the rise of celebrity culture, observes that '[television] is the primary force in breaking down the barriers that formerly existed between the well-known and the unknown' (2000: 9–10). This is because, he argues, of 'the way it brings famous folk into our living rooms in psychically manageable size. We see them not from the alienating distance of the stage, which is where we were forced to view them in the pre-electronic age' (ibid.). Through television, citizens could witness a political event, or watch politicians speaking thousands of miles away, in a variety of settings. It could be argued that leading politicians gained the status of celebrities (Evans, 2005; Street, 2003; West and Orman, 2003). Those in prominent public roles became familiar to a mass audience of non co-present citizens, as, also, did the settings of Capitol Hill and Westminster. Audiences could recognize the faces and the places just as they would recognize the people and locations in their neighbourhood. Newer outlets, such as the internet, have added to the process.

However, it is not only political leaders who have achieved a mediated public presence; over the twentieth century a wide spectrum of political actors became familiar to an audience of non co-present voters (Street, 2004; West and Orman, 2003). This list of recognizable actors includes those who have traditionally existed away from the public eye, such as spouses of leading politicians, their families and their media managers. Indeed, while the use of media managers by parties and politicians has been well documented, their visibility as a profession and as individuals has also grown. Key actors in politicians' private lives have, over time, been drawn into the mediated front regions of politics – their families, for instance, are now a key part of their public profile. As the visibility of elected politicians, especially those in leading positions, has already been documented in detail elsewhere (see Street,

2004; Thompson, 1995; 2000; West and Orman, 2003), this chapter focuses on those who find themselves in the limelight by virtue of their connection to leading politicians.

Visibility of the political leader's family

Over the course of the twentieth century, the visibility of the First Lady – the US President's wife – has grown. For most of the early part of the century, the First Lady was recognizable only from official photographs. Florence Harding was the first to assume a limited public role in the 1920s, appearing with her husband during official photo opportunities, and this trend continued with Grace Coolidge, who, in addition, made frequent appearances in women's fashion magazines (Ponder, 1999). Eleanor Roosevelt was the first to attain a media presence independent of her husband, but it was not until the advent of television and Jacqueline Kennedy – the first First Lady of the television age – that the President's wife obtained widespread visibility (Schroeder, 2004). Although many of the subsequent First Ladies have not attained Jacqueline Kennedy's high profile, they have all been more visible than their early and mid-twentieth-century predecessors. For instance, Nancy Reagan made regular media appearances, even starring in an episode of the sitcom *Different Strokes* (West and Orman, 2003). Hillary Clinton obtained particular media prominence (Winfield, 1997). According to one estimate, over a three-month period early in the Clinton presidency, she received more coverage than Vice-President Al Gore. She appeared for a total of 52 minutes on three network evening news bulletins, compared to Gore's 4 minutes (Diamond and Silverman, 1997). Laura Bush has maintained a high public profile, gaining widespread media coverage in a variety of roles. The position of First Lady now has a paid personal staff of 20, including two speech writers, and press officers (B. H. Patterson, 2000).

In the UK, the Prime Minister's spouse has also taken on an increasingly public role, especially since the 1990s. For most of the twentieth century, the Prime Minister's spouse remained firmly behind the scenes. Seymour-Ure (2003) notes that Mary Wilson and Dennis Thatcher, both of whom were satirized in columns of *Private Eye* magazine, are perhaps the main exceptions. Cherie Blair is arguably the most prominent spouse to date, her role being likened to that of the US First Lady. A search of the online BBC programme archive revealed that she made 811 appearances on BBC outlets, the vast majority since moving to Downing Street, substantially more than Norma Major's 448 or Audrey Callaghan's 66. Cherie Blair is the first Prime Minister's wife to have four assistants working for her, including a press secretary (Seymour-Ure, 2003).

Leading politicians' children have also assumed greater visibility in the media. They are now an integral part of a politician's public persona. The birth of a baby has become a public event, with baby and parents paraded in front of the cameras. The family holiday, whether it is on a Texan ranch or in a Tuscan villa, is treated as a further photo opportunity. Events in the lives of other family members have also become public: even siblings of Presidents and Prime Ministers have been known to receive wide coverage. For example, President Jimmy Carter's brother, Billy, was subject to seven times as many stories as the SALT II talks with the Soviet Union (T. E. Patterson, 2000).

Visibility of appointed political actors

All organizations engaged in public communication, especially political organizations, are staffed by unelected actors, appointed and charged with carrying out a support role. As the front regions of political institutions have become increasingly mediated, unelected actors involved in briefing the media have become much more visible to the voters. In addition, those who have traditionally played no formal front-region role – political and policy advisers, the pollster and consultants – have also become increasingly visible. Contemporary party politics is characterized not only by the well-documented rise of electoral professionals within political organizations, but also by their increased visibility.

Today, in both countries, these behind-the-scenes actors are not only covered in the news media but also appear in documentaries, films, magazines and books: their visibility is a key feature of contemporary mediated political communication (Diamond and Silverman, 1997; Kerbel, 1999). These actors, who previously tended to be anonymous, at least while in office, have become familiar to the public – in certain cases, even household names. For instance, take two roles in political organizations that we hear more and more about: the media manager and the campaign strategist. Mike McCurry, Ari Fleischer, Alastair Campbell and Bernard Ingham are all examples of media managers who have been the subject of intense media coverage and of books and documentaries, and have assumed a public visibility in a way that earlier media managers did not: for example, Stephen T. Early and James Hagerty in the US, and Francis Williams, William Clark and Alfred Richardson in the UK. Similarly, advisers and strategists, who form a strategic community around the President or Prime Minister, have been the subject of intense media coverage. Tim Bell, James Carville, Michael Deaver, David Gergen, Phillip Gould, Peter Mandelson, Dick Morris, Mark Penn, Gordon Reece, Karl Rove and George Stephanopoulos all achieved a prominence that pollsters and strategists of a previous generation, such as Albert Lasker, Warren Harding's chief of advertising, or Hadley Cantril, Roosevelt's pollster, or Patrick Cadell, Carter's pollster, never did. Kerbel (1999) gives an example of the attention heaped on James Carville and George Stephanopoulos in 1992, when both received a feature spread in *People Weekly* magazine: the *New Yorker* magazine did a biographical article on Carville and *Time* a feature on Stephanopoulos. In the British context, research shows that those in the strategic community around Blair since 1994 attracted a particularly large amount of media attention. Data on news coverage of the 1997 campaign showed that 58 per cent of all mention of spin doctors referred to these key actors (Esser et al., 2001).

It is not only the media managers, pollsters and strategists close to the President and the Prime Minister who receive the level of attention that their predecessors did not, but also the media aides to candidates, leading government ministers and party leaders. In a UK context, the media aides of leading government ministers have been subject to widespread media exposure, most notably Charlie Whelan and Jo Moore, but more recently, in 2005, the arrival of the Australian Lynton Crosby at the Conservative central office. In 2006, David Cameron's media guru, Steve Hilton, was the subject of media attention.

One could argue that, in certain cases, these actors have become political celebrities. Alastair Campbell is a clear example of the celebrity media manager. When Prime Minister Attlee's press secretary, Francis Williams, retired in 1947, it was not national news, no one wrote a book on him. Compare this to Alastair Campbell, whose resignation was front-page news in all the national media and who was also the subject of Peter Oborne's biography (Seymour-Ure, 2003). Indeed, in 1998 Alastair Campbell attracted more references in the national press than 29 cabinet ministers combined, including Stephen Byers, Alan Milburn, Clare Short and Margaret Beckett (Foley, 2000). George Stephanopoulos in the US achieved a similar level of attention, publishing a book and then hosting a show on ABC: *This week with George Stephanopoulos*.

But it is not just individual high-profile unelected political actors who are now recognizable in a way once reserved for leading politicians. As a group, the unelected actors, especially media managers and campaign strategists, have attained an unprecedented level of visibility. Through the news media, they have been introduced to the public as spin doctors, a whole new class of actor who populates the back regions of political organizations. The impression created is that behind the scenes in all political parties and governments is an army of spin doctors, and behind every candidate, a growing team of hired campaign consultants. Esser et al.'s research of six months of news coverage in broadsheet papers before the 1996 US presidential election revealed 464 articles on the campaign, with 647 references to spin doctors (2001: 29). In Britain, research over the same period, before the 1997 UK general election, revealed 444 articles and 527 references to spin doctors (ibid.). Indeed, McNair observes that one of the main frameworks for reporting the first Blair government was the 'ascendancy of the spin doctors' (2000: 55). The antics of these back-region actors have come to dominate the headlines of the British news media. One example concerns Jo Moore, the hapless adviser to a former government minister, who, an hour after the terrorist attacks of 11 September 2001, cynically suggested that this would be 'a very good day to get out anything we want to bury'. The row that erupted when the email was leaked to the media forced the government to try and diffuse ensuing critical coverage of the incident by reprimanding Moore and forcing her to issue a public apology (Wheeler, 2004). In February of the following year, further leaks emerged that revealed that Moore had emailed civil servants, suggesting that Princess Margaret's funeral would be a good day to 'bury bad news' about the railways. The subsequent furore over who leaked the email, and the public feud between Moore and senior civil servant Martin Sixsmith, was picked up by other news outlets and developed into one of the biggest stories of the year (Stanyer, 2003).

While the rise of 'process news' is clearly an important factor in understanding the visibility of behind-the-scenes activity in government and other political organizations, the exposure is not limited to news coverage but also includes current affairs documentaries, feature articles and books. Indeed, there has been a massive growth in the publication of insider accounts since perhaps the first, most well-known, accounts of campaigns in the 1960s. Theodor White's *The Making of the Presidency* (1960), McGinniss's book on Nixon's 1968 presidential campaign – *The Selling of the President 1968* – and Crouse's study of press packs' coverage of the 1972 presidential campaign, *The Boys on the Bus*, mark the beginning of a genre of behind-the-scenes disclosures. Today, Howard Kurtz's *Spin Cycle: Inside the Clinton Propaganda Machine* and Ben Fritz et al.'s *All the President's Spin: George W. Bush, the Media and the Truth* represent a very small sample of what is a large body of literature. In Britain, one of the most prolific writers on media managers has been Nicholas Jones, who published five books on the subject within an eight-year period. With titles such as *Soundbites and Spin Doctors: How Politicians Manipulate the Media and Vice Versa* and *Control Freaks*, they have raised the public profile of these actors. The behind-the-scenes activities of spin doctors is a theme picked up by other authors – for instance, Peter Stothard's *Thirty Days: A Month at the Heart of Blair's War*, and Lance Price's *The Spin Doctor's Diary*. As some of the subtitles show, these books claim to reveal what 'really goes on' behind the well-managed front regions of politics.

In addition to the books, there have been numerous documentaries. In the UK, several programmes were produced by *Panorama* about New Labour's media operation. In 1996 an entire programme was devoted to the spin doctors of the main parties. In 1997 there was a fly-on-the-wall documentary, *We are the Treasury*, which featured Gordon Brown's spin doctor at the time, Charlie Whelan (McNair, 2000). Documentary-maker Michael Cockerell has gained unprecedented access behind the scenes in Downing Street, producing, since 2001, programmes such as: *The Rivals, Cabinet Confidential, Hotline to the President, Road to War: The Inside Story, The Downing Street Patient, Do You Still Believe in Tony?* In the US, documentaries have included *Bush's Brain*, about George W. Bush's strategist Karl Rove, and *Diary of a Political Tourist*, a chronicle of the Kerry campaign screened on HBO. Websites have been developed, such as spinsanity.com in the US, with the aim of exposing the manipulation of the media by politicians. To these can be added the dramatized accounts of back-region activity that seeks to fill in the gaps in the factual record. These can be one-off dramatized 'factional' accounts of real events, such as *Primary Colors* in the US or *The Project* and *The Government Inspector* in the UK, or can be purely fictional, such as TV series like *The West Wing* in the US or *The Thick of It* in the UK.

It would be misleading to assume that the growing visibility of back-region actors and activity was solely the result of unwanted exposure. Politicians and their spin doctors have often been only too happy to grant the media access to, or to reveal to the outside world, the inner workings of party or government media operations. Although a lot of what is written or screened on back-region activity is produced without the cooperation of media managers and politicians, much is initiated by them, or produced with their cooperation. Back-region activity is revealed in the autobiographies of politicians and via documentaries. *The War Room* and *News from Number Ten* are examples of two documentaries where there was an extensive level of cooperation. In the US, D. A. Pennebaker and Chris Hegedus's *The War Room* focused on two campaign strategists behind Clinton's 1992 victory: George Stephanopoulos and James Carville. Screened in 1993, the film offered an insider's account of the Clinton campaign, from the first primary through to the November election; even so, the final 96-minute film was carefully controlled by the campaign team (Hayden, 2002; Parry-Giles and Parry Giles, 2002). In the UK, perhaps the most well-known film produced with the aid of Alastair Campbell was Michael Cockerell's *News from Number Ten*. Screened in 2000, the documentary followed Alastair Campbell, then Tony Blair's press secretary, as he went about his daily activities. It provided unprecedented insight into the activities of the government's media operation, including the informal relationship between Campbell and Blair.

The political actors appointed, employed and charged with carrying out a support role in political organizations and their activities have been rendered visible to the public in a way that would have been unimaginable even as recently as the 1970s. It could be argued that media coverage of conventional politics in the US and UK is characterized as much by the management of mediated visibility as the visibility of media management.

Intimate politicians

The familiarity of strangers – unknown others – and the rise of mediated visibility are interconnected. As mentioned, until the emergence of photography, leading politicians were largely unrecognizable to all but those who knew them. However, the image has been accompanied by increasingly personal information. Over time, citizens, through expanding media outlets, have been provided with detailed information about the persona of leading political actors. An important point needs to be made: not only has the rise of electronic media rendered various political actors visible – leading to their growing familiarity – but it has also led to a more intimate relationship between prominent political actors and the citizen. A distinction can be drawn between familiarity and intimacy. The familiar can be seen as the recognizable, but intimacy is more than this. The root of the word derives from the Latin, *intimus*, meaning 'inmost' or 'innermost' (Tomlinson, 1999). The public today are provided with increasingly explicitly personal information about a wide variety of 'political celebrities' that in the past would have been limited to those who personally knew them.

However, the dissemination of this personal information in the media 'produces a new kind of intimacy' (Thompson, 1995: 207), which is different from the intimacy between social actors who know each other. That form of intimacy is essentially reciprocal. With the growth of the media, individuals could, for the first time, 'establish a form of intimacy that [was] essentially non-reciprocal' and one which stretches across time and space (ibid.: 208). As Schickel observes, in relation to celebrities in general, 'thanks to television and the rest of the media we know [celebrities]. To a greater or lesser degree we have internalized them, unconsciously made them a part of our consciousness, just as if they were, in fact, friends' (2000: 4; see also Seaton, 2003).

Although not friends, the relationship between leading politicians and public has become intimate, but based on non-reciprocal intimacy (Thompson, 1995). Citizens not only recognize the image of leading politicians whom they have never met personally, but also know much about their personal life, thanks to the disclosure of information about those politicians in the media. In the past, this information was traditionally about their activities or intentions in parliament, or their role as political leader, information largely confined, in other words, to their public persona (Corner, 2003). However, in the latter part of the twentieth century, this non-reciprocal relationship became more intimate, fed by the flow of information from personal back regions into the media (Thompson, 2000).

Let us turn briefly to the distinction between front and back regions. If front regions are the mediated stages on which the performance unfolds, back regions remain places where actors 'can relax and allow themselves to lower their guard. They may ease the mechanisms of self-control, no longer requiring themselves to monitor their own actions with the same degree of reflexivity generally employed while acting in front regions' (ibid.: 63). In the context of leading politicians, we can also think of back regions as their private life and personal history – what Corner terms their 'private sphere' (2003). However, the 'bound-aries between front and back regions are relatively porous or leaky' (Thompson, 2000: 64). Their porous nature, of course, may have conse-quences – some no more than short-term embarrassments, whereas others may constitute much more, such as a full-blown scandal. The increasingly sieve-like quality of back regions means that personal information regularly finds its way into mediated front regions.

Information in the media about political actors has become highly personal. Members of the public know more about leading political actors' tastes, their families and their biographies than, say, their voting record. Through a process of disclosure and exposure, members of the public are provided with information about the private lives of prominent politicians, their families and appointed political actors. In the US, for instance, there has been a slow disappearance of, in Hillary Clinton's words, the 'zone of privacy' that surrounds the presidency (Parry-Giles and Parry-Giles, 2002: 198). Sexual revelations, drip-fed through gossip-based websites, published in the press and the Starr Report and posted on the web, provided an extremely intimate insight into the private sex life of President Clinton, perhaps the most obvious of many examples. In the UK, the zone of privacy around politicians is also fading. Seymour-Ure (2003) argues that there has, especially, been an erosion of the Prime Minister's privacy. This reduction of privacy is the result of a combination factors. First, politicians, especially the President and the Prime Minister, 'go personal' in an effort to shape public perceptions of them; Deacon (2004) observes that Prime Ministers have been quick to use their personal lives as a resource. Second, the shrinking zone of privacy is also the result of a media hungry for gossip and scandal.

In the US and Britain, as a result of growing self-disclosure and exposure, political actors, both elected and appointed, have moved from being the recognizable distant others to intimate strangers, of whom the public know a lot about their personal lives. The next section charts the disappearance of the zone of privacy around political actors and the growth of non-reciprocal intimacy.

Disclosing and exposing the personal

In contemporary politics, information regularly leaks from private back regions into mediated front regions. This might be information that politicians are keen to disclose (publicity), or information they might prefer to remain contained in the back region (counter-publicity) (Corner, 2003). The exposé is a key part of the media's coverage of politics. The tabloid exposé, in particular, makes visible aspects of a politician's private life that he or she might want to keep private. However, it would be wrong to focus solely on this form of leakage. Leading politicians publicize information to help construct a favourable impression of themselves. This form of strategic self-presentation sees political actors reveal and withhold information in order to ensure that spectators form an appropriate impression.

I want to distinguish between information leaked in these two different ways. Back region behaviour can enter mediated front regions because a politician has deliberately invited media coverage, or it can enter mediated front regions as the product of exposure, initiated by actors other than the politician in question. I want to examine both kinds of flow and argue that both have increased in recent times.

Self-disclosure

Leading politicians increasingly reveal aspects of their personal lives in the media which in previous generations would have been kept private. Private lives have become a resource on which politicians draw in constructing an identity (Corner, 2003). They have been keen to reveal aspects of their biography, allow media exposure of their family and even invite cameras into their homes and their daily lives. Much of this disclosure has not been through the traditional news media, but through non-news outlets (Street, 1997). Such outlets are often more interested in personal matters and provide well-known political figures with a platform to talk about their personal history, health, beliefs and values, taste in music, cars and clothes, hobbies and interests. Zoonen (1998b) argues that such outlets allow 'personalization', the construction of the politician as a human being with the peculiarities that includes.

The television chat show is one arena that has proved particularly conducive to disclosure (see Holbert, 2005). The first appearance of a politician on a chat show came in 1960 when both John F. Kennedy and Richard Nixon were guests on Jack Paar's show (Schroeder, 2004). By the early 1990s, in the US, self-disclosure on a chat show became routine for prominent political actors, especially during a campaign (Hayden, 2002). For example, in the spring of 1992, as part of an effort to get voters to connect with him, Clinton's campaign team launched the 'Manhattan Project', which involved Clinton using such shows to relay personal details about his childhood (Hayden, 2002; Stephanopoulos, 1997; Wayne, 2000). His opponent, George Bush senior, appeared on Larry King Live, MTV and also the Nashville Network. Ross Perot, the other candidate that year, appeared on a range of talk shows. In 2004, both presidential candidates were regular guests on various chat shows.

In 1984, Margaret Thatcher was the first serving British Prime Minister to appear on a chat show. During her term in office she was a guest on *Aspel and Company*, the *John Dunn Show* and *Wogan*, as well as appearing five times on the *Jimmy Young Show*. As a guest, she talked about a variety of issues, including growing up, her family life, family Christmases and her interests. Blair, as Prime Minister, made more appearances on chat shows than any of his predecessors. During his first term in office he was a guest on the *Jimmy Young Show*, *Frank Skinner Show* and *Des O'Conner Tonight* (Foley, 2000). In 2005, he appeared on ITV's *Saturday Night Take-Away*, being interviewed by the child duo, mini Ant and Dec, about a range of light-hearted matters, including underwear (Wring, 2005). In 2006, he appeared on ITV's *Parkinson Show*, where he talked about his heart operation and God and joked about gaffes he had made.

There are numerous lifestyle and special interest magazines, which offer another opportunity for self-disclosure. The music press and radio are frequently used outlets. In the UK, BBC Radio Four's *Desert Island Discs* has provided numerous leading politicians with an opportunity to reveal their musical taste. Each guest gets to play his or her eight favourite records while talking about their lives with the host. For example, when Tony Blair was a guest in 1996, he talked about his life career, the importance of his family, his son's schooling and how he met his wife. The new Conservative leader, David Cameron, spoke about similar subjects when he was a guest on the show in 2006. There is also a host of other music media outlets. In 1987 Margaret Thatcher appeared on the youth television show *Saturday Superstore*, hosted by DJ Mike Reid, where she gave her opinions on a series of pop videos. In 2005, Blair, in an interview for *Word* magazine, talked about his early musical years and the seventies rock group Atomic Rooster. In a so-called 'lad's mag', former Conservative Party leader William Hague revealed that as young man he liked the rock band Meat Loaf. Former Liberal Democrat leader Charles Kennedy made known that he listened to David Bowie and folk artist Karine Polwart, and his replacement, Menzies Campbell, that he liked the Arctic Monkeys. David Cameron, in an interview on Radio One, revealed the contents of his iPod, which included tracks by The Smiths and New Order. In 2004, in the US, the Bush team revealed his iPod play-list to a music magazine; it included songs by country and western singers Alan Jackson and Kenny Chesney, as well as tracks by Stevie Ray Vaughan and Van Morrison. Such revelations are further disclosed in other media, and may be seen as an attempt by politicians to show they are what Street terms 'cool' (2003: 96).

In addition, prominent politicians have become more willing to allow cameras and journalists inside their homes, even their wardrobes. They readily cooperate with magazine feature writers, authors of books, directors of documentaries and film producers in opening up their homes or official residences to the public. One area of notable back-region leakage concerns the official residences of the US President and the UK Prime Minister. In a regulated way, the media have been allowed to go behind the scenes. The White House television spectacle, established by Harry Truman in the early 1950s, has continued intermittently (Schroeder, 2004), perhaps most famously with Jacqueline Kennedy's 1962 Valentine Day tour of the redecorated presidential residence (Tebbel and Watts, 1985). Nixon invited cameras into the White House for a CBS Christmas Eve special in 1971, when he was interviewed while his family, clearly visible in the background, were putting up Christmas decorations (Schroeder, 2004). The tradition continued with Clinton when, in his last month in office in 2000, he gave a personal tour of the White House for the Fox TV show *The First Family's Holiday Gift to America* (ibid.).

In a similar vein, the media have been invited into the Prime Minister's home, Number 10 Downing Street. BBC Radio was invited inside in 1977 to talk to Audrey Callaghan about life in the house. Margaret Thatcher let a film crew in to film part of a series entitled *The English Woman's Wardrobe*, in which she talked openly about her taste in clothes and where she bought her underwear (Cockerell, 1988). In 2004, Tony Blair starred in a fly-on-the-wall documentary on Channel Four entitled *Tony and June*, in which youth TV presenter June Sarpong spent 24 hours shadowing the Prime Minister. In 2006, visitors to the Number 10 website could watch a short film about the Prime Minister entitled *A Day in the Life*. In the same year, Tony Blair invited BBC children's television show *Blue Peter* to look around Number 10. In sum, self-disclosure by politicians has become a taken-for-granted part of mediated political life, with politicians increasingly making public many aspects of their lives which would traditionally have been considered private.

Media exposure

While the seep of information into mediated front regions is the result of self-disclosure, in the media-saturated environment of contemporary politics, information and images that politicians would prefer to remain private are often exposed. This exposure of back-region activities has been justified in terms of a public–private disjuncture: for example, double standards – politicians not practising what they preach or living a double life – or a transgression or contravention of the high private moral standards expected from those who hold political office. However, in other instances, it is hard to tell why such behaviour contravenes norms or expectations. The revelations of impropriety concern private indiscretion rather than genuine wrongdoing. Often the revelation bears little relation to the actors' ability in their public role and does not necessarily generate any public outcry. The reasons given are flimsy and, in reality, are no more than an excuse to titillate audiences. For instance, in the US, Sabato et al. point to 'the obsessive focus on personal foibles' of politicians which manifests itself in reporting 'out of context references to political figures' personal conduct' (2000: 71). Similar points could be made about reporting in Britain (Deacon, 2004).

The news media is sensitized not just to transgressions, but also to sources of titillation, and are likely to give prominence and in-depth coverage to nearly all perceived 'sexually interesting' private lives. Indeed, a gamut of exposés occur with 'numbing frequency' (Thompson, 1995: 144). Scandal is probably the most high-profile outcome of a prominent politician's transgression of norms and expectations being made visible (see chapter 2). However, in the contemporary political communication systems, few of the exposés lead to a full-blown scandal. Most are short-term embarrassments that lead to resignation or are quickly forgotten.

One of the biggest factors behind the emergence of this scandal syndrome has been gossip-based tabloid outlets (Sabato et al., 2000). Such outlets are not new, with political gossip columns an established feature of 1930s newspapers (Schudson, 1978). Columns bearing titles such as 'Back stairs at the White House' and 'The man at the key hole', mild in comparison to today's headlines, 'revealed just enough information to keep readers vaguely interested and politicians vaguely nervous' (Summers, 2000: 839). Although not new, the number of tabloids has grown, and competition between them for readers has increased (Sabato et al., 2000; Sparks, 2000). The emergence of online gossip websites and blogs has been key to the growth of 'revelatory journalism', especially in the US (Williams and Delli Carpini, 2000; 2004). In Britain, competition between national tabloid newspapers has increased dramatically, as their circulation shrinks (Sparks, 2000; see also chapter 4).

Sex, sexual orientation and past misdemeanours

Whereas, once, extra-marital affairs, sexual orientation and allegations of transgression would have remained confined to the private sphere, now every indiscretion discovered, however small, about a politician from any point of his or her life is splashed in tabloid outlets. Private lives are dredged up by the tabloid media, with gossip and innuendo endlessly recycled, and treated as little different from fact. Parry-Giles and Parry Giles note that 'Lincoln's depressions, FDR's handicap, and LBJ's many idiosyncrasies would all be the stuff of talk and chatter on CNN and MSNBC, not hidden from view awaiting the diligent exposition of some future historian' (2002: 199). Having adulterous relationships does not distinguish today's politicians from their predecessors, but previously, disclosure was largely post facto – after the person had left office, or had died (Holmes, 2000). In the past, even if the adultery of a leading politician was widely known within journalistic circles, it was not reported (Seymour-Ure, 2003; Summers, 2000), and a comparison could be made between the non-coverage of a string of extra-marital affairs by past presidents and the coverage they would attract today. It is interesting to speculate how President Harding's affairs with Carrie Phillips and Nan Britton, Franklin D. Roosevelt's relationships with Lucy Mercer Rutherford and Missey LeHand, Eisenhower's romance with Kay Summersby, Kennedy's affairs with Marilyn Monroe and many others, and Lyndon Johnson's affair with Helen Gahagan Douglas would have been treated by the tabloid outlets that chronicled Clinton's various affairs (Sabato et al., 2000; Summers, 2000). In the UK, there is agreement that Lloyd George's relationship with Frances Stevenson or Dorothy MacMillan's affair and alleged illegitimate child by another politician would not have gone unreported today (Seaton, 2003; Seymour-Ure, 2003; Tunstall, 1996).

In the US, tabloid media have become the main source of unsourced and unsubstantiated rumour on politicians' sex lives (Sabato et al.,

2000). There is no consensus on when such reporting started; indeed, some have argued that it is nothing more than a return to nineteenth-century 'yellow' journalism (Summers, 2000). There were high-profile revelations during the 1970s: for instance, Chair of the House Ways and Means Committee, Wilbur Mills, resigned in 1974 after he was stopped by police and found to be drunk with a stripper in his car. House Majority Leader, Wayne L. Hayes, resigned in 1976 when it was revealed in the *Washington Post* that he employed a stripper, who could not type, as his secretary. However, it was the 1988 primaries, and the revelations surrounding Senator Gary Hart, that mark the start of the routine coverage in the media of extra-marital exploits. During the 1988 presidential primaries, Democrat front-runner Gary Hart's affair with Donna Rice was exposed in the *Miami Herald*, which staked out his Washington home; pictures of Hart with Rice on his knee aboard the boat *Monkey Business* were sold to the supermarket tabloid the *National Enquirer* (Witcover, 2001). In 1992, Bill Clinton's affair with Gennifer Flowers was also revealed in a supermarket tabloid, *The Star*, which paid $100,000 for her kiss-and-tell exclusive (Diamond and Silverman, 1997). Senator John McCain's womanizing was exposed during his bid for the Republican nomination in the 2000 presidential primaries. In the same year the *National Enquirer* published the story of a Texan woman who claimed to have had an 18-month affair with George W. Bush, which ended before the start of his campaign for president. It is not just presidential candidates who are targeted: Mike Bowers, candidate for the office of Governor of Georgia, had his extra-marital affair exposed in the media, as did Indianapolis Congressman Dan Burton, Californian Congressman Gary Condit, Pennsylvanian Congressman Don Sherwood and former House Speaker Newt Gingrich. These are just a few of what is a long list of names (see Sabato et al., 2000).

Websites such as the Drudge Report have regularly published rumours about the private lives of politicians, including John Kerry's alleged affair with intern Alex Polier. Drudge played a leading role in revealing the Clinton/Lewinsky affair. Allegations made on websites and in the tabloids are picked up not only by talk radio and gossip columns, but also by the 'serious' mainstream news outlets, and given credibility (Williams and Delli Carpini, 2000; 2004).

Currently in the UK, there are few qualms about reporting the sex lives of serving politicians, especially government ministers. Coverage in the tabloid press of the 1963 Profumo Affair perhaps marked the start of reporting on extra-marital exploits, but the coverage – at least until John Profumo, a government minister, resigned – was circumspect and the sex lives of politicians were, in the main, off-limits (Tunstall, 1996). By the 1970s the picture was changing. In 1973, the

News of the World entrapped government minister Lord Lambton by secretly recording his activities with call-girls with a camera and microphone hidden in a teddy-bear. The late 1980s onwards probably mark the beginning of the mass revelation of extra-marital exploits. In the 1990s there was a string of high-profile exposés of ministerial extra-marital affairs and other sex-related issues – too many to list all of them here. In 1992, the then Heritage Minister, David Mellor, resigned over revelations in the tabloid press about his affair with actress Antonia de Sancha. In the same year it was revealed that the then leader of the Liberal Democrats, Paddy Ashdown, had had an affair with his secretary. John Major, when he was Prime Minister, sued a magazine over allegations that he had an affair in 1993. In addition, in the early 1990s there were exposés of bizarre sexual practices and illegitimate children. For example, reports on the death of the MP Steven Milligan at his home, due to auto-erotic asphyxiation, included lurid details about him wearing women's underwear and the manner of his death – he was found prostrate on a table with an orange in his mouth. In 1994, government minister Tim Yeo resigned after the press revealed he had an illegitimate child. A change of government in 1997 made little difference. That year the then Foreign Secretary Robin Cook's decision to leave his wife for his secretary, Gaynor Regan, was printed in the tabloid press. In 2004, it was reported that the former Home Secretary, David Blunkett, was having an affair with a married woman, Kimberly Quinn. According to Blunkett, one tabloid paper even offered his ex-wife £50,000 to reveal all about their married life. In 2006, Deputy Prime Minister John Prescott's affair with his secretary Tracey Temple was exposed in the *Daily Mirror*. She was subsequently paid by the paper.

Another area concerns politicians' sexuality. Again, such issues, even when widely known within journalistic circles, have tended not to be made public until relatively recently. The 'outing' of homosexual politicians has now become a feature of political reportage. In the US, an elected representative's sexuality remained largely a private matter until recently. In 2004, the then New Jersey Governor, James McGreevey, was 'outed' in the media and forced to admit that he was having an extra-marital affair with a male aide. In Britain, had Tom Driberg – a well-known married homosexual MP – been an MP today and not 50 years ago, the chances are that he would have been outed by the tabloid press. Perhaps the first example of an MP being exposed as an alleged homosexual in the press concerns Liberal Party leader Jeremy Thorpe in 1970s. However, the tendency for the tabloids to expose leading politicians, married or single, has grown. Married Conservative MP, Jerry Hayes, was outed in 1996. In 1998, the then Secretary of State for Wales, Ron Davies, was revealed to be gay, when his mugging, while 'cruising' on Clapham Common, was widely reported. The sexuality of former government minister Peter Mandelson was revealed in a news broadcast after he had been outed by the *News of the World* (Barnett and Gaber, 2001). The same year, when threatened by the *News of the World*, government minister Nick Brown admitted he was gay (ibid.). The revelations prompted the *Sun* newspaper to run a front-page inquiry into whether Britain was run by a gay mafia, together with pictures of several gay ministers (McNair 2000). In 2006, during the Liberal Democrat leadership contest, married contestant Mark Oaten quit the race shortly before it was revealed in the *News of the World* that he had had a 6-month-old relationship with a 23-year-old rent boy. Coincidentally, in the same contest, another candidate, Simon Hughes, was forced after many denials to admit he was gay when the *Sun* confronted him with proof that he regularly used a gay telephone chatline. In the same year, the decision of married Conservative MP Greg Barker to leave his wife for a male interior decorator received widespread coverage.

Transgressions in politicians' past lives are also a source of tabloid speculation and revelation. As Sabato et al. (2000) note there is regular mining of politicians' past lives. All past indiscretions, 'every investment made, every affair conducted, every private sin committed from the college to the present' is liable to be reported (Sabato, 1991: 211). For example, Salon.com divulged that Henry Hyde, the Republican Congressman presiding over the House Judiciary Committee hearing articles of impeachment against Bill Clinton, had an extra-marital affair in the 1960s. There were also revelations about the extra-marital sex life of fellow committee member Bob Barr. Bob Dole, presidential challenger in 1996, was revealed to have had an affair in 1968, and the media brought to light in 2003 the fact that the pro-segregationist Senator, Strom Thurmond, had fathered a child with his parent's African American housemaid in the 1920s.

Another increasingly common focus concerns drug and alcohol use. In the past, alcoholism in particular has rarely been publicly discussed by the media. In the US, former House Majority leader Thomas Hale Boggs, former Senate Minority leader Everett Dirksen and former Armed Services Committee chair L. Mendal Rivers are just a few of the influential names whose drink problems went unreported (Williams, 1991). More recently, Bill Clinton's admission to smoking marijuana and George W. Bush's disclosure about his former drink problem were prompted in part by media speculation. While bringing such issues to the public's attention could be seen as beneficial, they are often covered in a prurient manner. In Bush's case, there was a media hunt for alleged pictures of Bush when he was a student, nude and cavorting on top of a bar in a drunken stupor (Sabato et al., 2000). In Britain, a similar situation exists. In 2006, Charles Kennedy was forced to resign as party leader by Liberal Democrat MPs because of a drink problem. His removal as leader and the scale of his alcoholism were the subject of intense media coverage. During the Conservative Party leadership election in 2005, there was much speculation in the media about whether David Cameron had used cocaine before he became a politician, speculation he has refused to comment on.

Family revelations

Media exposés increasingly involve the immediate family of prominent politicians: the private lives of spouses of political leaders, in particular, have come under scrutiny in an unprecedented way. In the US, in the wake of White House staff lawyer Vincent Foster's suicide, many rumours circulated in the tabloid media that Hillary Clinton had been having a long-term affair with him (Diamond and Silverman, 1997). Another rumour published was that she ordered the sacking of the White House travel office staff and handed out lucrative contracts to friendly firms. Perhaps the best-known allegation that dogged her throughout her time in the White House was about her property ventures, when her husband was Arkansas Governor. Her role in the Whitewater affair, as it became known, gained widespread media coverage during Clinton's term in office (Corrigan, 2000). Most of these exposés were justified on the pretext of exposing 'cronyism' in the White House.

In the UK, Cherie Blair's use of convicted conman Peter Foster – boyfriend of her close friend and lifestyle guru Carole Caplin – to negotiate a reduction in the purchase price of two flats in Bristol, generated a two-week press feeding-frenzy. The story broken by the *Mail on Sunday* was initially denied by the Prime Minister's spokespersons. However, after the *Daily Mail* published the content of emails between Cherie Blair and Foster, Number 10 was forced to admit that Foster had been involved in the deal. The story in the press then evolved, from the question of Cherie Blair's poor judgement to the honesty of Number 10. The story developed further by the second week of December 2002 when it was revealed that Cherie Blair had contacted Foster's solicitors to enquire about the progress of his pending deportation. This led to a raft of speculation in the press about whether the Prime Minister's wife had attempted to interfere in the proceedings of Foster's immigration case. The story finally reached a climax when Cherie Blair made a statement in front of the cameras, admitting she had made a mistake but denying any alleged wrongdoing (Stanyer, 2003). More recently, she has been widely criticized in the press for 'cashing-in' on her position as the Prime Minister's wife. In 2005, the press claimed she had charged £17,000 to speak at a charity fundraising event in Australia, a sum which left the charity out of pocket, and later in the year that she had billed the Labour Party £7,700 for her haircuts during the general election campaign.

The behaviour and activities of children of leading politicians is also the subject of media attention. The antics of prominent politicians' children gain attention, often in relation to sex and drug issues, but also concerning what school or university they might attend or want to attend. Mark Thatcher's activities were often an embarrassment to his mother, as were those of Ronald Reagan's daughter; the drunken escapades of President Bush's daughter Jenna, and the Prime Minister's son Euan, were both given widespread coverage.

Exposure is not solely the result of the growth of tabloid journalism: books have long been a source of revelation. The insider exposé is also not new (Summers, 2000). Clinton Wallace Gillbert's *The Mirrors of Washington* in 1921, was one of the first to attempt to lay bare, if in a very mild-mannered way, the activities of the Washington elite (Summers, 2000). This was followed by exposés by journalists Drew Pearson and Robert Allen in their 1931 book, *The Washington Merry-Go-Round*, and by Jack Lait in *Washington Confidential*, published anonymously in 1951. Both were tame, but *Washington Confidential* revealed the sexual activities of undisclosed senior politicians (Summers, 2000). Over recent years, the number of biographies and insider accounts published by those in, or close to, an administration has grown. Such accounts often seek to provide a behind-the-scenes account of life in the administration – to draw back the curtains that shroud the back regions of politics (Thompson, 2000). Gary Aldrich's *Unlimited Access*, Jeffrey Birnbaum's *Madhouse*, Bill Gulley's *Breaking Cover*, Ronald Kessler's *Inside the White House*, George Stephanopoulos' *All Too Human*, Dick Morris' *Behind the Oval Office*, Paul Scott's *Tony and Cherie: A Special Relationship* have all done this. In addition to books, a series of docudramas seek to fill in the gaps in the factual record by reconstructing recent events.

Self-disclosure and media exposure become intertwined. For instance, a political actor whose private life has been exposed, or who may have been involved in scandal, might subsequently go on to disclose his feelings and inner thoughts to the media in a further round of interviews. The events might also become the subject of a book, docudrama or film. In the US, 'outed' former New Jersey Governor, James McGreevey, went on to write a book about his life in politics and the events surrounding his resignation, entitled *The Confession*. In the UK, former Home Secretary David Blunkett, three months after he was forced to resign, made a return to public life, talking openly in the media about the events surrounding his resignation.

On Channel Four's day-time chat show, *Richard and Judy*, he spoke of his personal feelings about the events and about whether he was the father of Kimberley Quinn's young son. The affair subsequently became the subject of a film, *A Very Social Secretary*, and of a two-part documentary, *The Blunkett Tapes*, and was described in detail in his memoirs, which were serialized in the *Daily Mail*.

Conclusion

There has been a transformation of the visibility of not only leading political actors within political communication systems in the US and Britain, but also those connected to them. The band of familiar political actors is expanding to include others such as advisers and family members, who in previous generations would have remained largely invisible and behind the scenes. In addition, the media provide the public with a constant flow of personal information about these actors. Political celebrities have become 'intimate' strangers, their private lives widely known by millions of citizens. The 'zone of privacy' which once surrounded leading political actors is slowly vanishing, its disappearance driven by journalistic revelation and politician self-disclosure.

Conflict frequently arises between politicians and journalists about where the proper limits of privacy lie. If politicians choose to disclose their private lives to the public, can they complain when the media intrude into aspects of their lives that they want to remain hidden? As far as the tabloid press is concerned, if a politician courts publicity he or she cannot complain about bad exposure when it arises. But what about the families of politicians? Conflict over the visibility of Tony Blair's youngest child, Leo, raises an interesting case in point. Blair has been happy to be photographed with his son, but was angry about attempts by the *Daily Mail* to inquire into whether Leo had received the controversial MMR vaccination (Deacon, 2004). Such conflicts around the privacy of political celebrities are set to continue to be a feature of democratic political communication systems.

PART II

NEWS AND THE POLITICS OF MARKET-DRIVEN MEDIA

The News Media, their Audiences and Changing Organizational Roles: From Informing Citizens to Pleasing Consumers

T HE main news organizations in the US and Britain do not see their audiences today in the same way as they did 30 or 40 years ago. Traditionally, they have seen their audiences, first and foremost, as members of a national political community, and their own role as catering for the audiences' informational needs. Such an outlook has not been the sole preserve of public service media organizations; indeed, many commercial news organizations conceptualized their role in this way, and did so profitably (Hallin, 2000; Schudson, 1995). In general over the twentieth century, first newspapers, then radio and television news outlets, embraced their civic role, seeking to provide a community of citizens with information on which to make political decisions, and to act as a forum for the expression of public opinion (Hallin, 1992b; Seymour-Ure, 1991).

However, as this chapter shows, this citizen-centred outlook began to fade in the 1980s, the result of a combination of factors – the end of spectrum scarcity, digitalization, and re-regulation of the media environment. These factors led to an explosion of new news outlets and to an intensification of competition between outlets for a share of the available audience. This competition, combined with declining audience loyalty, especially for political output, and greater demands to be profitable, put the established news organizations under pressure. It is this pressure that has led to a reconceptualization of the news media's role vis-à-vis audiences. In this contemporary market-driven news order, audiences are increasingly regarded not as citizens first and consumers second, but first and foremost as consumers. The consumer model, which sees catering for customers' demands as key to financial success, has become the dominant model of audiences in the multi-billion-dollar global news business. This chapter does not argue that this transformation marks a 'dumbing-down' of news, or that news produced in this new environment is necessarily better, but it does argue that the rise of the consumer-centred model of audiences marks a shift in thinking by news organizations. This is a shift which has provided some benefits but also poses problems for democratic political communication systems.

News audiences as citizens

The news environment, through which conventional politics is filtered in contemporary political communication systems, has undergone a dramatic series of major changes in the last 50 or so years. These changes are encapsulated in Hallin's (1992b; 2000) notion of the passing of high modernism in journalism. In brief, Hallin observes that for much of the twentieth century – between the First World War and the 1980s – news journalism in the US could be said to have been in its high modern phase. This period, he argues (2006), was characterized by a particular approach to news reporting, and, one could add, also by unique market and technological configurations. In Britain, despite differences, a case can be made for the rise and decline of a similar phase in journalism, and similar market and technological configurations (Seymour-Ure, 1991; Tunstall, 1996). For both countries, then, the passing of high modernism is a useful metaphor that encapsulates the wide variety of changes that have taken place from the late twentieth century onwards.

In relation to the role of news organizations within democratic political communication systems, one could argue that the high modern epoch, broadly defined, was characterized by a particular role conception, one which differs from those that currently dominate. This notion of the news media's role and the needs of audiences were not only shared by news outlets but also, in certain instances, reinforced by regulation (see Blumler and Gurevitch, 1995; Dahlgren, 1991; Hallin, 2000). It is worth exploring in more detail how the press and broadcast news perceived their role and their audience.

The press

Newspapers were the predominant news outlet for much of the high modern epoch. In the main, especially amongst the serious or broadsheet press, editors' conception of their organization's role was shaped by notions of social responsibility and dominant professional values (Calabrese, 2000; Seymour-Ure, 1991). This conception was fostered by certain external variables. In both countries, news outlets were largely sheltered from direct economic pressures. In the US, many newspapers were, in effect, regional monopolies and faced limited or no competition (T. E. Patterson, 2000; Zaller, 1999). In Britain, competition amongst the national press was less intense, and the readership much larger than today (Tunstall, 1996). In addition, in both countries, there was a secure source of income from advertisers, with little or no competition with broadcasters for advertising revenue (T. E. Patterson, 2000; Seymour-Ure, 1991). There were also stable patterns of newspaper consumption. Readership was high, often habitual, with the choice of paper reflecting the readers' socio-economic background or region.

The broadsheet press saw their audience as citizens, as members of a political community that needed to be provided with accurate and factual information. The US saw the emergence and flourishing of an 'objectivity movement' within news journalism (Schudson, 1978; Zaller, 1999). For example, in the 1920s, the American Society of Newspaper Editors adopted a code of practice which emphasized that journalists were to strive for truth and justice (Attaway-Fink, 2004). There was a move away from partisan reporting, which had characterized the nineteenth century (Schudson, 1978; Zaller, 1999). Indeed, press partisanship declined slowly, and had almost disappeared by the 1950s (Hallin, 2000). In Britain, while press/party parallelism remained, partisan opinion was very much removed from reporting, restricted to the editorial or op-ed pages of the newspaper (Seymour-Ure, 1991). While there was a clear attempt by the broadsheet press to separate partisan opinion from straight news reporting ('fact'), it should be noted that this practice was less robust in the popular press (Sparks, 2000).

In addition, journalists saw themselves as providing a service (Hallin, 2000; McChesney, 1999). In the US, Thomas Patterson notes that the 'yellow journalism' of the nineteenth and early twentieth centuries had all but disappeared by the high modern era (T. E. Patterson, 2000; Underwood, 1998). Newspapers could be seen as 'a privately owned public utility' (Carper, 1997: 63). The newspaper journalists of the time saw it as their role 'to serve the public as a whole and not particular interests' (Hallin, 2000: 220). The drive to serve citizens can be seen further in the emergence in the 1960s of investigative journalism (Schudson, 1978). Investigation was not an abandonment of civic obligation but rather a reinterpretation of it.

In Britain, the approach to audiences differed between serious and popular outlets. The broadsheet press sought to serve a mainly middle-class audience. Investigative journalism, as in the US, was an important part of this service, especially from the 1960s onwards (Tunstall, 1996). While the broadsheet press catered for an upper- and middle-class audience (social grades A and B – see chapter 6), the popular press's audience was predominantly working class (social grades C1, C2, D and E). The popular mass circulation press conceived its role as being less abstract, not so much informing citizens as entertaining and championing the political interests of the working-class audience (Sparks, 1992; Tunstall, 1996).

Broadcast news

The role of broadcast news was shaped by an ethos of public service. Radio, followed by television news, saw the audience as members of a political community that needed to be provided with information upon which to make political judgements. In the case of Britain, broadcasting was, from its inception, a public service, designed to inform, educate and entertain (Franklin, 1997). News was an essential part of the BBC's remit and was well guarded, in this respect, from financial pressures (Curran and Seaton, 2003). For the BBC, and ITV when it arrived in the 1950s, the audience was seen as consisting of citizens with political needs that news organizations should serve. This view permeated broadcast journalism and shaped professional practice. Impartiality was an essential aspect of broadcast news, and one that distinguished it from the partisan press, especially at election times. Audiences were seen as citizens who needed an unbiased reflection of developments in public life (Seymour-Ure, 1991). In Britain, these organizational values were buttressed by regulation. Broadcast news was tightly regulated, its civic role defined carefully in law. The BBC's charter, and the legislation that gave rise to ITV, carefully set out the role that broadcasters should perform, a role that was subject to regular reviews (Curran and Seaton, 2003).

In the US, although the networks were run along commercial lines, competition was orderly and competitive pressure generally low (Hallin, 1992b; T. E. Patterson, 2000; Zaller, 1999). The news divisions of the main networks, through the 1960s and 1970s, were largely sheltered from direct economic pressures; they were seen as the 'prestigious' part of the network (Calabrese, 2000; Hallin, 2000). This 'buffer' shaped their focus in no uncertain terms: news departments saw their role as providing audiences with the information needed to function as citizens (Hallin, 2000) and Hallin talks of network journalists conceptualizing their roles as 'public servants' (1992b). Journalism was seen as a profession and, like other professions, it developed its own code and practices that were important in shaping news (Hallin, 2000). Local television news, now the subject of much criticism, in the main saw its role as a provider of hard news with a local political angle (Zaller, 1999). From the late 1960s onwards, the three networks – ABC, CBS, NBC – provided a platform for investigative reporting in the shape of magazine programmes such as *Sixty Minutes* (Zaller, 1999).

In both countries, the notion of journalists as public servants, and the media as providing a public service, became a dominant set of ideas framing reporting (Seymour-Ure, 1991; Hallin, 2000; McChesney, 1999). Such a journalistic culture was part of a wider consensus about the role that broadcast news should play within a democracy. This consensus was reinforced via national regulation. In the UK, as already mentioned, news was seen as a prestigious part of the network, essential for the fulfilment of public service obligations. In the US, although broadcasting was not as heavily regulated as in the UK, it was highly regulated (T. E. Patterson, 2000). Hallin notes there was a 'regulatory injunction that broadcasters serve the public convenience and necessity' (1992b: 16). The Federal Communications Commission placed further regulatory requirements on the amount of news that networks should broadcast. In both countries, therefore, the regulatory environment reinforced the broadcasters' conception of their role vis-à-vis their audience.

This view was further reinforced by the nature of broadcast technology. With the quick rise of radio and TV ownership, audiences were large – by the mid-1960s 90 per cent of households in both countries had a television set (Putnam, 2000; Seymour-Ure, 1991). Audiences were not only large, but also, with a limited number of channels to watch, they were captive. Patterns of consumption for news bulletins were relatively stable. Further, the rolling format of news meant that, unlike the press, the audience was not free to skip between features according to interest. As Sunstein observes, audiences were exposed 'to material that they would not have chosen in advance' and, further, citizens could tune in at the same time each day (2001: 8).

It is important to note that audiences were also seen as members of a national community of citizens, sharing consumption of political information (Katz, 1996). Schudson observes that the primary trend in the media from the late 1950s onwards was a 'nationalizing of the American consciousness' as television took a central role in the minds of elites and public alike (1995: 95; see also Abrahamson et al., 1990). The vision behind public service broadcasting was in part to reach beyond the social and regional divisions that existed in British society, emphasizing a common identity (Crisell, 1997). As the historian Eric Hobsbawm notes of broadcasting, 'for the first time in history people unknown to each other who met knew what each other had in all probability heard . . . the night before' (cited in ibid.: 62). The national community of viewers, as it became, irrespective of class or partisan

background, was subject to national political information, at set periods in the television and radio schedules.

During the high modern epoch, therefore, the network news bulletin and the broadsheet press formed the centrepiece of the political communication system. By the 1960s, it is possible to talk about a serious news sector, centred on the network news bulletins, with current affairs and the broadsheet press seeing their role as providing 'objective' information to members of a national political community. All citizens, regardless of partisan background, were provided with access to serious news with little competitive distraction. In the US, the press and then television remained the main sources of political information for the citizenry (Schudson, 1995). In Britain, broadcast news informed both tabloid and broadsheet readers, providing an impartial rock in a partisan sea (Seymour-Ure, 1991). However, it is important to make explicit some of the criticisms of the old order. As Hallin notes, it was never clear how independent journalists were from their government sources. US journalism of the period could be termed 'establishment journalism' (Hallin, 1992b), characterized by deferential reporting of elites, and the often close relationship between journalists and parties and government; a similar observation could be made of the relations between journalists and political elites during this period in Britain (Blumler and Gurevitch, 1995).

The end of the old order

The passing of high modernism, and the conception of audiences which accompanied it, is the result of a combination of factors, which have been widely examined (see for instance, Golding and Murdock, 2000; Murdock, 2000), but are worth briefly re-examining. In the US, Hallin (1992b, 2006) argues its passing was due to several interrelated factors: a collapse of the Keynesian/New Deal political consensus; a move to more assertive forms of reporting from the late 1960s onwards, challenging political authorities; and a declining confidence in state institutions in the wake of Vietnam and Watergate. In Britain, one could point to similar range of factors. In both countries, however, one could argue that certain systemic factors were also responsible for the change: factors such as government policy, the rise of new technologies, and changing habits of news consumption.

Government regulation

The first key factor concerns government regulation of broadcasting. In the US, in the 1980s, the Federal Communication Commission removed the requirement that networks had to devote 5 per cent of airtime to news, completely removing any notion of serving 'public convenience and necessity' (Hallin, 2000: 224; McManus, 1994). Further deregulation saw a relaxing of laws on mergers and acquisitions in the media industry, leading to a wave of take-overs (McChesney, 1999). Each of the three networks was acquired by new profit-hungry owners in the 1980s (Boyd-Barrett, 2005; Zaller, 1999). In the UK, the process of deregulation began with the 1990 Broadcasting Act, which reduced content regulation, increased competition and eased ownership restrictions (Franklin, 1997). The Thatcher government turned a blind eye to Murdoch's Sky television, which increased its market share throughout the 1990s (Curran and Seaton, 2003). The 2003 Communication Act has continued the deregulation process, removing nearly all content regulation and opening up the once-regulated world of broadcasting to the global market.

The impact of new technology

The neo-liberal agenda of the Thatcher and Reagan administrations needs to be seen alongside a second factor – new communication technology. While technology has been an ever-present part of the news industry, it has had a profound effect on the news environment. In both countries there has been a well-documented process of channel multiplication. In the UK, in 2004, 55 per cent of households received digital television; by 2005 that figure had risen to 63 per cent – the equivalent of 15.7 million households (Milano, 2005). In the US, multiple-media outlets have been well established for some time. In 1970s around 10 per cent of homes had cable, by the early 1980s that figure had grown to 20 per cent and by the late 1990s it had reached 72 per cent (Norris, 2000; T. E. Patterson, 2000).

The number of people who use the internet has also grown. Estimates suggest the number of adults online in the US stands at 65 per cent. This represents a sharp rise from 21 per cent, the proportion of Americans who surfed the web in 1996 (Pew Research Center, 2004f). In the UK, the number of homes using the internet has increased since 1997 from one in twenty to slightly more than one in two in 2006, with roughly 14 million homes having access to the internet (Office for National Statistics, 2006).

This has led to several changes. First, the sheer volume of news output has increased. In the UK, not including the main 24-hour news channels, output increased from 22 hours in 1985 to 110 hours in 2002 – an increase of 88 hours (Shaw, 2003). According to one estimate, the viewer in multi-channel homes has access to a possible 243 hours of news a week compared to 30 in 1986 (Hargreaves and Thomas, 2002).

There is a similar picture in the US (see Project for Excellence in Journalism, 2006). In 1990 only seven newspapers could be accessed online in the US; by 2002 that figure had grown to 3,400 newspapers and 2,000 non-US papers (Gunter, 2003: 143). In Britain, in 1995 no newspapers were on the internet; by 2006 all national newspapers are online, with the *Guardian* becoming the first to break news on its website rather than in hard copy.

Second, technology has allowed news channels to become interactive: audiences can choose the news they are interested in, and let journalists know their opinions (see chapter 7).

Changing consumption patterns

News remains one of the main sources of political information for the public, but the patterns of news consumption are changing fast. When citizens can access news is no longer limited to several half-hour slots a day, but is available at any time of day or night. In the age of 24-hour news channels, new stories hit the headlines and 'old' ones are updated every half-hour, or sooner. And the traditional news outlets are no longer necessarily the first port of call for citizens: in the US, between 1993 and 2004, one trend in news consumption was particularly clear, namely that the traditional news outlets were rapidly declining as the main source of news for audiences (Pew Research Center, 2006b). The public seems to be losing the habit of tuning into the main evening news outlets. One of the most glaring declines has been in the numbers who regularly watch the local news and the main network newscasts.

Table 4.1 shows that those saying they regularly watch nightly network news has fallen from 60 per cent in 1993 to 28 per cent in 2006. This is reinforced by data which reveal that the number of viewers of evening news bulletins has halved over a 25-year period. In 1980 the three main evening network news bulletins attracted an average of 52 million viewers nightly; by 2005 that figure stood at 27 million (Project for Excellence in Journalism, 2006; see also Davis and Owen, 1998). Table 4.1 shows too that the proportion of respondents saying they regularly watch local news has also dramatically fallen. In the UK, there is similar evidence. Since about the mid-1990s, the consumption of terrestrial news has fallen from an average of nine hours per month in 1994, to eight hours per month by the beginning of 2002 (Hargreaves and Thomas, 2002). The main television news bulletins have witnessed a decline in audiences: in 1989 the combined ratings for the two main evening new bulletins – BBC's *Nine O'clock News* and ITV's *News at Ten* – was on average 15 million; in 2002, the combined viewing figure for their replacement evening bulletins was 7.9 million

Table 4.1 Regular news consumption in the US by outlet, 1993–2006 (% who regularly consume)					
Medium/year	1993	1996	2000	2004	2006
Evening network news	60%	42%	30%	34%	28%
Local television news	77%	65%	57%	59%	54%
Newspapers	58%[a]	50%	47%	42%	40%
Cable television news	–	–	33%[b]	38%	34%
Online news	–	2%	23%	29%	31%

[a] 1994 figure

[b] 2002 figure

Source: Compiled from Pew Research Center, 2006b

(British Audience Research Bureau, cited in Shaw, 2003); and by 2005 that figure had fallen even further to an average of 7.1 million (BARB, cited in Tryhorn, 2005).

Another dramatic trend is the extent to which the public no longer uses newspapers as the main source of news. In the US, the average weekday newspaper circulation has fallen by 7 million in approximately 15 years, from 62 million in 1990 to 55 million in 2004. There have been big declines in the readership of newspapers in major cities like Washington, DC, Los Angeles, Boston, San Francisco, Atlanta and Philadelphia (Project for Excellence in Journalism, 2006). Table 4.1 reinforces this picture, showing that the number of people who regularly read a newspaper has fallen consistently between 1993 and 2006, from 58 per cent to 40 per cent. In the UK, in 1973 47 per cent of those asked said that newspapers were their main source of news; this figure has fallen steadily and stood at 9 per cent in 2001 (Towler, 2002). Further, patterns of consumption in both countries have become more unstable. In the US, the 'seven-day-a-week subscriber has been replaced by the occasional buyer' (Project for Excellence in Journalism, 2006). In the UK, subscriptions have also declined and multiple readership of newspapers has effectively died out (Sparks, 1992, 2000; Tunstall, 1996).

In the US, the number of people who regularly consume cable and online news sources has grown as the number of cable outlets grows. In 1996, as shown in table 4.1, 2 per cent of those asked regularly gained their news from the internet; in 2006 that figure had risen to 31 per cent. Table 4.1 also shows that those frequently watching cable has risen, if only slightly. In the UK, too, the public are getting their news from a greater variety of sources. According to the British Audience Research Bureau (BARB), 6.6 million people in 2002 had access to 24-hour news channels, compared to around 3 million in 1996 (Hargreaves and Thomas, 2002; see also Lambert 2002). The reach (the percentage of viewers who watch more than three continuous minutes) of 24-hour news was 23.3 per cent of multi-channel homes in 2001. During the first part of 2002, an average of 10.6 million people per month were accessing news websites – an increase from 7.1 million in November 2000 (Hargreaves and Thomas, 2002).

Who watches: changing demographics

The traditional news media's audience is ageing. In 1995 in the US, the main newscasts captured 46 per cent of the desirable 18–49 age group; in 2002 the figure was 29 per cent; and by 2005, the average age of the viewers of the three main newscasts was 60, with only 9 per cent of viewers in the 18–49 age bracket (Kurtz, 2002; Project for Excellence in Journalism, 2006). A survey by the Pew Research Center (2000a) shows that network news appeals to older viewers, as do news magazine programmes such as *Sixty Minutes*, *20/20* and *Dateline*. A similar situation exists in the UK, where the evidence reveals that in 2002 the over-45s accounted for 66 per cent of the total terrestrial television news audience, up from 64 per cent in 1994 (Hargreaves and Thomas, 2002). Newspaper readership demographics produce a similar picture. In the US, 29 per cent of those under 30 read a newspaper compared to 63 per cent of those 65 and over (Pew Research Center, 2004b). In Britain, the picture is not much different (Tunstall, 1996). The young, in both countries, increasingly gain information from a variety of sources. For instance, in the US, the internet was the main source of news for 20 per cent of those between 18 and 29 years, compared to 7 per cent of those over 50 (Pew Research Center, 2004b). In the UK, the internet was the main source of news for 41 per cent of 18–34 year olds, compared to 13 per cent of those over 55 (BBC/MORI Citizenship Survey cited in Schifferes, 2006).

Shrinking markets, hyper-competition and profit pressure

The outcome of these developments has been a shrinking of the established news organizations' audience share and an increase in competition for those audiences, especially certain demographics. In the UK, the audience share of the two main terrestrial channels has declined steadily: between 1999 and 2003, ITV's average audience share fell from 31.2 to 23.6 per cent, while BBC 1's share fell from 28.4 to 25.6 per cent. This trend seems set to continue with the spread of the digital terrestrial network Freeview. In 2004, cable and satellite had a 25 per cent share of the national audience (BARB cited in Deans, 2004).

In the US, in 1959 the three main networks (ABC, CBS and NBC) had a roughly equal audience share, followed by the press. The audience share of the press began to decline in comparison to the main networks, with the dominance of the three networks lasting until the 1980s (T. E. Patterson, 2000). In the mid-1980s the networks' newscasts attracted more than three-quarters of the viewing public; today they attract around a quarter (Kurtz, 2002; Macedo et al., 2005). In the UK, the combined evening audience share for broadcast news in 1989 was 70 per cent of those watching television; in 2002 the evening bulletins gained a 42 per cent audience share (Shaw, 2003).

With more entrants in the news field, competition for the shrinking audiences increases. In the US, from the 1980s onwards competition in the broadcast sector increased (Hallin, 2000): the once-dominant news-casts of the three main networks faced growing rivalry from cable news providers like CNN, and then Fox News, which challenged the dominant position of the three networks (T. E. Patterson, 2000). In the new millennium, competition became more intense with the advent of internet news. In the UK, since the 1990 Broadcasting Act, commer-cial news providers such as ITN have come under pressure to provide a value-for-money, cost-effective news service for the networks – one that maximizes audiences. This pressure has intensified with the presence of three British-based 24-hour news channels, an advertising recession and shrinking audiences (Barnett and Gaber, 2001). The BBC, since the 1990s, has also faced competition from a host of international providers, such as Sky News and CNN. In both countries, the networks have found themselves having to compete harder to be profitable or, in the BBC's case, to legitimate its licence revenue. In sum, the traditional news providers face a triple whammy of audience uncertainty, more competition and greater pressure to be profitable.

Reconceptualizing the role of news in uncertain times

The consequence of uncertain patterns of media consumption and greater emphasis on profitability has been the abandonment of the citizen-centric model of news that dominated the so-called high modern era and the adoption of a market-oriented one (Hallin, 2000; Stepp, 2000). Such a process has also been, in part, given credibility by the rise and dominance of neo-liberal thinking within government and the media industry at large (Curran, 2000). This change is some-thing that has occurred over a period of time and is more obvious in some news organizations than others. For example, a market-oriented approach can be seen more clearly in the British tabloid press and commercial news broadcasters than in licence-funded broadcasting. That said, though, traditional news organizations no longer see their audiences in the same way as they did back in the 1970s – the rethink stretches across the divide between popular, serious news media and between commercial and licence-funded media. From about the 1980s onwards, some traditional outlets began to view their audiences primarily as consumers with a series of wants that they needed to address. While this process started earlier in the US than in Britain, in both countries this market-oriented approach began to spread to more traditional news organizations throughout the 1990s (Franklin, 1997; McManus, 1994; Underwood, 1998). By the new millennium, this consumer-centric approach had become taken for granted by almost all large news organizations (Attaway-Fink, 2004; Beam, 2001). Catering for the vagaries of the 'floating' consumer, allied to the organizational bottom line, has become the central driving force of most news organizations, serious or popular. This in turn has forced them rethink their role, with notions of informing an audience of citizens being replaced by the idea of maintaining profitability by uncovering and responding to consumer wants.

News organizations and market research

The news audience has gone from being seen as members of a political community, which news serves, to a footloose customer with individual wants, which news organizations need to meet. As one US observer put it, 'it is not uncommon to hear editors refer to [audiences] as "customers" now', a view not unusual in the UK either (Carper, 1997: 49). Economic success is now seen as dependent on understanding the motivations of the audience, and the drive to understand audience interests has seen broadcast news organizations employ market research (Beam, 2001). This trend, which started in the late 1970s, is now routinely used, especially in the US (Carper, 1997). As one author observed: 'not so long ago it was unheard of for an editor to serve on a marketing or advertising committee or think of a reader in terms of what he or she might desire. . . . Today the practices have become so common place' (Attaway-Fink, 2004: 150). By the 1980s, news organizations in the US were devoting greater resources to determining audience wants, regularly employing consultants to view and critique stories (Calabrese, 2000; Underwood, 1998). Market research companies are used to poll readers on a wide variety of layout and content matters, the dominant view amongst editors in the US being 'find out what readers want and give it to them', with the logic that this will increase circulation and profitability (Carper, 1997: 48). According to McManus (1994), one survey discovered that key likes include humour and human interest stories, and key dislikes include labour and government news. The advice given to the client who had commissioned this survey was to pander to audience prejudices if they wanted to be successful (ibid.).

Market research in the UK has become more important for the news broadcasters since the 1990s: since 2004, for instance, BARB has provided profiles of viewers' interests, passions and beliefs, in addition to information on their leisure activities, home and car ownership, and other media consumption (Gibson, 2004). The information allows news organizations to target audiences more exactly. The licence-funded BBC is less able to ignore the findings of market research if it is to continue to justify the fee to government. The BBC has sought to find new ways to attract a younger audience to its news programmes after research revealed that nearly two-thirds of the *Six O'clock News'* audience was over 55 (Holmwood, 2006). Market research recently forced Sky News to reconsider the way it presents the news, reducing the number of anchors used to front its rolling 24-hour news bulletin. In Britain, the press has adopted a similar approach; focus groups and polling are an important element in determining readers' opinions on a variety of newspaper-related matters.

Market research combines with increased pressure from advertisers to attract a particular customer. Advertisers are interested in attracting a particular group of consumers and are prepared to pay to reach such demographics, while news organizations, with their ageing audience profile, have found themselves under intense pressure to capture younger customers. The success in capturing this audience is measured in ratings scores, with continuous research seeking to determine these customers' wants. Where market research and ratings point to the direction of less hard news, news producers have often been quick to follow.

The consumer's political appetite

The very idea of a news bulletin or newspaper as solely a source of political information for citizens has largely been abandoned. The assumption, reinforced by market research, is that the news consumer has a limited appetite for news on conventional politics. In this view, to continue to treat the audience to conventional political output would be 'financial suicide'. This opinion has come to dominate the news room and has impacted on news output (Underwood, 1998). In simple terms, with the shelter from economic pressure removed, the function of the news bulletin is primarily to attract an audience of consumers, not to inform citizens. This is especially the case in the US, where there is a widespread belief amongst editors and journalists 'that the public won't sit still for serious news' (McManus, 1994: 169). For example, in the US, the agenda of local news outlets has changed dramatically since the 1970s, moving from one of hard news to one mainly focused on entertainment (Hallin, 2000; Zaller, 1999). The 'serious' news magazine programmes, once the centrepiece of the network current affairs output, have been superseded by rating-grabbing magazine programmes; one estimate suggested that they account for around 14 hours of primetime news output a week (Hallin, 2000). The popularity of these ratings-driven local news and magazine programmes has had a major effect on the agenda of networks' news bulletins. The agenda of these popular shows – 'human drama, celebrity, scandal and crime' – has, in Calabrese's words, 'infected the mainstream' (2000: 45). There has been nothing less than an erosion of the 'walls' constructed between public affairs and entertainment (Williams and Delli Carpini, 2000, 2004). Soft news is no longer the preserve of news magazines: McManus notes that news reports are now briefer, with greater emphasis on emotion and visuals (1994). The style of these 'rating success' shows have been emulated; this ratings conscious approach can be seen in the way network news covers politics.

Coverage from Washington, DC has changed on the three oldest networks' early evening newscasts. Hess's examination of Washington reporters has produced a revealing snapshot of some the changes in US political reporting. According to Hess (2000), in 1998 the three main networks used their Washington correspondents in different ways compared to 1978. He observes that the networks are less committed to breaking news and have adopted a more 'lifestyle' angle on the news, plumping for 'soft' news over 'hard' political news (ibid.: 233). These have been combined with efforts to make output more appealing to particular demographics (Boyd-Barrett, 2005). Efforts by ABC to attract younger audiences included hiring Leonardo DiCaprio to interview President Clinton about the environment, and paying a Washington lawyer to smooth the way for Monica Lewinsky's interview with Barbara Walters (Helmore, 2000).

Hess's study also found that news from Washington no longer dominates the news media's attention to the same extent as it did in 1978 (2000: 227). On the main network news programmes, lead stories from Washington fell from an average of twelve out of fifteen in 1978 to seven out of fifteen in 1998 (ibid.). This finding is reinforced by other research: between 1969 and 1997 the proportion of stories on network news devoted to government and foreign affairs fell from an average of 58 per cent to 36 per cent (Zaller, 1999: 15); the coverage of politics on local news has virtually disappeared (Underwood, 1998); in local news, the proportion of stories on government, education and politics fell from 54 per cent in 1976 to 15 per cent in 1992 (Zaller, 1999: 7): and hard news, which used to be the mainstay of news bulletins, has become a commodity for a particular customer group, a minority, one that can be catered for through the 24-hour outlets or, increasingly, online. The very notion of a mixed audience, sitting down at a set time to watch a traditional 30-minute news bulletin, is disappearing fast in the US.

In Britain, news broadcasters have largely come to regard their viewers as having a limited political appetite. The traditional politics-centred news agenda is increasingly seen as unlikely to attract audiences. Pressures from the commercial networks to maintain audience share, in face of competition, has led ITN to adopt a more popular news agenda. The attention paid to political institutions as-of-right has given way to a more news-value-driven approach, where political institutions are given coverage according to whether they are deemed newsworthy. The treatment of the activities of politicians is now firmly based on 'assessments of their intrinsic newsworthiness . . . [so] that consequently the prominence given to the stories reporting these activities, the amount of time or space allocated to them will be determined by a strict consideration of news values' (Blumler and Gurevitch, 1995: 84). ITV has already suggested that ITN should put more emphasis on 'leisure, consumer and show business news' and 'big political stories' and minimize coverage of 'day-to-day politics' (Stanyer, 2002). The BBC has not been immune from the increased competitive pressures in the news market: BBC bulletins compete head-to-head for audience share with the other networks and the BBC has been forced to adapt its news values in the face of competition (Harrison, 2000).

As with network news, the view, reinforced by market research, is that the newspaper reader has a limited desire for news on conventional politics. This view dominates press news rooms and has impacted on news output (Underwood, 1998). It has led, first, to a reduction in the coverage of traditional politics. As one observer notes, the frequent casualty of this view is government, and foreign news (Carper, 1997). In Britain, the traditional tabloids have largely abandoned coverage of subjects that do not attract readers, leaving conventional politics to serious outlets (Rooney, 2000). The extent of the decline in the amount of space tabloid news outlets devote to national political institutions and public affairs has been well documented and, in Britain, the diminishing news coverage of public affairs, especially in the tabloid press, has caused much alarm (Franklin, 1997; Sparks, 2000). Curran and Seaton (2003) suggest that there has been a 'de-politicisation' of the tabloid press, with a marked reduction in the amount of space devoted to public affairs. In the US, tabloid news outlets have enjoyed a resurgence: the old muck-raking virtues are now found in supermarket magazines like the *National Enquirer* and the *Star*. These tabloids, like the tabloid press in Britain, devote no coverage to everyday conventional politics.

It is not just the tabloids. In Britain, studies by Franklin (1997) and Straw (1993) have shown that coverage of parliamentary debates has declined in the broadsheet press. Straw showed that coverage of parliament in the *Telegraph* and the *Guardian* fell from 400–800 lines in 1988 to fewer than 100 lines in each paper in 1993 (cited in Franklin, 1997). Franklin found that *The Times*, for instance, reduced its parliamentary coverage from 148 reports in 1990 to 87 in 1994 (ibid.: 235). In the US, Hess showed that there was an average of twelve Washington stories in the daily newspapers surveyed in 1978; however, in 1998 the average had fallen to six. He notes that on Sundays the decline is even starker: whereas in 1978, Washington stories dominated the Sunday press, and were more numerous than on any other day, in 1998 the picture had reversed, with more Washington stories during the week (2000: 227). Pugnetti observes that in 1991–2, there were some 51 per cent fewer legislative news items in six Washington dailies than in 1981–2 (cited in Underwood, 1998).

Second, 'walls' constructed between public affairs and entertainment, as mentioned, are crumbling. The tabloids have sought to attract readers through a diet of celebrity, human interest and sports stories (Franklin, 1997; Williams and Delli Carpini, 2000; 2004). The tabloid media's political coverage, if it can be called that, focuses largely on leading political personalities, a political celebrity class, rather than policy (see chapter 3). In Britain, Bromley observes that in the 1990s there was a convergence in news values between the tabloid and broadsheet press (1998: 26). All too often, the broadsheet press follow the tabloid-driven news agenda, leading on the same issues.

Third, there have been changes in presentational style: in the US, the 1990s saw the use of more graphics, more space devoted to photographs and to human interest stories and the emergence of papers like *USA Today* (McManus, 1994); in Britain, there is more emphasis on photohgraphs – especially colour pictures – and a growth in the size of headlines (McLachlan and Golding, 2000). In addition, broadsheet newspapers have shrunk in size in an effort to boost circulation. The *Independent* has been at the forefront of the transformation, reducing its size to that of a tabloid newspaper; *The Times* has followed, and the *Guardian* has moved to the slightly larger Berliner format.

Investigative reporting and muck-raking

One of the key roles of the media has been to act as watchdog on behalf of the citizen: a fourth estate able to scrutinize and hold to account government and politicians. From its birth in the 1960s, investigative journalism has sought to expose impropriety by political and corporate elites and many of the leading US newspapers invested in teams of journalists to conduct investigations (Schudson, 1978). In Britain too, the 1960s saw the emergence of investigative reporting. However, some argue that the nature of investigatory journalism has now changed (Franklin, 1997; McManus, 1994). The charge is that the high aims of investigative journalism, of revealing the abuses of power for citizen audiences, have been subsumed by low-cost 'muck-raking', aimed at attracting consumer interest. Such a charge requires unpicking. Investigatory reporting has not disappeared: investigations by broadcasters and broadsheet press continue in both countries; indeed, investigations by leading broadsheet newspapers have led to some major scandals (see chapter 2). However, there has also been an explosion of muck-raking (Franklin, 2004; Sabato et al., 2000). Long, painstaking and expensive investigations cannot hope to be as frequent or as 'cheap' as dirt-digging. Examining the private lives of public officials, government ministers or candidates, to find some kind of less than exemplary behaviour in terms of personal conduct, is often dressed up in the guise of public interest, and, increasingly, investigation into serious or potentially serious transgressions takes place in a news environment that is saturated with exposés of questionable merit. Private lives, as chapter 3 has shown, are dredged up by the tabloid press, and gossip and innuendo printed – treated in some sectors as little different from fact. Private sexual misdemeanours are treated in the same way as acts of dishonesty and financial malpractice in public life. This is most in evidence in tabloid coverage of politics, which focuses largely on a cast of leading political personalities rather than on process and structure. However, there are those who observe that the same charge can be levelled at the coverage by the so-called 'serious' outlets, in that they have not eschewed coverage of private lives, if not themselves breaking stories, then in their coverage of tabloid exposés (Kerbel, 1999).

Politics on demand

News organizations see their audiences as a group of consumers, not only with limited political appetite but also with different tastes and patterns of consumption. Aided by new technology, news organizations increasingly seek to cater for diverse consumer tastes and modes of consumption. The internet allows the news organizations to provide for different audience interests and tailor news output accordingly. As in the US, hard news in the UK has become a commodity for a particular customer group. Increasingly, commercial news organizations see the web as a tool to deliver niche audiences to advertisers. Users are encouraged to subscribe, their choice of stories regularly monitored, and subscribers are offered opportunities to receive news directly.

The notion of the half-hour bulletin watched by a large audience is under pressure, as we have already discussed above. In the UK, there is a growing divergence between popular news bulletins and more in-depth, longer programmes that cater for the different audiences (Harrison, 2000). Increasingly, the customer is offered short headlines of a few minutes on Channel Five: according to one Channel Five producer, 'they vastly out rate our main set piece news programmes [and] consistently score higher in terms of audience appreciation' (Shaw, 2003: 61). For the moment, Channel Four persists with its in-depth 50-minute newscast.

The broadsheets have sought to cater for different audience interests through introducing a legion of new supplements. As McNair notes, newspapers are 'larger, denser . . . [more] accessible to more people than at any previous point' (2000: 39). The broadening of the news agenda has also led the serious press to address new lifestyle and consumer concerns, and new fields of journalism, catering for a variety of interests, are backed up with an increasing online presence, where consumers can follow up their particular interests. Newspapers in both countries have made a significant investment online (Project for Excellence in Journalism, 2006). In both countries, the web provides further scope for newspapers to cater for particular audience tastes. The networks also seek to reach different audiences by a variety of other means: podcasts of stories and bulletins can be downloaded on demand on a personal computer or sent direct to a viewer's mobile phone (ibid.; Shaw, 2006). The BBC, alarmed that it was failing to attract 16–24 year olds to its news programmes, teamed up with youth radio station, Radio One, and with its own children's channel to look at ways of reaching this audience via mobile phones (Holmwood, 2006). ITN now provides 24-hour news to all Vodaphone 3G mobile customers (Deans, 2006). In the US, CBS has pioneered a watch-on-demand news service, CBS.com, where audiences can choose from a selection of stories; the other networks provide similar services, ABC providing a pre-edition of its evening newscast for download (Project for Excellence in Journalism, 2006).

Finding new roles: from news to views

The distinction between news and comment, once a cornerstone of the broadsheet press, is fading. In both countries pressure from competition has meant the high modern notion of providing 'objective' information, on which a civic-minded public can make political decisions, is being abandoned. The changes have been driven in part by advertisers, interested in reaching a particular audience. With the reporting of politics now conducted on a 24-hour basis, almost in real-time, newspapers are no longer the public's first port of call to gain the news. Palmer observes that each of the news outlets is seeking a new role in the 24-hour news environment: while 'the five Ws' are now the domain of the 24-hour news media, the press has had to readjust and find a new role; there is very little point for news outlets to repeat what the audience has seen the day before (2000).[1]

The broadsheet press increasingly sees its role as that of a commentator on events, acting as an interpreter for their readers. There has been a tremendous growth in the 'value-added' that the news media provide for their readers and viewers. In the US, Patterson observes that the press have adopted a more interpretative style of reporting: the proportion of interpretative reports in the *New York Times* between 1960 and 1992 rose from 8 per cent to 80 per cent (T. E. Patterson, 2000: 250) and journalists have moved, in Patterson's words, from being an observer relaying events to being an analyst interpreting events for the audience. Moog (2001) similarly notes that news is increasingly engaged in interpreting events and reactions to interpretations. According to a survey of journalists in 2003, concerns about the blurring of the boundaries between reporting and commentary increased from 53 per cent in 1993 to 64 per cent in 2003 (Pew Research Center, 2003b).

In Britain, McNair notes that there has been a tremendous growth in the amounts of analysis and commentary; beyond simply reporting events, the media provide an interpretative space for their audience: 'spaces where evaluation of an opinion about either the substance, the style, the policy content or the process of political affairs replaces the straight reportage of new information' (2000: 61). Palmer (2000) observes a large recycling process, with the printed press increasingly commenting on events in the news. This process has been fuelled by growth in the number of columnists (McNair, 2000; Tunstall, 1996), who have been called a 'commentariat' (Kronig, 2004). Opinion-led front pages amongst broadsheet press, once a rarity, have grown. The editor of the *Independent* has suggested that broadsheets are becoming 'views-papers' (Tryhorn, 2004); he noted: 'the view behind the news, is more and more what newspapers must do. We cannot compete with electronic media and immediate news' (ibid.).

In both countries, blogging has added a new dimension to the interpretative environment. Key journalists express their opinion on issues not only in newspapers but also online. The blogs allow newspaper columnists to provide running, real-time commentary on political events, almost as they unfold, and readers to respond to the comments. The leading broadsheet press has also moved in to the field of podcasting (Marriner, 2006). Using podcasts, the press is now able to break news. Like 24-hour news channels, it takes live agency feed and can have correspondents on hand to interpret events.

Cost-cutting

Both the press and the networks have had to reduce their costs considerably in order to maintain their profitability. One of the main casualties has been staff. The BBC had to make 30 per cent 'efficiency savings' to fund its new 24-hour news channel (Harrison, 2000), and with further plans to shed some 6,000 posts including 415 in news and current affairs (Plunkett, 2005). There were also redundancies at ITN when it closed ITV's 24-hour news channel after five years, even though the channel had won the best 24-hour news programme award at the 2005 Monte Carlo TV festival (Conlan, 2005). In the US in 2004 the number of network news correspondents had fallen by a third compared to 1985 and there were 2,200 fewer journalists; the number working in radio fell by 44 per cent from 1994 to 2001 (Project for Excellence in Journalism, 2006). CBS's high-profile and longest-running weekly current affairs show, *60 Minutes*, also saw a decline in ratings and responded accordingly by cutting staff (Hodgson, 2001).

Serving the voter?

Elections are significant events in the life of any democracy, and news plays an important role in election campaigns. It is the main source of political information for citizens, enabling them to make an informed choice about which candidate or party to vote for, and is also traditionally the main conduit through which citizens co-witness such democratic rituals. However, the transformation in the way news organizations conceptualize their role has impacted on election coverage in a significant way. The notion of an engaged citizen needing campaign information has been largely replaced by the perception of a consumer with little political appetite – a consumer likely to desert worthy but dull coverage. While in the days of limited outlets and competition such concerns were less pressing, in the increasingly competitive contemporary media environment this lack of appetite puts pressures on news organization. News outlets need to consider how much time and space they can afford to devote to campaigns, which have limited appeal, and how they can best package them to ensure audience interest. Research tends to suggest that the perception of an audience with a limited enthusiasm for campaign coverage, combined with competitive pressures, is having potentially damaging consequences for democratic political communication systems (Blumler and Gurevitch, 1995; Deacon et al., 2001; 2005; Franklin, 2004; Kerbel, 1999).

Framing campaigns

Worried about falling audiences, the established news organizations have sought to change the way elections are covered to maintain audience interest. The large body of research on news coverage of first-order election campaigns in both countries has detected a number of significant changes (see, for example, Gitlin, 1991; Franklin, 2004). One key trend that has attracted concern is the changing focus of campaign coverage, which, according to various studies, has been shown to have shifted from a concentration on substantive issues to portraying the campaign more as a game (Blumler and Gurevitch, 1995; Patterson, 1993) or horse race (Gitlin, 1991), in which the findings of the latest opinion polls are highlighted in an attempt to inject excitement into the proceedings. In the US, Kaplan and Hale found that 55 per cent of campaign stories during the last month of the 2000 presidential campaign on the 74 affiliates focused on candidates' tactics and the race aspect, and only 24 per cent involved candidates talking about the issues (2001: 2). In the UK, the conduct of the campaign now attracts more coverage on TV news than ever before. A study by Goddard et al. (1998) showed that campaign-oriented coverage had doubled on the main BBC evening news bulletin from 13 per cent to 26 per cent between 1992 and 1997, while it increased to 30 per cent from 24 per cent on the ITV evening news bulletin. Deacon et al. (2005) revealed that the amount of coverage concerned with 'electoral process' had risen from 33 per cent in 1997 to 44 per cent in 2005.

In the US, Cappella and Jamieson argue that campaign coverage in the news media is increasingly dominated by what they call the strategic frame. Strategy coverage has several features: '1, wining and losing as the central concern; 2, the language of wars, games and competition; 3, a story with performers, critics, and audience (voters); 4, centrality of performance, style, and perception of the candidate; 5, heavy weighting of polls and the candidates standing in them' (1997: 33). Patterson similarly notes that in covering politics, journalists interpret events 'within a schematic framework according to which candidates compete for advantage' (1993: 57). 'The core principle of the game schema is that candidates are strategic actors whose every move is significant' (ibid.: 58); they are 'continually adjusting to the dynamics of the race', 'driven by a desire to win' and so their every move can be seen as an 'effort to acquire votes' (ibid.: 60–1). The notion of the race is lent weight by the reporting of polls, which are now a key part of media coverage in both countries. So for Patterson (1993) and Cappella and Jamieson (1997), the game schema, or strategy frame, portraying politics as a competitive process between self-interested vote maximizers, becomes the dominant frame subsuming other interpretations of events and politicians' behaviour.

Elections as a niche interest

Many of the older news organizations, which traditionally transmitted political information to citizens, have reduced the amount of coverage they devote to campaigns on their main outlets so as not to risk alienating their readers and viewers, while at the same time placing coverage in niche supplements and online to be accessed by those interested. In both countries, news broadcasters have reduced their reportage of first-order elections.[2] Campaign coverage has become more episodic, concentrating more on newsworthy events, such as gaffes, overheard remarks and rows, only to fade when things return to the routine of the campaign (Sabato et al., 2000). The coverage of second-order elections has virtually disappeared, or has been limited to specialist sections of news organizations' websites (Patterson, 2002). In the US, research has shown that coverage of the presidential campaign by the main networks in the year leading up to the November election declined by some 863 minutes, from 3,401 minutes in 1988 to 2,538 minutes in 2004 (Tyndall Report; see also Norris, 2001b). These findings are supported by research from the Center for Media and Public Affairs, which found that evening network newscast coverage of the 2000 presidential campaign was down by roughly a third from 1996, which was down 50 per cent from 1992 (Taylor, 2000; see also Macedo et al., 2005). It is not just national campaign coverage that has declined; so too has coverage of campaigns for state governor. In California, in 1998, research at the Annenberg School of Communication showed that 'the state's major television Channels devoted less than half a percent of their of their total news coverage to the governor's race in the three months leading up to the election' (Taylor, 2000).

In Britain, the picture is similar. Research shows that news coverage of the general election campaign on the main terrestrial channels has fallen since 1992; in 2005 the main evening news bulletins on BBC1 and ITV devoted almost half the time to election stories compared to the 1992 campaign (Deacon et al., 2005). In 1987, the BBC evening flagship news bulletin was expanded by some 25 minutes during the election campaign; during the 1992 and 1997 campaigns, this had fallen to 15 minutes; the bulletin was only expanded by 5 minutes in the 2001 campaign and not at all in 2005 (Stanyer, 2002).

General election campaign coverage in the British popular press has fallen even more dramatically. The tabloids have almost become an election-free zone in the UK, with very little prominence given to the election: the *Sun*, the *Mirror* and the *Star* carried campaign news on their front pages in 2005 on seven, five and three days respectively, out of a possible 21 days. The *Daily Mail* and the *Express* did little better, devoting eleven and eight days respectively to the campaign. Even key events receive little coverage in the tabloids. Research by the *Guardian* on press coverage of the Liberal Democrat and Labour manifesto launches in 2001 found that the tabloids and mid-market press – with a combined circulation of 9.2 million – devoted little space to their content: the Liberal Democrat manifesto received no coverage in the *Express* or the *Star*; the *Mirror* devoted four paragraphs to it, the *Sun* just a hundred words and the *Daily Mail* half a page. Labour's manifesto fared marginally better, receiving a line in the *Star*, less than a page in the *Mirror* and the *Sun* and two pages in the *Express* and the *Daily Mail* (Stanyer, 2002). In Britain, there is a growing gap between the broadsheet newspapers that provide more coverage, but segmented in special sections, and the tabloid press. Coverage of second-order contests such as the European elections or local elections is virtually non-existent in the tabloid press and limited in the broadsheet press, with most of the attention focused at the end of the campaign.

In both countries, the reduction in coverage on the main news outlets has been mirrored by the growth of more coverage on the web and in 24-hour news channels. The websites of news organizations have become a deposit for a large quantity of information on the contestants and their policies and the web has been used effectively in both countries to offer additional information to the electorate. However, such sites tend to attract a minority of citizens. In 2004–5, 29 per cent of the population in the US and 27 per cent in the UK went online to get news and information about elections (Pew Internet, 2005a; BBC/MORI Citizenship Survey cited in Schifferes, 2006). Of these around 80 per cent in the UK, and 40 per cent in the US, visited the websites of major news organizations like the BBC, CNN, MSNBC, and the *New York Times* (Pew Internet, 2005a; BBC/MORI Citizenship Survey, cited in Schifferes, 2006). In sum, as fewer citizens come together to witness democratic rituals, so the coverage of such rituals shrinks on the traditional mass news channels. Detailed election coverage, once a feature of mainstream news, is now treated increasingly as a specialist interest, there if the consumer wants to access it.

Conclusion

This chapter has sketched the changing way established news organizations understand their role and perceive their audiences. For much of the twentieth century, audiences were largely seen by news media through a civic lens, and journalism was largely driven by norms of objectivity and public service (Calabrese, 2000; Hallin, 2000; T. E. Patterson, 2000; Schudson, 1978; Seymour-Ure, 1991). This, combined with spectrum scarcity and the universal monological nature of communication technology, provided a unique channel for the flow of civically nourishing information, which reached audiences of all partisan shades. As the high modern phase passed, conceptions of audiences primarily as citizens have gradually been replaced by notions of audiences first and foremost as consumers. While catering for the needs of an audience of consumers does not necessarily mean less or poorer quality political coverage – although some evidence suggests that it might well do – it does pose serious questions for the health of the political communication system in several other respects.

First, as audiences fragment, the tendency is for news organizations to seek to cater for the different niches that arise, segmenting their output accordingly. The essential role of the 'general interest intermediary' (Sunstein, 2001) providing a shared experience for members of a political community is abandoned in favour of catering for the different tastes of consumers. Of course, there are key news events to which all citizens are exposed, but outside this any sense of shared political experience is slowly disappearing; it could be argued that democracy is gradually being deprived of a last common meeting ground for diverging views (Katz, 1996: 22; see also Macedo et al., 2005: 43).

Second, news organizations tend to marginalize the worthy but dull. If a particular event or issue is perceived to be of limited interest, such as election campaigns, the tendency is move it to the margins and perhaps invest less money in its coverage. This is not to say that the service on the margins is necessarily poor: it might well be excellent in places, but it is a service that is reliant on being accessed. While the mass news media of the high modern era exposed audiences to views that they had largely not pre-selected, contemporary consumer-driven journalism recoils for fear of losing audience share. Civically nourishing news is there for those who want to be nourished, but it is, increasingly, little more of an option than gardening or sport in the multichannel environment.

Third, there is a tendency for advertising-sponsored news media to be interested only in certain niche audiences; for example, they are interested in the young or the comparatively affluent rather than the old or those with low disposable incomes. The pressure is on news programmes to deliver these audiences to advertisers, not to provide political information for a mass audience.

If the nexus of technology, journalistic values and regulation conspired to generate a particular conception of the audience and the organizational role, then regulatory reforms, new technology and market logic have combined to produce another – the news consumer. With the end of captive audiences, monitoring political life is an opt-in activity for those who are interested; conventional political news, and election news in particular, is in danger of becoming a consumer interest like gardening or horse-racing, a state of affairs that will have real consequences for the health of the political communication system.

CHAPTER
05   The Media and the
Populist Political Impulse

IDEOLOGICALLY charged, sometimes partisan, media outlets are an important feature of the political communication systems of the US and Britain. In the US, while some have remarked on the decline of press partisanship (T. E. Patterson, 2000; Wattenberg, 1996), others have observed the emergence of a partisan electronic media (Hallin, 2006). Indeed, Hallin notes that the 're-emergence of partisan media' is one of the most significant trends in the US in recent years (2006). Aided by the abolition of the Federal Communication Commission's 'fairness doctrine', the notion of objectivity, once central to US broadcasting, has been challenged by the rise of overtly partisan outlets. Channels such as Fox, the Clear Channel and Sinclair Broadcasting, and a host of talk radio shows, have sought to produce output for media consumers with specific political views (ibid.). These outlets, however, are not partisan in the traditional sense of the word; more accurately, they share a conservative or liberal ideological outlook and agenda. They may support the Republican Party, or in some instances the Democrats, but they are not run or funded by either party, their content is not determined by parties or candidates and they can be equally critical of candidates of either party.

In Britain, there has been a loosening of the connections between political parties and the press (Seymour-Ure, 1991). The 'key trend' has been dealignment 'often expressed as diffuse disenchantment with the two major parties' (Deacon and Wring, 2002: 207). But this has not meant that the press has become apolitical – far from it. National newspapers overtly express their opinions, but their outlook is not set and controlled by a political party. They are regularly critical of government and political parties, especially where their agenda departs from those of the papers. The majority of the national press is situated on the right of the political spectrum. Tunstall (1996) argues that the Thatcher premiership saw the emergence of a 'new right press', broadly supportive of Thatcher's agenda, and highly critical of any opponents, especially on the left. Even though Margaret Thatcher has left the scene, the 'new right press' remains.

What is occurring, as this chapter will elaborate, is not the re-emergence of partisanship, as some have argued, but the appearance and spread of ideologically charged populist politics in the media. New and traditional news outlets have emerged as populist political actors at the centre of popular reaction to a variety of factors impacting upon lives of citizens in both countries, such as taxes, immigration, security, crime, global trade and European integration, to name but a few. In both countries, these outlets take a stance on the issues that resonate with their audience; they not only frame developments for their audiences but also seek to campaign on their behalf, and articulate their concerns to politicians about the issues mentioned and a host of others. However, while ideologically charged, such a stance is also driven by the economic realities of the media environment in which these outlets operate; it is the need to maintain audience share in a competitive market place that motivates these outlets to campaign. In reality those opinions out of tune with readers' concerns are soon changed. They may 'rant and rave', but do so in part to maintain an audience and the revenue that comes with it.

While the previous chapter detailed the way and extent to which audiences are treated as consumers, this chapter examines the way in which the media also appeal to audiences as members of a variety of communities. It looks at examples of right-wing talk radio in the US and the right-wing national press in Britain. It explores the rhetoric of both, looking at the process of 'Othering', and the way in which these reactionary populist media outlets portray those that their audience see as a threat. It argues that the right-wing media increasingly stereotype actors and institutions that pose a threat to what they see as the ordinary, decent, law-abiding, hard-working and god-fearing citizen, both denigrating and demonizing them. The media not only reinforce audience prejudices, ignorance and fears of the Other, but also seek to maintain and build ratings. The chapter argues that, as audiences fragment in a competitive media marketplace, there is a danger of divisions and prejudices in society being reinforced by commercially driven profit-pressured media organizations hungry for audience share.

Political populism

Populism has been called 'a difficult slippery concept' (Taggart, 2000: 2), and there are many definitions (for a synoptic account, see ibid.). It is a label often attached to a wide variety of activities, actors and rhetoric, in a fairly indiscriminate way. As Mazzoleni notes, perhaps much of the 'conceptual uncertainty' derives from the fact that populism has taken 'different directions in different historical eras' (2003: 4). Although difficult to define with any precision, political populism has a long tradition in both countries (see Kazin, 1998; McWilliam, 1998). Both left- and right-wing, democratic and autocratic movements and actors can adopt a populist approach to politics, but, while their values may differ, the approach remains the same: political populism can be recognized by a central binary.

The populist political actors and movements claim to represent and speak on behalf of one group and against another – for example, on behalf of the poor, the law-abiding or the moral majority, and against big business, government or criminal minorities. So, as Betz notes, they not only 'claim to speak for the unarticulated opinions, demands and sentiments of the ordinary people', but also channel those sentiments against a range of opponents (1998: 4). Populism may also define itself in opposition to the other groups, values, religions, races and nations that are seen as a threat. One characteristic of populism has been its anti-establishment nature: the anti-establishment populist rejects any insider status, claiming to speak on behalf of the 'people' against the 'power bloc' (McGuigan, 1992). The 'power bloc' includes a wide range of actors, such as politicians, big business, the media and other authority figures who represent a potential or real threat, or an obstacle, to the particular group. In American political culture, as Huntington observes, there is a long tradition of 'suspicion of government as the most dangerous embodiment of power' (1981: 33). There is a fear of federal tyranny, anger at the bloated state and at liberal elites, exemplified by anti-government armed militias such as the American Militia and the Patriot Movement, which in 1996 had an estimated membership of 250,000 and the support of five million people across 30 states (Boggs, 2000; Castells, 2004). But there are also more mainstream popular reactions against 'big government', for example, the Proposition 13 campaign in California in 1978, which was a revolt by middle-income home-owners and small businesses against 'local property taxes' and welfare spending (Boggs 2000). Anti-establishment populism can also be seen in British politics; government taxation has been the source of popular protest and the European Union has also been the object of much hostility.

The populist political actor is often a charismatic individual who has 'distinctive public speaking skills' and 'mediagenic personal qualities' (Mazzoleni, 2003: 5). The language used is often emotionally charged and draws on 'traditional kinds of expression, tropes, themes and images to convince large numbers [of people] to join their side, endorse their views or particular issues' (Kazin, 1998: 3).

Right-wing populism

Populist politics takes reactionary or progressive forms (Kazin, 1998). Although there is a long history of progressive populism in both countries, in recent years right-wing populism has become dominant in the US and the UK (ibid.; Taggart, 2000). Indeed, Mazzoleni notes that the populism that has become firmly established in advanced industrial democracies is on the 'conservative reactionary spectrum of political ideology' (2003: 4). It can be seen as a reaction, or opposition, to the threat, or perceived threat, of the Other. It is reactionary, small 'c' conservative in nature, seeking to conserve a way of life, particular values, valued institutions and practices against a series of Others. Its reactionary nature stems from a perceived threat to shared value systems, ways of life – the nation even, whether that comes from terrorists, asylum seekers, government bureaucrats or supra-national bodies such as the European Union or the United Nations; it taps into concerns and fears of the audience that arise from the perceived threat to their community or way of life. Progressive populism, in contrast, does not seek to conserve but to change particular values, valued institutions and practices. The Other is seen as an obstacle to achieving their aims.

A key characteristic of populist political rhetoric is the central binary of 'us' and 'them'. In simple terms, the 'us' can be seen as those who belong, those who are known, familiar people, places and culture, those who share values; the 'them', the Other, those who do not belong, who do not share these views, values and beliefs. The 'us' may vary in size and in other ways; it may be the nation, a local community, a particular class, an age group, those who hold a certain belief or value. But whatever it is, it is intimately connected to belonging and shared identity. Whosoever the 'us' is, the populist outlook, to borrow Pickering's words, 'presumes a direct I/we reciprocity of identity despite internal differentiation' with any group (2001: 89). The Other may similarly vary. However, the Other is defined as different, as being apart, as not belonging (Pickering, 2001). 'Symbolic boundaries' are therefore constructed around the group, which serve to differentiate it further from the Other (ibid.). Thus, populism defines itself in opposition to one or a variety of 'Others', whether from above, below or outside the group and, in doing so, it appeals principally to the shared identity of its audience, to their sense of belonging to some imagined community – in national terms it appeals to the audience's sense of patriotism, and the need to respond to outside threats.

Whatever any 'real' nature of the threat posed by the Other there may be, populist actors seek to amplify it. They play on the fears and beliefs of community members, exploiting any distrust. The right-wing populist reinforces the fears that exist between communities, between the 'us' and the Other. The Other is framed as a real or potential threat, to the community, to a way of life, livelihood or a moral order etc. – or at the very least a cause of concern. The threat becomes an important frame for interpreting the actions of the Other: their actions are framed as yet more evidence of their intentions. Ultimately it is the audience's fears of the Other, real or imagined, on which the populist advocate plays.

The media and political populism

The role of the media in the development of populist movements, while central, has often been overlooked. All populist political movements rely on the media in some way, especially the popular mass audience media outlets, where they are likely to receive coverage and the popular media are more likely to provide favourable coverage or give space for the articulation of populist views (Mazzoleni, 2003). Mazzoleni conceives of the media as being separate from the populist actors or movement: neo-populist political movements or actors seek to get their message across to an audience and the media covers them. However, outlets can be populist political actors in their own right, articulating their audiences' concerns and fears but also seeking to campaign on their behalf (see Conboy, 2006).

The populist media outlet is not in itself new, but there has been a flourishing of such populist outlets in both countries. This growth has been the result of several factors. First, there has been a transformation of the media environment: the end of spectrum scarcity and the spread of the internet have lead to a growth of outlets for populist political actors, and the unregulated web has proved a particularly fertile ground for populist movements in both countries. Second has been a transformation of the regulatory environment (see chapter 4). In the US, a spur was the Reagan administration's removal of the Federal Communication Commission fairness clause for broadcasting (Davis and Owen, 1998; Johnson, 2001); this had the effect of enabling the formation of a series of politically partial and partisan radio and television outlets. Third, there has been a transformation of the party political environment. In Britain, with no such regulatory relaxation on balance, partisan politics has largely been limited to the press. However, with a growing disenchantment in the main political parties, the tabloid press, in particular, has adopted its own position on issues, irrespective of the main parties' views, a position given further impetus by circulation wars. These outlets are not a movement in the formal sense of party and in many respects benefit from not being seen as politicians or as political parties.

The right-wing media

A substantial section of the populist outlets in both countries can be described as right wing. The number of the outlets and the size of their audiences mean that, individually and collectively, they play an important political role in political communication systems. While there are different shades of right-wing views expressed in these outlets, all share a characteristic of right-wing populism outlined in the previous section: they are conservative in nature, seeking to conserve a way of life, particular values and valued institutions and practices against a series of 'Others'. However, they go further, seeking to exploit their audiences' fears and concerns about a range of Others and the threats they pose. They pander to their prejudices, feed their arrogance and hystericize the threat of the Other; the Other is stereotyped and lampooned, and the threat they pose is exaggerated. Their rhetoric can be seen as negatively 'epideictic', denigrating the Other (Finlayson, 2006). Right-wing media are routinely involved in the construction of myths about the insider community and the Other and the threat they pose – myths that resonate with the chosen audience – and the media act as a channel for the collective anxieties of the listener or reader community. It is important to note that audience interaction is a key element of populist media: they encourage audiences to show their anger and resentment, to target their elected representatives. This process is not one-off, but continuous, there is always an opportunity to phone, text or write in response to a particular issue that is being discussed (see chapter 7). The media and the audience they entertain are linked; they are part of the same community, sharing the same values, concerned about the same threats.

It should be noted that the right-wing media operate within a commercial framework. While the format varies, the aim is the same: to maximize audiences. Profitability is central to these outlets' survival and they have to maintain ratings and circulation. Championing various causes that resonate with their listeners or readers, defending their values and way of life, often proves good for ratings, and in a ratings-driven media environment such a strategy has sound economic reasoning. Combined, these outlets, in both countries, reach an audience of millions. The next section explores two of the highest-profile reactionary populist media actors: talk radio in the US and the right-wing national press in the UK.

Talk radio: the voice of the people or channels of resentment?

Talk radio is a visible and raucous part of the US political communication system, broadcasting at least 6 hours a day, 5 days a week, 52 weeks a year (Barker, 1998). Talk shows dominate the AM radio frequencies, and are both local and nationally syndicated to a host of local affiliates. According to one estimate, the number of talk shows tripled between the 1980s and the late 1990s, from 200 to 600 (Diamond and Silverman, 1997). Others note that the number of shows had risen to 1,000 in the same period, trailing behind only country music stations (Barker, 1998; Johnson, 2001). Whatever the exact figures, there is a plethora of talk stations producing hours of output, which has grown even further with online narrowcasting. The expansion of talk radio is due in small part to political talk shows that discuss 'politicians, elections and public policy issues' (Barker, 1998: 83). The number of those gaining political information from talk radio has increased: in 2000, 15 per cent of those sampled learned about the presidential campaign and the candidates from talk radio; in 2004 that figure had risen to 17 per cent of those sampled (Pew Research Center, 2004b).

The shows follow a set format, usually starting with the host introducing the topic for discussion. In the introductory monologue, which could be anything from two to twenty minutes depending on the audience response, the host gives his or her opinion on the topic and invites the audience to respond. Often, shows also have a guest, who will usually, along with the host, take calls for part of the programme. This phone-in is the key element of the show and the host continually makes appeals to his or her audience to phone in, and will reintroduce the topic at intervals throughout the show (Davis and Owen, 1998; see also chapter 7). However, while audience participation is the life-blood of shows, it is ultimately the host's show and he or she controls the direction and flow of the show, determines the agenda and invites callers to respond.

The politically oriented talk shows across the US are hosted by often outspoken and provocative hosts. These larger-than-life characters label themselves in such a way as to attract listeners – conservative, independent, liberal. Hosts are encouraged to be outspoken and to sound passionate about an issue (Davis and Owen, 1998). That said, their political stance is backed by audience considerations; they are entertainers seeking to hold an audience and attract listeners – ratings determine the focus of the show (ibid.). Most of the nationally syndicated talk radio hosts are conservative. There have been hosts on the left – Jim Hightower, Mario Cumo and, more recently, the former *Saturday Night Live* star Al Franken – but they have often failed to build the same kind of audiences as their right-wing counterparts (Silver, 2005). The right-wing host's political outlook has been described as 'Reaganism with a rock and roll beat' (Diamond and Silverman, 1997: 121). This reflects the fact that a majority of listeners tend to describe themselves as conservative and identify with the Republican Party (Davis, 1997; Davis and Owen, 1998). Davis and Owen note that talk radio audiences predominantly share the right-wing views of their hosts and research by Bolce et al. (1996) found that in 1994, 29 per cent of listeners identified themselves as conservative, and 26 per cent as Republican. A National Election Studies survey in 1996 found that those who listened to talk radio were largely conservative – 57 per cent – and more likely to identify with the Republicans – 37 per cent – compared to 32 per cent for the Democrats (Davis and Owen, 1998). The numbers identifying with the right seems to be increasing: more recent research found that 48 per cent of listeners in 2004 identified themselves as Republicans and 38 per cent as Democrats (Pew Research Center, 2004b).

The most widely listened-to shows are those by so-called 'liberal-baters' (Davis and Owen, 1998). Of these, the most well known are Rush Limbaugh and G. Gordon Liddy, with a further group of national hosts such as Oliver North, Michael Reagan, Chuck Harder, Ann Coulter and a series of local hosts. The shows are events-driven; they tend to follow the national news agenda, drawing on other news media and talk shows. The issues discussed are often so-called 'water cooler topics', issues which the public discuss at work or home (Davis and Owen, 1998). A content analysis on three sample days of conservative talk radio in 1996 found that 16 per cent of time was devoted to crime and punishment, 15 per cent to military and foreign affairs, 11 per cent to federal budget and taxes, 12 per cent to the Republican primaries, 9 per cent to minorities and 6 per cent to Clinton; the rest were on a range of subjects, including the media, health, business and technology and Congress (Cappella et al., 1996).

As noted, one of the hooks of the shows is that the host is controversial, that his opinions, or those of his guests, are meant to generate a response. While the show may be events-driven, the host will also identify him- or herself on the side of the listeners, the ordinary hard-working, god-fearing citizen, in opposition to a variety of Others. These include an assortment of 'outsiders'; for instance, since 11 September 2001, the Other has been the Islamic fundamentalist or the wider Arab world. In the immediate aftermath of the terrorist attacks, shows 'buzzed with talk of dropping nuclear bombs on Afghanistan and exterminating all Muslims' (Kellner, 2002: 147).

It is not only outsiders who are targets, but also establishment figures such as politicians, and government in general. Hosts regularly amplify issues which they see as being ignored by 'establishment politics', express their opposition to government policy, their outrage at politicians' behaviour or certain moral issues or consider conspiracy theories about the activities of government. One particularly long-standing target attacked by these shows is the 'liberal Other'. The liberal Other is a stereotype constructed by right-wing hosts for the benefit of the talk show listener – a person or institution whose liberal beliefs, values and motivations are totally at odds with those of their listeners. President Clinton proved a particular hate figure of talk show hosts, along with the liberal cultural elite and the liberal mainstream media, including Hollywood and the networks. Many on the right have, since the 1970s, been convinced that the mainstream news media were hostile to their views (Kazin, 1998). Further, the liberal Other's beliefs and values are framed as a threat to the community of listeners. Post-9/11, the liberal Other is portrayed as unpatriotic, weak on terror and ready to capitulate to America's enemies and to jeopardize America's security. Both the stereotyped Others and the threat they pose are continually reinforced, day after day, show after show. This can be seen clearly in the example of Rush Limbaugh's show.

Rush Limbaugh and the liberal Other

Rush Limbaugh's show went from being syndicated to 50 stations nationwide in the early 1990s to 500 in four years (Diamond and Silverman, 1997). His show reaches an average weekly audience of 20 million listeners (Barker, 1998; Silver, 2005). Limbaugh issues a monthly e-bulletin to his listeners and he has a web-presence in addition to the show. His listeners are largely conservative: research found that in 2004, 77 per cent of those who listen to Rush Limbaugh described themselves as conservative, up from 72 per cent in 2002 (Pew Research Center, 2004b). Many listeners are also pro-Republican: a survey of listeners in 2004 found that 88 per cent approved of the way George W. Bush was doing his job as President and only 12 per cent disapproved (National Annenberg Election Survey, 2004). Limbaugh and his 'ditto-heads', as some of his listeners are called, represent a dissonance community. Limbaugh's views are reinforced by those who call in; his audience hears a 'stream of callers who corroborate the host's message' and reinforce their own views (Barker, 1998: 86), and the prejudices of his conservative listeners are reinforced by the show's host.

The liberal Other is a key stereotype in Limbaugh's shows. Those labelled liberal include mainstream organizations, such as the Democrat Party and the news media, feminist and pro-choice groups, and high-profile politicians and members of the cultural elite. There is little distinction between the shades of opinion on the left; they are all given the liberal tag. Limbaugh's show repeatedly questions the motivations and values of liberals, and in the wake of 9/11 and the invasion of Iraq, the patriotism of the liberal Other has come under particular attack. For example, in 2004, after the publication of the prisoner abuse photographs from the Abu Ghraib detention centre in Iraq, Limbaugh attacked the liberal media for sensationalizing events and deliberately misrepresenting what the photos showed, which in his view was nothing more than a 'skull and bones' fraternity initiation (Smucker, 2004). In one monologue about the media coverage of Abu Ghraib, he reflected, 'there are people in this country who may not be on the side of the terrorist in Iraq, but their actions wouldn't be any different if they were, and those are Democrats and liberals, who are anti-US military and anti-victory' (ibid.: 3). Later in 2004, at the height of the presidential campaign, he persistently linked the Democrats to Al-Qaeda, suggesting a vote for candidate John Kerry was a vote for terrorism (Media Matters, 2004).

High-profile liberals are regularly singled out for attack. During the 1990s, the Clinton presidency proved a 'god-send' for many talk show hosts and Limbaugh spent many of his shows attacking the administration (Diamond and Silverman, 1997). Indeed, a content analysis of his show found that around 9 per cent of output during February and March 1996 focused on the Clinton administration and scandal (Cappella et al., 1996). Even after 11 September 2001, Limbaugh blamed Clinton for not doing enough to prevent the attack while he was President (Kellner, 2002). Barker (1998) identifies one rhetorical technique used by Limbaugh – 'name-calling' – and found that Limbaugh made extensive use of derogatory name-calling, for example, calling Hillary Clinton a 'femi-nazi' – a stereotype that 'stirred the target audience's worst fears' (Diamond and Silverman, 1997: 70); President Clinton, during the Lewinsky affair, became 'philanderer in chief' (ibid.). It was not just the Clintons who were the subject of name-calling: presidential candidate John Kerry was frequently called a 'gigolo' or 'skirt chaser', and Howard Dean a 'truly sick man'; other favourites for Limbaugh's ire have included Senator Ted Kennedy, Jane Fonda and actor Michael J. Fox – whom he accused in 2006 of exaggerating the extent to which he was suffering from Parkinson's disease. Environmentalists are regularly called 'water-melons' – green on the outside, red in the middle – and feminists are 'femi-nazis' (Davis and Owen, 1998); in Rush's words: 'I love the women's movement especially when I'm walking behind it' (Davis, 1997: 325).

Humour plays a key part in the reinforcement of the liberal stereotype; different liberal figures become the material for jokes, which reaffirm the prejudices of the listeners. A typical show intercuts audience calls and Limbaugh monologues with taped songs produced by the show's team. Diamond and Silverman provide typical examples:

> The Andy Williams version of the wildlife anthem *Born Free* was punctuated with machine gun fire and mortar explosions ('gotcha! animal rights wackos'); Dion's *The Wanderer* was retitled the Philanderer, and sung by an Edward Kennedy impersonator ('Cause I'm a Kennedy, yes I'm Ted Kennedy / I sleep around, around, around . . .'); and Hillary Clinton was ridiculed in a mock trailer for the motion picture *Single White Female* ('. . . the terror coming to your neighbourhood soon'). (1997: 121)

Behind the name-calling and humour, the liberal Other is constructed as a threat to his listeners and their beliefs and values. The threat liberals pose is of course exaggerated through a series of myths, such as that liberals are unpatriotic, or that liberal big government is eager to take the money of hard-working Americans through taxes, etc. As Barker observes, Limbaugh's show 'operates from the perspective that government activity in the domestic realm poses a threat to freedom, and that any government interference with markets results in inefficiency, waste and degradation' (1998: 86). The 'threat' becomes an important frame for interpreting the actions of the liberal Other, and while their actions and views might be considered 'zany', the threat they pose to the listeners and the wider country is real.

Political talk radio in the UK

In the more regulated world of British broadcasting the phenomenon of political talk radio is not as well established, but if London and other large cities are anything to go by, it is a form of mediated populism that may well become more established. Recent expansion of commercial local radio has seen the growth of talk shows. Many of the shows, as in the US, focus on key issues, and the audience is encouraged to phone in and let their views be known and to vent their frustrations. The right-wing populism of Limbaugh and Liddy is manifest in shows by James Whale on *TalkSport*, Scottie McClue on *Forth2* (an Edinburgh radio station) and James Stannage on Manchester's *Magic 1152* (Muir, 2003).

In London the activities of its left-wing mayor, Ken Livingstone, has attracted constant attack from several talk show hosts; Jon Gaunt and Nick Ferrari – former *Sun* executive turned talk show host for the London station LBC – have been particularly hostile. In 2003, the mayor's refusal to sanction a victory parade for British troops after the Iraq war led to the right-wing Ferrari to urge his listeners to jam the switch boards at City Hall. In another incident, after Ferrari was censured by the broadcasting standards commission for a show on asylum seekers, the mayor wrote to LBC management enquiring what action LBC were going to take. Ferrari responded by telling his listeners about the incident, but framing it as an attempt to get him sacked by the mayor. Listeners jammed the switchboard to denounce the mayor's behaviour (Muir, 2003).

The British press and reactionary populism

Unlike talk radio, the press is not a new addition to the British political communication scenery. As mentioned, the national press, while becoming less attached to political parties, is increasingly ideologically charged. The ideological alignment of the British press can be understood by looking at the position of national newspapers along two imaginary axes. The vertical axis marks levels of party support and runs, to borrow Deacon and Wring's words, from staunch Labour through to staunch Conservative, with a corridor of uncertainty or ambiguity in between. That axis is bisected by a second, an ideological continuum between left and right. The national press is, then, mainly in the corridor of partisan uncertainty or ambiguity, but increasingly polarized along the ideological continuum with a majority on the right of the ideological continuum. Like talk radio hosts, a significant number of these papers have a reactionary agenda. The right-wing tabloids are often overtly xenophobic, and highly critical of those they see as posing a threat to the nation and community. The right-wing tabloids account for just over half of daily national newspaper circulation: the *Daily Mail*, the *Express* and the *Sun* have a combined circulation of approximately 6.3 million – based on February 2006 figures – representing around 56 per cent of total daily circulation. In addition, there are the right-wing Sunday tabloids, the *News of the World*, the *Mail on Sunday* and the *Sunday Express*, with a combined circulation of approximately 6.5 million, which represent 55 per cent of total Sunday circulation – based on February 2006 figures.

Tabloid newspaper readers are treated to a brand of pernicious populism. As members of a community – whether this is the hardworking tax-payer, the law-abiding citizen or the moral majority or the nation – they are continually bombarded with a variety of stereotyped Others, welfare scroungers, trade unions, teenage single mothers, drug addicts, paedophiles, young criminals, asylum seekers and Islamic terrorists. These are but a few of the stereotypes portrayed as a threat to the taken-for-granted moral order, way of life, societal norms, etc. Research on moral panics and the media, too large to examine in detail here, clearly shows how the right-wing tabloid press, and the press more generally, routinely exploit the shock value of transgressions by the Other (see Cohen, 1973; Critcher, 2005). Atypical events and stereotyped folk devils are placed against the backdrop of the normal everyday, and decent ordinary people (Pickering, 2001). The reaction to those posing the threat can be ferocious.

Like talk show hosts, the tabloids seek to encourage feedback. Readers are regularly given the opportunity to participate in a phone poll, email or write in response to a particular issue that is being discussed, and enabling attitude-expression – and then publishing the results – reaffirms the newspapers' initial strident tones. In the ensuing climate of outrage the newspapers attack politicians for not doing enough, and campaign for tougher sanctions against the Other, often demanding new legislation to curb transgressions (Aldridge, 2003; Cross, 2005). For example, the *News of the World* campaigned for so-called 'Sarah's law' – an equivalent of 'Megan's Law' in the US – which would require communities to be notified if a convicted paedophile takes up residence.

There is also a strong nationalistic element to tabloid populism, which is manifest in the coverage of numerous events from sport to international affairs. They are 'belligerently British', expressing hostility toward the outsider (McGuigan, 1992); the nation becomes the site of mutual reader and newspaper political identification. This shared 'banal' national identity can be seen in the coverage of immigration and asylum seekers, radical Islamists and the European Union (Conboy, 2006). Asylum seekers are seen and framed as not belonging to the homeland: they are Othered, characterized as 'bogus spongers'. In one editorial in March 2000, the *Sun* raged: 'Scroungers, illegal immigrants and criminals are sucking this country dry. The cost of this multi-billion pound packet is staggering. And it is hard-working taxpayers who are footing the bill' (Conboy, 2002: 157). The juxtaposition between the 'us' and the 'them' could hardly be clearer. The hot topic of asylum is rarely out the tabloid press, and is often combined with other 'red button' issues such as social security fraud (Conboy, 2006). Governments, in turn, are attacked for doing little to prevent the 'flood' of those seeking to come into the country, or being unable to do anything, due to 'venal' lawyers, 'high-minded' judges or human rights legislation undermining the immigration system. Government intransigence or ineffectiveness is 'counterpoised to the reasonable expectations of the taxpayer' for effective government action (ibid.: 96).

The tabloids seek to mobilize their readers to express their opinions on the issues they have identified. For example, the *Sun* launched its 'End this Asylum Madness Now' campaign in January 2003, running on from an earlier campaign about asylum seekers, entitled 'Britain Has Had Enough' (see Conboy, 2002). A key part of the campaign was a reader petition or phone hot line: in 2003 the *Sun* provided a cut-out form, which could be easily filled in by the reader and returned free-post to the *Sun*. The paper claimed to have received 400,000 petitions, which it delivered to Downing Street.

The threat to the national community is not solely external: the British Islamic Other has become portrayed as threat to the homeland, especially since the 7 July 2005 bombings in London. The radical London-based Muslim cleric, Abu Hamza, has been a particular target of tabloid vitriol; the adjective 'evil' is regularly attached to his name, and his prosthetic arm, ending in a hook, the source of his tabloid nickname – Hooky. For the tabloids and their readers the 'evil Hooky' has become the personification of the irrational Islamic fundamental-ist (Conboy, 2006). Hamza and the acts of an extremist minority are prima facie evidence in the tabloids of the threat Islamists pose to the nation and, as with the case of asylum seekers, the government is attacked for its failure to act, or human rights legislation blamed for protecting such a minority. In turn, the tabloids call for ever more draconian measures to curb terror, with stringent restrictions on civil liberties justified as the only appropriate response.

It is not just groups and individuals that are portrayed as threats to the homeland; the European Union has been constantly presented in the right-wing press as a threat to the nation and British values. The next section examines the representation of the European Union in the press in more detail.

The European Other

Nationalistic populism, illustrated above, is manifest not only in the tabloid coverage of the European Union (EU), but also in coverage by the right-wing broadsheets, which have also pursued an anti-EU agenda. The right-wing Euro-sceptic press dominates national news-paper circulation in Britain: the *Daily Mail*, the *Express*, the *Sun*, the *Daily Telegraph* and *The Times* have a combined circulation of approxi-mately 7.6 million – based on February 2006 figures. This represents around 68 per cent of total daily circulation. In addition, there is the right-wing Sunday press – the *News of the World*, the *Mail on Sunday*, the *Sunday Express*, the *Sunday Telegraph* and the *Sunday Times*, which repre-sent 72 per cent of Sunday circulation – based on February 2006 figures. The 1990s saw a growth of opposition to both the EU and to the project of European integration and the formation of a federal Europe, and the right-wing press has been at the forefront of this opposition. The EU (a term often used loosely) is framed as a threat to 'British' values and way of life. Editorials and the opinion columns in the right-wing press have adopted the classic 'people versus the power bloc' dynamic; they claim to speak on behalf of the British 'people' and against the distant, remote and foreign 'power bloc'. They continually provide a crude and politically charged assessment of the activities of the 'power bloc'. The European Union and its initiatives, plans and policies are framed, at best, as the work over-zealous faceless, often 'barmy', bureaucrats bent on changing the British way of life and, at worst, as representing 'overweening bureaucracy attempting to wrest control of Britain into its own hands'; a threat to the sovereignty of the British nation state (Dougal, 2003: 29). The papers seek to keep in touch, not only with their readers' views on European integration, but also with public opinion. The *Sun* and *The Times* have regularly commissioned public opinion surveys on EU matters: between 1996 and 2005, together they commissioned 13 polls from MORI, asking questions about leaving the EU, replacing the pound with the Euro and the EU Constitution.

Euro-myths

The right-wing press regularly ridicules the EU for constructing silly and petty rules. One of the most popular forms of reporting EU matters is the so called Euro-myth. These are exaggerated stories or even inventions about the activities of EU bodies, or EU directives which defy 'common sense', such as the banning of mince pies, curved bananas, busty barmaids, soya milk, mushy peas, vitamin supplements – to name a few of numerous examples; indeed, the European Commission, which has been monitoring such stories, has logged 126 separate Euro-myths propagated between 1995 and 2003 (see <www.cec.org.uk>). In 2003, for instance, the *Daily Mail* printed nine Euro-myths, the *Daily Telegraph* and the *Sun* printed seven each, the *Express* six, the *Times* four, the *Sunday Telegraph* three and the London *Evening Standard* two, with a host of other papers printing one or two each.

One example of a story that featured widely in 2003 was a local council's demolition of a set of swings in a children's play area because they did not conform to EU legislation. Among the headlines in January that year were: 'You could just swing for them! – EU officials shut playground favourite' (the *Express*); 'Children pushed off swings by EU' (*The Times*); 'Village loses swings that are 22 inches too high for EU' (*Daily Telegraph*); 'Children pushed off swings by EU' (the *Sun*). Dougal notes:

> [I]n reality the whole affair was based around an entirely voluntary measure, set by a non-EU body, and already adopted by the British Standards Institute some years ago. But because the relevant body, the European Standardisation Committee, contained that generic

affirmation of nuisance, 'European', the stories ran with the EU firmly positioned in the role of villain. (2003: 33)

The main propagators of these myths were the right-wing press.

The threat of European integration

The right-wing press has adopted an extreme Euro-sceptic frame when reporting the process of European integration: any aspect of integration – the single currency, the rapid reaction force and the European Constitution – is roundly attacked. The integration process is painted as a threat to the very community, of which newspapers and readers are a part, while the British government is portrayed as continually ceding sovereignty to a new supra-national body, which would eventually leave Britain as a region of a European super-state. The notion of integration as a threat is constructed and reconstructed in a continuous stream of stories on EU activities (see Wilkes and Wring, 1998).

Take the example of the launch of the Euro in 1999. The research by Computer Aided Research and Media Analysis analysed 1,695 articles on the Euro in nine British newspapers and found that coverage not only misinformed readers, but was overtly critical (MacArthur, 1999; see also Firmstone, 2003). While the right-wing broadsheets provided more coverage than the tabloids, like the *Sun* and the *Daily Mail*, a majority of stories on the Euro in both were deemed unfavourable (MacArthur, 1999: 40). After the event-free launch on 1 January 2002, the *Daily Mail* warned, 'don't fall for this Euro magic trick', and the *Sun* that 'everything costs more than it does in pounds' (ibid.). An analysis of the *Sun*, the *Daily Mail* and *The Times*, between 15 December and 31 January 2002, found a total of 22 editorials hostile towards the Euro, nearly a third more than supportive editorials in other papers over the same period (Firmstone, 2003). Disparaging the Euro is matched by continued campaigns to keep the pound.

The framing of integration as a threat can be seen in a more personalized way in the coverage of a court case involving a Sunderland greengrocer who insisted on weighing his fruit and vegetables only in pounds and ounces – in defiance of the law. His case became a *cause célèbre* for the right-wing press; his conviction, in April 2001, came to symbolize the threat of continuing EU integration to the 'British' way of life. For the *Daily Mail*, 'the implications of the Sunderland court ruling were so immense' that they ran the headline: 'The day selling a pound of bananas became a crime like burglary or rape'. For the *Sun* it was 'a sad day for Britain . . . we can now see that the wishes of the people and parliament come second best. What the EU wants, the EU gets. No one voted for pounds and ounces to be made illegal. Kilos and grams have been imposed on us by Brussels bureaucrats. How they would love to do that with the Euro too.' For the *Daily Telegraph* this was 'outrageous on so many levels that it is difficult to know where to begin' (Cole, 2001). Despite the fact that the government had agreed to single weights and measures, and that Steve Thoburn did not receive a custodial sentence, he was framed as the 'metric martyr', a symbol of defiance against the EU bureaucrats.

Of course, the press encourages their readers to phone and write in on such matters. The right-wing press acts as a channel for the collective anxieties of their readers on European integration: for example, in the wake of the launch of the single currency, in 1999 the *Sun* ran a reader phone-in poll, where readers were asked to vote whether they were 'for or against Britain joining the single currency' (Barnett and Gaber, 2001: 20). The result of the poll was, of course, a lead news item.

Conclusion

Reactionary populism is an established feature of the political communication systems of both countries. As this chapter has shown, right-wing media outlets are at the centre of popular reaction to a variety of issues. Like populist movements, they play on their readers' anxieties and fears about a host of Others. The individual listener or reader is addressed as a member of a wider community whose values and way of life are confronted by a variety of threats. Although the Others identified by the media are always changing, they are all seen to pose a threat. The Other is stereotyped, prejudices held by their audience are reinforced and resentment against the Other continually mobilized through a combination of phone-ins, letters or emails. Indeed, the mobilization of audiences is a key tactic of populist media outlets. However, unlike traditional populist political movements, they do not want audience votes, they want their custom.[1]

The chapter has argued that the market-driven media environment is an important factor in the addressing of audience concerns in such a way. The right-wing media outlets address political issues that attract and maintain audience share: they are ratings-conscious entertainers as well as populist political actors. Challenging the political fears of the audience might mean losing audience share, whereas pandering to their prejudices might maintain or even build audience ratings. In a market-driven media system, this will be an increasingly important consideration.

PART III

COMMUNICATIVE ENGAGEMENT AND THE EXERCISE OF POLITICAL VOICE

Turning On, Tuning Out?

THE media is now the main point of connection between citizens and the world of representative politics. The majority of citizens engage with conventional politics 'as members of the media audience' (Mancini and Swanson, 1996: 16), spectators on events rather than being directly involved and witnessing those events at first hand. As Denton and Woodward observe, the 'political world is not experienced first hand. Instead it is more the product of impressions that we gather from the vast information sources that incessantly sell, entertain and inform' (1998: 145). It is through television in particular that the public witnesses events in Westminster or on Capitol Hill, or the activities of the President or Prime Minister. However, while citizens have never had access to so much information on conventional politics, there is growing evidence that certain sections of the audience increasingly view politics with a sense of 'boredom and detachment', or have stopped viewing altogether (Dionne, 1992: 9; see also Worcester and Mortimore, 2002).

Drawing on the evidence from a range of sources, this chapter seeks to establish whether such concerns about communicative disengagement are warranted (see McKinney et al., 2005). It starts by looking at the data on political engagement, which shows increasing differences in voter turnout and interest in politics between citizens of different age groups, and from different socio-economic and racial backgrounds. It then examines the evidence of disengagement from coverage of conventional politics – what Neveu (2002) terms the 'cogs of representative democracy'. This includes the activities of government, political parties and candidates; the legislature; election campaigns; and other activities associated with governance. It seeks to ascertain whether both countries are witnessing the emergence of 'communicative engagement gaps' between an engaged citizenry who participate and regularly tune in to conventional politics, accessing information from a variety of sources, and a less-engaged citizenry, who are, at most, episodic spectators on national political life, and increasingly likely to tune out, avoiding output completely. It also tries to determine the extent to which the engaged tend to be richer, better educated, members of ethnic majorities and older than those who are less engaged with all aspects of conventional politics.

A diverse but unequal citizenry

There is a tendency within political communication research to see the citizen audiences, at least tacitly, as largely homogenous. Indeed, the notion of an undifferentiated 'mass citizenry' processing a stream of political information is perhaps one of the most pervasive. It is a view that has persisted from the inception of the study of political communications to the present. Such an assumption has often blinded studies not only to the diverse background of citizens in contemporary democracies, but also to the divided background of audiences. Class has always been one of the main cleavages of industrial society: the mass audience for political output was indeed divided along class lines, yet the role of socio-economic background in shaping mediated political experience has traditionally been examined in a more high-profile manner outside the field (see Morley, 1980). The make-up of both the US and the UK is increasingly ethnically diverse, the UK especially so in the post-war period, and both countries continue to be shaped by immigration. Both also exhibit significant racial divisions. In the US the long history of racial division can still be seen in geographical segregation and the racial dividing lines of the urban environment on both sides of the Atlantic are widely taken for granted (Munck, 2005): ethnic minorities tend to inhabit the often poor inner-city areas, while their white counterparts live in the 'boutique' suburbs (Macedo and Karpowitz, 2006). New immigrant populations, in particular, generally inhabit the deprived inner-city areas of the large gateway cities, and urban areas are now increasingly racially 'balkanized', especially in the US (Macedo and Karpowitz, 2006). Indeed, such stark divisions were revealed in New Orleans in the aftermath of Hurricane Katrina in 2005 (Bartels, 2006). Economic inequalities cut across ethnic lines: the most economically deprived are often ethnic minorities and, in both countries, unemployment rates amongst these groups are higher than amongst the majority population. For example, in the US, the unemployment rate amongst African American men is almost twice that of white males (Munck, 2005). Ethnic minorities also tend to occupy predominantly low-paid jobs.

Citizen audiences not only need to be recognized as heterogeneous, characterized by difference and division, but also as increasingly unequal. One of the biggest challenges facing both countries is the rise of wealth disparity (Jacobs and Skocpol, 2006). Munck (2005) observes that by the 1990s many western societies had become increasingly polarized between rich and poor and Brandoleni and Smeeding note that there has been a significant rise in income inequality in both countries since the 1980s (2006: 25; see also Stonecash, 2006). Wealth has become more concentrated in the hands of a few citizens, while the number of those living below the poverty line has increased (Boggs, 2000; Castells, 2000; Jacobs et al., 2004). The US and the UK are now more unequal than at any other time in the post-war period (Jacobs et al., 2004; Hill, 2002). In the US, higher-income earners receive roughly five-and-a-half times more than low-income earners, and in the UK it is five times more (Brandoleni and Smeeding, 2006). Not only is the divide sharper than at any time previously, but it also has a geographical profile (Castells, 2000); the contrast between the deprived inner-city areas and the affluent suburban areas has never been so stark (Munck, 2005). In addition, generational differences cut across these divides; differences in values and attitudes impact upon new and established communities, rich and poor communities alike. As this chapter will show, such differences are also important.

Discussion of such divisions is not abstract, but has real implications for political engagement and communicative engagement. The different spatial locations and economic experiences of citizen audiences, and hence the divergent lived experiences, have to be seen as important aspects, shaping audience interest in politics and its coverage. Research increasingly shows that the economically marginalized are likely to become the politically marginalized, uninterested in and disengaged from the political process and, one could argue, from media coverage of politics.

The interested and the disinterested citizen

Political interest and political engagement go hand-in-hand. The engaged are more likely to be interested in politics, and those interested, as Verba et al. (1995) point out, are more likely to be politically engaged. From the available research in this area, this chapter draws on surveys of political interest and data on voter turnout and voter registration as indicative measures. In both countries, data on citizen interest in politics and various measures of political engagement reveal significant differences between citizens in terms of socio-economic status (income levels and education), ethnicity and age. Take the example of those from different socio-economic backgrounds expressing an interest in politics: in 2000, in the US, the American National Election Studies found that 35 per cent of those in the top 5 per cent of income earners said they were interested in public affairs 'most of the time', compared to 12 per cent in the bottom 15 per cent of income earners. According to the American National Election Studies, in the US since the 1950s, blue-collar and unskilled workers and those with low educational attainment have been consistently less interested in public affairs than their better-off, professional, counterparts. Since 1960, those in the top income bracket have been, on average, more than twice as likely to be interested in public affairs 'most of the time' compared to those in the bottom income bracket. A similar pattern can be seen in relation to education: since 1960, those with a college degree have been, on average, more than twice as likely to be interested in public affairs compared to those who have dropped out of high school (American National Election Studies). A similar picture can be seen in the UK: in 2005, 63 per cent of A, B and C1s said they were interested in politics compared to 36 per cent of C2, D and Es (Electoral Commission, 2005b; see also Pattie et al., 2004).[1] In terms of education, 24 per cent of those who had been in education past the age of 19 were very interested in national politics compared to only 10 per of those who left school at 15 (Pattie et al., 2004).

Voter turnout data reveal similar variations between socio-economic groupings. In the US, according to one piece of research, in the early 1990s 'half of those Americans with family incomes under $15,000 cast a ballot, compared to 86 per cent of those with incomes of $75,000' (Norris, 2002b: 92). In 2006, only 26 per cent of those earning less than $20,000 voted regularly, compared to 44 per cent of those making $75,000 or more – a gap of 18 per cent (Pew Research Center, 2006c; see also Hill, 2002). Research by Doppelt and Shearer (1999) in the US, found that non-voters tended to have lower family incomes and be less educated than voters. In the UK, general election turnout was lower in those constituencies with a high proportion of 'poor, socially deprived and unemployed voters' (Whiteley et al., 2001: 215). Those least likely to vote were the working poor and the very poor, earning less than £10,000, and those with the fewest number of years of education (Pattie et al., 2003a: 627; see also Electoral Commission, 2005e). In 2005, turnout amongst social classes A and B was 70 per cent – compared to 56 per cent amongst C2s and 54 per cent amongst D and Es – a gap of 14–16 per cent (MORI, cited in Rogers, 2005). The propensity to turn out is similarly skewed – 52 per cent of A and Bs said they would vote, compared to 44 per cent of C2s and 42 per cent of D and Es (Electoral Commission, 2005e; see also Sanders et al., 2005). In 2005, the turnout level was 76 per cent of those with a post A-level qualification, compared to 63 per cent for those with fewer qualifications (ibid.).

Those on higher incomes in the US are also more likely to register to vote: registration levels in households with an income level of $75,000 or above stands at 84 per cent, compared to 60 per cent for households earning $20,000 or less (Pew Research Center, 2003a). American National Election Studies data on voter registration confirms that those on the lowest incomes are least likely to register. Non-registration, while rising only slightly amongst professionals, has notably increased in blue-collar occupations: between the 1950s and 1970s, it was an average of 16 per cent, rising to an average of 29 per cent through the 1980s and 1990s. The unskilled have always been least likely to register, but non-registration rose from an average of 20 per cent between the 1950s and 1970s to around 33 per cent through the 1980s and 1990s (Pew Research Center, 2003a). Voter registration is also higher amongst college graduates, standing at 85 per cent, compared to 54 per cent for high school dropouts (ibid.).

The economically deprived often consist predominantly of certain ethnic minority groups (Heclo, 1996; Munck, 2005). Such groups traditionally have less interest in conventional politics than their white-majority counterparts and, in the US, turnout amongst African American, Hispanic and Asian voters is generally low (Freedman, 2000). Doppelt and Shearer (1999) found that 30 per cent of non-voters were from minority groups. Turnout is particularly low where the majority of a community consists of recent immigrants: in the Hispanic community, for instance, 60 per cent voted in 2000 (Segura et al., 2001). In certain districts with high levels of Hispanic immigration, such as in San Diego, turnout for local elections, such as city council elections, has been consistently low: between 1983 and 2001 it ranged from 7 to 30 per cent of registered voters (Le Texier, 2004). In the UK, turnout amongst white British citizens was 60 per cent in 2001, 13 per cent higher than amongst members of ethnic minority communities (Electoral Commission, 2005d). A study of turnout during the 2005 general election found that it was 68 per cent amongst white British citizens – 12 per cent higher than amongst members of ethnic minority communities (Sanders et al., 2005)

Ethnic minority groups are also less likely to register to vote compared to their white counterparts. In the US, while registration by white Americans falls above the average, at 75 per cent, registration by minorities falls below: the numbers of African American registered standing at 72 per cent, Hispanics at 58 per cent and Asian Americans at 47 per cent (Pew Research Center, 2003a). In the US, certain groups can be excluded by state laws: disenfranchised ex-felons are one of the largest groups of Americans denied the vote (Manza et al., 2004). While 13 states have liberalized laws on ex-felon disenfranchisement, 11 have passed further limitations (ibid.); according to some sources, nearly five million Americans cannot vote because of the laws which disenfranchise those with criminal convictions (Campbell, 2004). African

American communities are disproportionately affected: according to some estimates, 13 per cent of African American males are unable to vote (ibid.). In Florida, for instance, former felons are excluded from voting until officially pardoned by the Governor. Thousands of felons currently await an official pardon. It was estimated that 600,000 ex-felons were disenfranchised in the 2000 presidential election (ibid.).

In the UK, the number eligible, but not registered, to vote has risen slightly (Electoral Commission, 2005a). In 2004, 17 per cent of ethnic minority groups were not registered to vote compared to 6 per cent of their white British counterparts. The unemployed were also more likely not to have registered – 18 per cent of the unemployed compared to 6 per cent of the employed were unregistered. The unskilled, similarly, were more likely to be unregistered compared to the skilled – 10 per cent compared to 5 per cent for the skilled. Amongst those with no qualifications, non-registration was 8 per cent, compared to 4 per cent amongst those with a higher education qualification (Electoral Commission, 2005a).

In both countries, variations in the levels of political interest between those from different socio-economic backgrounds have hardened and widened. Take the example of those expressing an interest in politics. In the US, the gap between the top 5 per cent of income earners who said they were interested in public affairs 'most of the time' and the bottom 15 per cent of income earners has widened: in 1980 roughly twice as many in the top 5 per cent of income earners than in the bottom 15 per cent said they were interested in public affairs. In 1990 that figure remained roughly the same, but by 2000 about three times as many in the top 5 per cent of income earners than the bottom 15 per cent said they were interested in public affairs (American National Election Studies). Indeed, the proportion of the bottom 15 per cent of income earners who said they were interested in public affairs 'most of the time' has halved, falling from 24 per cent in 1980 to 12 per cent in 2000 (ibid.).

In the UK, in 2003 and 2005 nearly twice as many A, B and C1s said they were interested in politics compared to C2, D and Es (Electoral Commission, 2005b). When a comparison is made between A, B and C1s, and C2, D and Es living in deprived areas, the difference becomes over two-and-a-half times greater (Electoral Commission, 2005d). Without further figures it is not possible to paint a fuller picture, but these findings are reinforced by data on voter turnout; as noted already, turnout amongst social classes A and B in the 2005 general election was 14 per cent higher than amongst class C2 and 16 per cent higher than classes D and E (MORI, cited in Rogers, 2005). This represents an increase on the 2001 general election, where voter turnout amongst social classes A and B (68 per cent) was 12 per cent higher than amongst C2s and 15 per cent higher than amongst D and Es (MORI, cited in Electoral Commission, 2005d). In the 1997 general election, the turnout gap between social classes A and B and classes D and E was 13 per cent (MORI, cited in Rogers, 2005). These engagement gaps are not limited to socio-economic and educational status but are also generational.

Generational differences

In both countries young people are less likely to be interested or engaged in conventional politics than previous cohorts and, when surveyed, young people tend to express less interest in politics than older generations. Patterson observes that 'today's young adults are less politically interested and informed than any cohort of young people on record' (2002: 210). In the US, Wattenberg found that the number of 18–29 year olds interested in public affairs steadily declined between 1964 and 2000: in 2000, 38 per cent professed an interest, compared to 64 per cent of those over 65, a gap of 26 per cent; in 1964 that gap was 7 per cent (2002: 89; see also Delli Carpini, 2000). In the UK, 20 per cent of 18–24 year olds professed a great deal or quite a lot of interest in politics in 2001, compared to around 40 per cent of the over-65s – a gap of 20 per cent (Bromley and Curtice, 2002). This gap is growing too. In the UK, the number of 18–24 year olds not interested in politics has risen from 47 per cent in 2001 to 64 per cent in 2004, a rise of 17 per cent (Electoral Commission, 2004b; see also Henn et al., 2002: 175).

An examination of voting shows that the young are less likely to turn out and vote than previous cohorts. In the US, the number of people voting under the age of 30 has fallen from 55 per cent in 1972 to 42 per cent in 2000, though rising slightly to 51 per cent in 2004 (Patterson, 2004). In the UK, the percentage of 18–24 year olds who vote fell between the 1997 and 2001 general elections by 18 per cent, from 61 to 43 per cent. In comparison, turnout for those over 65 only fell by 5 per cent, from 87 to 82 per cent (Bromley and Curtice, 2002). MORI estimated the 2005 turnout figure for the 18–24 age group at 37 per cent, down on the previous election by 2 per cent and by 12 per cent on 1997; and 30 per cent less than an estimated 70 per cent turnout of those aged 65 and over (Electoral Commission, 2004b, 2005e). In local elections only 21 per cent of 18–24 year olds said they voted, compared to 49 per cent of those over 55 (Electoral Commission, 2003).

In the UK and US, turnout gaps have emerged between young and old citizens. Turnout amongst the 18–29 age group averaged 55 per cent in the UK and 53 per cent in the US, while for the over-65s, turnout levels were 87 and 84 per cent respectively, a gap of 32 and 31 per cent, one of the highest levels amongst advanced industrial democracies (Electoral Commission, 2004b). Wattenberg's research confirms this picture. In the US, he found that the difference between those over 30 reporting having cast a ballot and those under 30 was 31 per cent. In the UK, the difference between those over 30 reporting having cast a ballot and those under 30 was 21 per cent (Wattenberg, 2002).

Such gaps are not confined to turnout: in the US, 50 per cent of young people were not registered to vote in 2004, a much higher figure than for those over 65 (Patterson, 2004). In the UK, 18 per cent of 18–24 year olds were not registered to vote compared to 7 per cent of those aged 35–44 and 2 per cent of those 65 and older (Electoral Commission, 2005a). These findings are in line with those of a study of political activity by age in 15 European democracies, including the UK. This found 'only half of all the younger people (under 30) reported having voted in an election during the previous 12 months, in sharp contrast to over three quarters who reported casting a ballot among the middle aged and older groups' (Norris, 2003: 11).

Similar gaps were visible, according to Norris, in respect to party membership: 3 per cent of young people were party members compared to 8 per cent of older citizens. In terms of party affiliation, only 41 per cent of young people (under the age of 30) feel close to any particular party, compared to two-thirds of older citizens (2002b: 14). In the US in the 1970s, one in five young adults 'could see themselves working in a campaign' but in the last decade or so that figure has dropped to around one in ten (American National Election Studies).

In sum, there is clear evidence of different levels of political interest and engagement between different socio-economic groupings, between the majority and ethnic minorities and between generations. However, are citizens that are wealthy, better educated, older and members of an ethnic majority more likely to consume mediated political output than those who are relatively poor, less educated, young and members of an ethnic minority?

Communicative engagement gaps

This section tries to establish the extent to which the differences in political interest and engagement outlined above are mirrored in the patterns of communicative engagement.[2] From the available data, a divide between citizens can be seen in terms of the attention paid to the coverage of conventional politics and the coverage of specific events, such as election campaigns. In the US, since 1968, when TV ownership reached saturation, more of those in the top income bracket have followed election campaigns on TV than those in the

Table 6.1 The highest and lowest earners saying they watched the US presidential campaign on TV, 1968–2004

Income/year	1968	1976	1980	1992	2000	2004
Income percentile 96–100	88%	94%	96%	94%	96%	94%
% difference	*5%*	*13%*	*15%*	*11%*	*19%*	*12%*
Income percentile 0–16	83%	81%	85%	85%	77%	82%

Source: Compiled from American National Election Studies

Table 6.2 Those with the highest and the lowest levels of educational achievement saying they watched the US presidential campaign on TV, 1968–2004

Education/year	1968	1976	1980	1992	2000	2004
College graduate	92%	97%	92%	93%	88%	94%
% difference	*6%*	*14%*	*12%*	*9%*	*13%*	*17%*
Grade school, some high school	86%	83%	80%	84%	75%	77%

Source: Compiled from American National Election Studies

Table 6.3 Those with different levels of educational achievement, in the US, saying they paid attention to hard news in 2004 and 2006

Education/year	2004	2006
College graduate	43%	39%
% difference	*27%*	*23%*
No high school	16%	16%

Source: Compiled from Pew Research Center, 2004b; 2006b

lowest income bracket. Table 6.1 shows a gap between the top and bottom income earners, a gap which, although fluctuating, has widened. Similarly, since 1968, more of those with a college degree have watched presidential election campaigns on TV compared to those who have dropped out of high school.

Table 6.2 shows a widening gap between the most educated in American society – those with a college degree – and the least, one which has grown from 6 per cent in 1968 to 17 per cent in 2004. These findings are reinforced by research on the viewing of the presidential debates on television in 2000 and 2004, which found that those who watched the entire programme were 'more educated [and] had higher incomes' than those who did not (Kenski and Stroud, 2005).

What about outside election campaign periods? Are similar gaps evident when it comes to watching, for instance, political news? Table 6.3 shows the level of attention paid to 'hard news',[3] and reveals a marked difference in communicative engagement between the most and the least educated. A much greater number of those with a college degree consistently focus on hard news stories compared to those with no high school qualifications. Similarly, when it comes to viewing the political channel, C-Span, there is a nearly 20 per cent gap between college graduates and those with no qualifications (Pew Research Center, 2004f).

The consumption of conventional political output is also noticeably lower amongst certain ethnic minority groups compared to their white counterparts. For example, amongst US citizens of Hispanic descent, a survey revealed that 47 per cent paid 'quite a bit or a great deal of attention to political news', while amongst Hispanics who were not yet citizens, those paying attention stood at 35 per cent (Segura et al., 2001). Research by the Pew Center (2004b) also showed that 23 per cent of Hispanics consistently focused on hard news, compared to 32 per cent of white Americans – a gap of 9 per cent. This disparity is replicated in the viewing of C-Span, 74 per cent of whose regular viewers were white Americans, compared to 11 per cent Hispanic and 8 per cent other non-white – a gap of over 60 per cent (Pew Research Center, 2004f).

In the UK, surveys conducted by the Independent Television Commission (ITC) and Ofcom have also focused on the attention paid by different socio-economic groups to election coverage on TV. In 2001, an ITC survey showed that the avid viewers were mainly from the upper end of the social spectrum, and the least avid were from the lower socio-economic groups (Sancho, 2001). In 2005 the picture was the same.

Table 6.4 shows a gap between different social classes when it comes to avoiding news coverage during and after the 2005 general election campaign. A greater proportion of the unemployed and those of lower social status sought to avoid coverage. Hargreaves and Thomas's (2002) findings suggest that such patterns are not limited to campaign periods; they found the groups most likely to be uninterested in political output were C2s – with 35 per cent of those sampled not interested. Of the A, B and C1s sampled, 31 per cent agreed with the statement 'Much of the news is not relevant to me', compared to 37 per cent of lower social classes C2, D and E. Those members of social class categories A, B and C1 had a greater interest in politics and business news, while those in classes C2, D and E were more interested in entertainment news. This disparity can also be seen in respect to race: 46 percent of black British agreed with the statement 'Much of the news is not relevant to me', compared to 34 per cent of whites (ibid.).

When it comes to use of the internet to gain political information, those citizens in the US who go online to acquire political news tend

Table 6.4 Those of different social class and employment status switching channels or switching off TV news coverage of the 2005 UK general election

Social class	During campaign	Post-campaign
A, B	24%	23%
C1	20%	27%
% difference A,B and D,E	*4%*	*7%*
C2	25%	34%
D, E	28%	30%
Full-time employed	22%	28%
% difference	*10%*	*7%*
Unemployed	32%	35%

Source: Compiled from Ofcom, 2005

Table 6.5 The highest and lowest income earners and those with different levels of educationa achievement going online to gain news on US mid-term elections 1996–2002

Income/year	1996	1998	2002
$75,000+	7%	12%	29%
% difference	*5%*	*10%*	*23%*
<$20,000	2%	2%	6%
College graduate	9%	12%	27%
% difference	*8%*	*12%*	*23%*
No high school	1%	0%	4%

Source: Compiled from Pew Research Center, 2003c

to be the wealthy and the well educated. Table 6.5 shows that a greater proportion of the well educated and higher-income earners go online to gather electoral information. In 2003 the gap between the most well-off and the least and between those with and without a college degree was stark, and seems to be widening, and this is not just with respect to election news: Washington news was among the top three news interests amongst college graduates surfing the web, but did not feature in the top five news interests of those with a high school education or less (Pew Research Center, 2004b). Ward et al.'s (2003) survey of internet use in the UK found that those using the internet for political purposes, including looking for political information, were, in the main, well educated and from higher socio-economic groups (see also Gibson et al., 2005). A survey by MORI in 2005 confirmed this picture. It found that those earning £30,000 or more accounted for 50 per cent of the online election news audience – double the number earning

Table 6.6 Those from different social classes and those with different levels of educational achievement engaging in online politics (including looking for political information) in the UK in 2002

Social Class	Engaging in politics online
A, B and C1	73%
% difference	*46%*
C2, D and E	27%
Years in education	
Highest, age 19+	37%
% difference	*15%*
Leave school at 16	22%

Source: Compiled from Ward et al., 2003

£15,500 or less (BBC/MORI Citizenship Survey, cited in Schifferes, 2006).

Table 6.6 shows that 37 per cent of those engaging in online politics had been in higher education, or had been in education up to the age of 19, compared to 22 per cent who had left school at 16 or before. In relation to social status, 73 per cent of social classes A, B and C1 engaged in online politics, compared to 11 per cent of C2s and 16 per cent of D and Es (Ward et al., 2003).

A generation apart?

In both countries, young people are less likely than previous generations to consume media coverage of conventional politics. Fewer of today's young seek out 'political' coverage compared to older cohorts; the young actively seek to avoid exposure to national, international and local political news and other political output. Stephen Bennett observes that amongst Americans under the age of 30 there is 'a clear cut pattern of youthful indifference to news about national, international, and local affairs' (1998: 5), a view echoed by some studies in the UK (see Buckingham, 2000). Table 6.7 shows that 18–24 year olds have consistently paid less attention to hard news stories compared to those aged 50–64.

Election news is one element of mediated politics that the young seek to avoid. A survey by the Pew Center in the US found that there was a lack of interest in the election campaigns amongst the young. Table 6.8 shows that young people (18–29) were not as interested in media coverage of presidential election campaigning as those over 65. It also shows that there has been a consistent gap over the last decade between 18–29 year olds and those over 65. It is not just election news:

Table 6.7 Attention paid to hard news in the US by age, 1996–2006

Age/year	1996a	2004	2006
18–24	10%	16%	14%
% difference	12%	26%	22%
50–64	22%	42%	36%

ᵃ 1996 attention to political news was measured. Age ranges were 18–29 and 50+

Source: Compiled from Pew Research Center, 1996, 2004b, 2006b

Table 6.8 Those saying they followed presidential election news very closely by age in the US, 1996–2004

Age/year	1996	2000	2004
18–29	22%	16%	21%
% difference	10%	17%	15%
65+	32%	33%	36%

Source: Compiled from Pew Research Center, 2004b

Table 6.9 Those switching channels or switching off TV election news during the 2005 UK general election, by age

Age/year	During campaign	Post-campaign
18–24	30%	37%
% difference	8%	14%
65+	22%	23%

Source: Compiled from Ofcom, 2005

coverage of specific events seem a turn-off to the young. Wattenberg (2004) observes a growing gap between the young and older citizens when it comes to watching televised presidential addresses; in 1979, 60 per cent of 18–29 year olds tuned in to watch Jimmy Carter's 'crisis of confidence' speech, compared to 73 per cent of the over-65s – a gap of 13 per cent. In 2001, 67 per cent of 18–34 year olds watched Bush's speech on 11 September – a small increase on 1979 – and 86 per cent of over-65s watched. The gap between them had widened to 19 per cent.

In the UK, young people seem estranged from political coverage: a survey by the ITC found that the groups least likely to be interested in election output were 16–24 year olds (33 per cent of these were not interested) and those most likely to be interested were the elderly (Sancho, 2001). Table 6.9 shows that 18–24 year olds were more likely to switch off or change channels to avoid election coverage compared to those over 65. When they did watch, the young also paid less attention to campaign news than their older contemporaries. In 2005, 59 per cent of 18–24 year olds watched the general election campaign closely, compared to 68 per cent of those over 65 – a gap of 9 per cent (Ofcom, 2005; see also Electoral Commission, 2003).

In addition, fewer of the young draw on the news media for their political news: in the US, 23 per cent of 18–29 year olds gleaned information from newspapers in 2004, compared to 40 per cent of the over-50s; and 23 per cent of 18–29s gleaned information from network news, compared to 46 per cent of the over-50s (Pew Research Center, 2004c). The number of young people gaining information from traditional outlets has also fallen over time: in 2004, 16 per cent fewer gained information from network TV than in 2000; and 9 per cent fewer gained information from newspapers than in 2000 (Pew Research Center, 2004c). The 18–29 age group was also less likely than the over-50s to watch a dedicated political channel such as C-Span (Pew Research Center, 2004f).

In the UK, audiences for television news are concentrated in the older age groups. Of those aged 16–34, 39 per cent read a daily newspaper compared to 64 per cent of the over-55s – a gap of 25 per cent (Hargreaves and Thomas, 2002). The same research also shows that the age groups 16–24 and 25–34 consumed less news in 2001 than in 1994 (ibid.). However, the question arises as to whether young people are tuning out completely or gaining their political news from other sources.

Engaging with alternative sources of political information

The available data does show that the young are increasingly getting their political information from 'alternative' sources (ibid.). Research from the Pew Research Center (2004c) in the US has shown that, in 2004, 21 per cent of young people regularly learned about the campaign from TV comedy shows, compared to 5 per cent of 50–64 year olds and 2 per cent of the over-65s. Table 6.10 reveals that the number of 18–29 year olds learning something from alternative sources grew between 2000 and 2004, while the number learning something from traditional sources declined. Although not directly comparable, research in the UK found that 50 per cent of 16–24 year olds sampled regularly learned something from topical comedies, and 23 per cent something from the internet (Hargreaves and Thomas, 2002).

In the UK, the use of the internet to gain political information has generally been higher amongst the young than the old, with 21 per cent of those aged 18–24 using the internet to find electoral information, compared to 12 per cent of those aged 55–64 (Coleman, 2001). In 2002, 30 per cent of those who engaged in online political activity were

Table 6.10 Young people's sources of presidential campaign information, in the US in 2000 and 2004 (18–29 year olds)

Shows/year	2000	2004	Change %
Comedy TV shows	9%	21%	*+12%*
TV news magazines	8%	26%	*+8%*
Late-night TV shows	13%	13%	*0%*
Network news	39%	23%	*−16%*

Source: Compiled from Pew Research Center, 2004c

aged 15–24 and 28 per cent were 25–34; this compares to 11 per cent of those aged 45–54 and 8 per cent of those over 55 (Ward et al., 2003). In the US, use of the internet to gain political information continued to be higher amongst the young than the old: in 2000, 22 per cent gained political information on the web compared to 16 per cent of those aged 50–64; by 2004 that figure had risen to 57 per cent of the young, compared to 45 per cent of those aged 50–64 (Pew Internet, 2005a).

It is worth noting that habits learnt by one cohort may endure over time as that cohort ages (Gans, 2005; Nie et al., 1996). Franklin shows that the disparity between cohorts in turnout is not eliminated when a new cohort of voters ages. He likens this disparity to a 'footprint' that, once made, persists over time (2004: 82). Wattenberg observes that 'a whole generation has grown up in the narrowcasting age' and it is hard to persuade 'a generation that has channel surfed all their lives that they ought to tune into what the president has to say' (2004: 560). It may be too early to assert, but the differential generational consumption patterns of conventional political output might well continue, with the younger cohorts failing to gain an interest in the coverage of conventional politics by traditional channels, and increasingly relying on non-news outlets. Caution needs to be exercised though; communicative engagement through 'alternative' non-news sources should not be seen as the same as watching or logging on for news coverage of a political event. The persistent gap in news consumption between age groups is an important signifier of differing attitudes towards conventional politics, not simply the outcome of utilizing 'alternative' sources.

The evidence presented in this section is suggestive rather than conclusive, but it does reveal a political output consumption gap between the wealthy and the less well-off, between the well educated and the less well educated, to some degree between the majority and ethnic minorities and, to a certain extent, between the young and the old. This mirrors the political engagement gap detailed earlier in this chapter. To conjure up two extreme stereotypes: those who are most likely to consume conventional political output tend to be aged 45 and over, well educated and white, come from a higher socio-economic background, with a higher salary, vote regularly and live in the suburbs. Those least likely would tend to be 18–24, with low levels of educational attainment, be a member of an ethnic minority, come from a lower socio-economic background – being unemployed or on a low wage – be non-voters and live in the inner cities. The size of the gap between the most likely and the least likely is difficult to pin down with any certainty, but it could be 10 per cent or lower, or as high as 30 per cent. Either way, it is a gap that seems set to become a permanent feature of both countries, and one that could widen.

The vicious circle

So far, the chapter has shown that political engagement – and hence the consumption of political coverage, in its various forms – is concentrated amongst certain groups in society and is increasingly absent in others. That is, it is focused, other things being equal, amongst high-income earners, members of the majority community, the well educated and older cohorts and is increasingly absent amongst low-income earners, members of ethnic minority communities, the less educated and younger cohorts. The economic and racial divisions in both countries are reflected in the patterns of political engagement and communicative engagement – as represented in the consumption of political coverage.

In addition to the 'virtuous circle' identified by Norris (2000), which sees the affluent citizen increasingly engaged in and attentive to political coverage, there is a 'vicious circle' working in the opposite direction. This disproportionately impacts upon those on lower incomes, on ethnic minorities and younger citizens, reinforcing their communicative disengagement. Many in these marginalized groups feel alienated from the political process and have little incentive to pay attention to media output. They have largely lost interest in the politics of governance and almost entirely in the rituals which accompany it, such as elections. It is not surprising that if conventional politics is seen as having little bearing on their lived experience, mediated conventional political output will not hold any relevance either. Political and social exclusion experienced in everyday life go hand-in-hand with communicative disengagement, forming ghettos of the excluded, marginalized from conventional politics, not mobilized by the media and not interested in its coverage of the rituals of representative democracy. For the poorly educated, low-income, welfare-dependent single parent, or the newly arrived immigrant, often in social housing, living in areas of high unemployment, politics, politicians, political institutions and processes are distant. Mediated coverage of Westminster and Capitol Hill, or the campaign trail, bears little relevance to their everyday lives. They are part of a second-hand world of conventional politics, which is remote and of little concern (Thompson, 1995).

In the UK, recent focus group findings on the attitudes of those who do not vote reinforce this point: these individuals saw conventional politics as 'familiar but at the same time . . . as being distant, as having little direct relevance to, and impact on, their lives' (Diplock, 2001; see also Hargreaves and Thomas, 2002; Nestlé Social Science Research Programme, 2005; Sancho, 2001). Commenting on watching politics in the news, one non-voter noted: 'I think they [MPs] are argumentative, when I flicked on the telly and saw them in parliament . . . you see people arguing and laughing, I don't want to listen to this' (Diplock, 2001: 5; see also Addley, 2003). Doppelt and Shearer's (1999) work in the US found the same sense of alienation from political life in some of the non-voters they interviewed (1999; see also Eliasoph, 1998; Patterson, 2002). Similar expressions of alienation were made by young people: a focus group conducted with young non-voters in the UK, after the 2001 general election, found that they felt 'bewildered by the alien culture of electoral politics' (Coleman, 2002a: 247). This view is not one-off. Henn et al. note that 'a consistent message expressed in all of the focus groups, was that politics is not aimed at young people' (2002: 175). In the UK, 41 per cent of 16–34 year olds agreed with the statement 'Much of the news is not relevant to me', compared to 30 per cent of those aged 55 and older – a gap of 11 per cent (Hargreaves and Thomas, 2002). Young people perceive the world of formal politics to be distant from their lives, and broadly irrelevant' (Henn et al., 2002; see also Buckingham, 2000).

Conclusion

This chapter has shown that political interest and political engagement, as measured by voter turnout and registration, varies by socio-economic status, ethnicity and age, and that a gap exists between the civic habits of high- and low-income earners, between members of ethnic minority ethnic majority communities and between generations. Further, it has shown that the attention paid to political coverage differs along the same lines. The viewing of political programming varies between a largely politically interested and engaged 'majority', and a politically disengaged 'minority'. Gurevitch and Blumler are right to note 'not everyone in the audience for political communication is a political animal, nor is obliged to be' (1990: 271), and we have seen that certain audience members are clearly less interested in coverage of politics than others.

In both countries, existing communicative engagement gaps may widen in the future and may well become self-perpetuating. For example, for the poorly educated, low-wage, welfare-dependent, ghetto-dwelling citizens, from an ethnic minority background, conventional politics may continue to have little relevance to their lived experience and be of little interest, and the fewer the incentives to engage, the less likely they are to become engaged. In contrast, for university-educated, suburb-dwelling middle-class citizens, conventional politics may seem to have greater relevance and interest to their lives and there will be more incentives to be, and remain, engaged. If Franklin (2004: 60) is right, and new cohorts retain the habits of their early political experience, then a permanent footprint may have been cast which will continue with new cohorts as they grow older. For the young growing up in deprived environments there are few, if any, incentives to gain the habits of citizenship of their wealthier counterparts. This group may not become interested in the political messages of the main parties, or the media. In contrast, a young person growing up in affluent surroundings will more than likely go on to be part of a new generation of 'critical citizens', not only engaged in conventional politics but also prepared to engage in alternative forms of political activity, as chapter 7 will show (Norris, 1999; Pattie et al., 2003a, 2003b).

The Rise of Self-Expressive Politics

Mᴇᴍʙᴇʀꜱ of the public in the US and the UK not only receive information and form opinions but also express their views on political matters in a variety of ways. Traditionally, public opinion has been conceived of as entering political communication systems through certain set channels: protest repertoires, such as strikes, public meetings and demonstrations; the ballot box; the media, in the letter columns of newspapers; and opinion polls (Coleman, 2002b; Davis and Curtice, 2000; Hart, 2001; Inglehart, 1997b; McNair et al., 2003; Manin, 1997; Norris, 2002b; Pattie et al., 2003a, 2003b, 2004; Verba, et al., 1995; Wahl-Jorgensen, 2001). These various channels were viewed as fairly stable routes through which members of the public could express their views on political matters. For the majority of the public, though the exercise of political voice has been confined largely to voting in a variety of elections (Dalton et al., 2003). This picture, however, is changing fast.

Public political attitude-expression is undergoing a transformation. It is no longer confined to certain events such as elections, nor does it necessarily require the co-presence of others. The public can articulate its views on political matters through a greatly expanded series of protest repertoires and media outlets, and via new technologies (Bucy and Gregson, 2001; Davis, R., 2005; Ferguson and Howell, 2004; Hill and Hughes, 1998). Further, members of the public now inhabit a political environment where they are continually encouraged by various actors to vocalize their views, whether this is in opposition to the activities of governments or transnational corporations, support for environmental regulations or complaints about a company or local government services. As the number of issues coming to the public's attention has increased, attitude-expression is less and less confined to national issues and conventional politics.

This growth in opportunities for verbal forms of expression via the media, and non-verbal forms of expression through symbolic action, means that public opinion now saturate political communication systems as never before (Blumler and Gurevitch, 2000). Both countries are witnessing the emergence of what some have termed a 'self-expressive culture' (Coleman, 2004) and others have called a 'new' opinion environment (Bennett, 2003a) or an 'advocacy democracy' (Dalton et al., 2003); in other words a culture where the exercise of political voice is continually encouraged, enabled and facilitated, by a series of individuals and organizational actors, and through new repertoires and communication technology.

This chapter explores the emergence of this self-expressive political culture. It maps the ways in which members of the public seek to express their views. It examines the growth of opportunities for attitude-expression and the attempts to mobilize opinion by various organizational actors. Based on data from several sources, it reveals that certain types of attitude-expression are increasing and that certain sections of both societies are more likely than others to take advantage of opportunities to express themselves publicly. Finally, it concludes that while this environment offers new opportunities, it is far from the deliberative picture some have painted.

Opportunities for self-expression

In the US and the UK over the last 50 years there has been a dramatic growth in the opportunities that members of the public have to express their political views. This growth of opportunities has been aided by two main factors: the emergence of new repertoires, and the emergence and diffusion of new communication technologies and programme formats. Each factor needs to be examined in more detail.

Political repertoires, new and old

Citizens do not need to wait for elections or referenda in order to express their opinions, or to be asked by pollsters. They can communicate their views on government activity and a whole series of other matters through less routine and more immediate ways. There are traditional repertoires such as strikes, occupations, demonstrations, voting and donating money, all of which have a long history and remain important forms of attitude-expression. In addition, 'newer' repertoires have become a taken-for-granted part of political attitude-expression over the past 40 years or so. The public can make a statement through many acts: boycotting a product or joining a 'buycott' of ethical goods; signing a petition; joining a chain letter; wearing a t-shirt, badge, cap or coloured ribbon or wristband; handing out leaflets; raising funds;

donating money to a telethon appeal or a Live Aid-style fundraiser. This is by no means a comprehensive list; new, hybrid, online versions of protest repertoires have appeared in recent years – the public can, for instance, join an email letter chain, or sign an e-petition.

Protest voting and mid-term ballots

The public uses traditional repertoires in new ways: elections are used to register a protest against the policies of the incumbent administration; or express antipathy towards the main political parties. Such protest voting occurs at general elections, although it is a key feature of a host of mid-term, 'second-order elections' (Rallings and Thrasher, 2000; Southwell and Everest, 1998). The public often utilizes second-order or mid-term elections to send a message of general unhappiness, disaffection or anger on particular issues. These elections can be seen as informal referenda on government policy and performance.

Although turnout is often low in second-order and mid-term elections, the recipients of protest votes are the government's main opponents or sometimes single-issue parties. In the US, in 1994, apprehension about President Clinton's policies led to a mid-term electoral backlash against the Democrats (Davies, 1999). In 2006, disquiet about Iraq led to a mid-term electoral rejection of the Republican Party. In the UK, for instance, the Liberal Democrats are regularly the recipients of anti-government protest votes in local authority elections and by-elections. Some times the recipients of protest votes are candidates campaigning on a particular cause, or anti-establishment protest candidates – in other words, candidates who symbolize the concern felt: for instance, concern about the closure of a school or hospital might lead to support for a candidate opposing its closure. In the UK, concerns about immigration and asylum led to sections of the electorate to vote for the far right anti-immigrant nationalist parties. These anxieties are not only local but can also be national and international. A worry about the ongoing process of European integration and the new European Union Constitution led to a large increase in those voting for the UK Independence Party in the 2004 European parliamentary election – they gained 16 per cent of the vote.

New communication technology and public access media

The emergence of public access discussion-based media outlets and new communication technologies allows further public opinion expression to occur on a variety of issues, with, in addition to traditional channels such as telephone land-lines and public-access television, new technologies such as mobile phones, digital television and the internet. The onset of interactive digital television has allowed viewers to interact with programming through their remote controls; although take-up is more limited than other technologies, digital viewers can register their opinions directly with ease and SMS texting has enabled members of the public to communicate their views from any location. The internet has had a particularly well-documented impact: as Castells (2004) observes, in general the internet has enhanced the public's ability to mobilize around an issue. The growth of email, for instance, has increased the ease with which the public can enunciate on issues; although the public can, and do, still write letters, email provides an almost instantaneous way in which messages can be sent to government, elected representatives and the media (Margolis and Resnick, 2000). The internet has created yet further opportunities for self-expression through chat rooms and Usenet groups, which have grown in abundance: Usenet groups, for instance, offer members opportunities to post their views and for fellow members to comment (R. Davis, 2005; Hill and Hughes, 1998). The widespread availability of specialist easy-to-use software has led to a proliferation of web-logging or blogging: in 1999, it was estimated there were fewer than 50 blogs (Drezner and Farrell, 2004); by 2004, according to another estimate, there were more than 2.5 million (Technorati, 2004; cited in Ferguson and Howell, 2004). Other, more recent, estimates have put the figure still higher, at 10 million and rising, although it is difficult to estimate accurately overall numbers (Henning, 2004). Blogs are the online equivalent of a journal or diary, with regular entries made by the site host, which often include video clips and photos as well as text. Many have a facility that allows visitors to respond to the messages (Ferguson and Howell, 2004). In addition, websites such as YouTube and Bebo-TV have become popular forums for the public to post their own video material. In the UK alone it was estimated that such sites had around 3.6 million users in 2006 (Harris, 2006). This is not to say that the content of blogs or Usenet bulletin boards is always political, but that they offer the opportunity for political expression which is often taken up (Cornfield et al., 2005).

Modes of attitude-expression

It is clear that there are a large number of opportunities for political self-expression; however, the growth has been in a certain type of expression. It has been in what can be termed 'individualistic' as opposed to 'collective' forms of expression.[1] Individualistic forms of attitude-expression, unlike collective forms, do not require the simultaneous co-presence of others. Individualistic forms rely on cumulative input to make an impact – the numbers signing a petition, for instance,

Table 7.1 Modes of political attitude-expression

	Traditional	Non-traditional
Collective	Demonstrations	Street protest/festival
	Strikes	Swarming
	Occupations	
Individualistic	Voting	Signing a petition
	Leafleting	Boycott
	Writing a letter	'Buycott'
	Donating money	Email letter chain, blogging, vlogging,
		Usenets, chat rooms
		Wearing t-shirt/badge, coloured ribbon or wristband
		Email, SMS, telephone-views to media

Source: Complied by the author

grows over time. However, more than this, the expansion has been in 'non-traditional' individualistic modes of expression. Non-traditional modes differ from traditional in several respects.[2] First, they are quicker; non-traditional forms are fairly instant, especially those aided by communication technology. Second, they require little commitment; in the main they do not involve time-consuming activity, expenditure of resources or membership of an organization. Third, they are more convenient; members of the public do not need to wait to vote, or for some one to organize a demonstration or ballot to express their views. There is no need to travel physically; they can express themselves at the time or place of their choosing and not one decided by another.

As the bottom right-hand corner of table 7.1 shows, the growth in opportunities in the last 30 years or so has been in non-traditional individualistic modes; there are more opportunities for citizens to quickly and conveniently convey a message of opposition or support with little or no commitment to a cause. Of course, non-traditional individualistic forms are used with collective and traditional ones: individuals may choose to express their views on one issue through blogging, calling or texting talk radio shows and joining a demonstration or a strike, or by voting, but can just as easily merely text a talk radio show on another issue.

'Let us know what you think': encouraging attitude-expression

The growth in opportunities has been coupled with widespread encouragement of the public to express itself. Manin observes that for much of the twentieth century public attitudes were channelled largely through party or partisan outlets. He argues that during the era of party-dominated democracy, citizens had no voice other than that of the party and its affiliated organizations (1997: 215). In both countries today, however, there is a plethora of organizations and individuals inviting members of the public to express themselves. They are urged, almost continually by some actors and organizations, to indicate their views on a whole series of issues. It is no longer the case that the public only expresses views on key events and remains silent the rest of the time; citizens can vocalize their opinions on political injustice, famine in the developing world, as well as environmental, lifestyle and culture, and a host of other material and post-material concerns. In addition, actors and organizations have realized that encouragement needs to be complemented by efforts to make expression quick and convenient. For instance, since the 1960s, issue entrepreneurs have used not only traditional repertoires, but also non-traditional individualistic repertoires to register opinion.

Issue entrepreneurs, whose numbers have proliferated over the last 40 years or so, have been particularly successful at introducing a wide range of issues to the public's attention. These new social movements, religious groups, cause groups and celebrities not only play a consciousness-raising role, but also, importantly, seek to facilitate reactions through traditional and non-traditional means. They regularly organize opportunities for public enunciation, mobilizing the public through continual appeals (see Bennett, 2003a). Such reactions can have various triggers; in both countries, the activities of local and national government, new taxes or tax rises, have acted as catalyst for the outpouring of feeling (see chapter 5). The policy and the activities of the US government, as well as the policies of global bodies such as the World Trade Organization and the International Monetary Fund and the G8 nations, have been another stimulus (Bennett, 2003b). Anti-globalization groups have planned, advertised and coordinated concurrent demonstrations in various world capitals (Castells, 2004). During the so-called 'Battle in Seattle' in November 1999, it was estimated that protests were simultaneously organized in 82 other cities (Lichbach and Almeida, cited in Bennett, 2003b). In 2003, the invasion of Iraq acted as a huge mobilizing device. Demonstrations in the UK against the invasion were designed to send a message of opposition as much to George W. Bush as to Tony Blair. In 2005, there were protests at the G8 summit, the centrepiece being the 'Live 8' concert. These issue entrepreneurs, in the various guises, stress the cause, whether it be local, national or global, the type of direct action under way and its goals.

The growth of non-traditional individualistic forms of expresion

Where there has been a real emphasis by issue entrepreneurs is in encouraging responses through non-traditional individualistic means. If members of the public are not willing to attend a demonstration, they may be willing to sign a petition, wear a ribbon or t-shirt, or engage in some other form of expression. Some recent examples are particularly illustrative: popstar Bono, with a series of leading corporations, launched 'Red' products to help fight poverty in Africa, with all the products, from mobile phones to clothes and accessories, symbolically coloured red; cause group Liberty joined forces with fashion designer Vivienne Westwood to produce a series of t-shirts to highlight the plight of those held without charge by US and UK governments in the 'War on Terror', each shirt displaying the words 'I'm not a terrorist'; in 2005, following an idea by American cyclist Lance Armstrong's cancer charity, numerous pressure groups and charities launched their own coloured wristbands embossed with a slogan.

In many cases advocate groups have utilized the web to provide online versions of off-line repertoires. Websites such as thepetition-site.com, ipetitions.com or pledgebank provide browsers with information and access to petitions and pledges of action on a wide variety of issues in numerous countries, not just the UK or US; as with an off-line petition, members of the public are provided with an overview of the issue and encouraged to leave their name and email address. However, unlike an off-line petition, it is more immediate, allowing the pronouncement of opinion quickly; there is no need to rely on the good fortune of meeting an activist in the street (Gurak and Logie, 2003; Johnson, 2005). Through such sites, petitions can be found on local, national or global issues, and quickly signed; as Gurak and Logie observe: 'online protests far outstrip their counterparts in terms of speed and reach. Internet protest efforts are often measured in days and hours, whereas paper-based protest efforts move no faster than postal carriers' (2003: 44–5). In this way, the internet is often used in tandem with a consumer boycott, a demonstration or other forms of direct action.

While these issue entrepreneurs are important informal mobilizers of public opinion, they are by no means the only ones. Public bodies and elected officials have also moved towards encouraging and facilitating public comment. While the increased use of referenda has been well documented (see Dalton et al., 2003), the frequent use of non-traditional individualistic means has been less so. In both countries local and central government in particular have been some of the key actors encouraging public attitude-expression as part of being seen to be responsive. In the UK, at the level of local government, an increasing number of councils now ask members of the public for their opinions on a wide range of issues, through focus groups, polls, citizen panels and citizen juries (Pratchett, 1999). In both countries there have been various initiatives since the 1980s aimed at facilitating public reaction on a range of issues. The governments of both countries also believe that the internet will enable a re-engineering of the relationship between government and citizen (Chadwick, 2006) and both governments have internet portals: FirstGov in the US and DirectGov in the UK. These allow citizens to contact ministers and civil servants in the various government departments through email. Both governments have also started to use the web to make the public consultation process on legislation more inclusive, allowing ministers and civil servants to hear from the public. The aim is to ensure that all central government public consultations are accessible through the web (Chadwick, 2006). A similar scheme to encourage young people to express their views to parliamentary committees of inquiry was launched in 2006 in the UK by the Home Affairs Committee and the Hansard Society – an independent non-party organization. The specially designed website for the 'Citizen Calling' project provides young people with a phone number and asks them to text their views on a variety of issues being considered by the Committee.

Writing to an elected representative or meeting him or her face-to-face have traditionally been the main channels through which members of the public could communicate their views on an issue. Elected representatives in both countries now also encourage email communication, with nearly all representatives' websites providing contact. Some even encourage text-messaging and have message-board facilities for constituents to leave their views (Ferguson and Howell, 2004; Johnson, 2004). The President and the Prime Minister both encourage contact. In the US, the White House website asks members of the public to 'choose from a menu of options, such as seeking assistance, extending a speaking invitation or expressing agreement of disagreement with a White House position' (Davis and Owen, 1998: 125) In the UK, in addition to the usual features, the Downing Street website provided the public with an opportunity to design and sign an e-petition.

In addition, mainstream media outlets actively encourage members of the public to voice their views, and there has been a dramatic growth in the number of shows specifically engaging the public, where a non-co-present audience are encouraged to express their opinions. Political talk shows on radio are perhaps one of the most high-profile facilitators, encouraging listeners to get in touch and 'let them know what they think' and the call-in (text-in, email-in) has become one of the defining aspects of talk media (Herbst, 1996; Ruddock, 2006). These programmes represent a relatively new opportunity for the public to enunciate on issues; as McNair et al. observe in the UK, 'no one partic-ipated in *mediated* political debate' before 1948 (2003: 77). The radio phone-in programme was not part of commercial radio in any major way until the 1970s (Davis and Owen, 1998; McNair et al., 2003). In the US by the 1980s, Christian Radio, NRA Radio and numerous political talk radio hosts, such as Rush Limbaugh and G. Gordon Liddy, had arrived (see chapter 5).

In the UK, although there were a few programmes that used a public question format, these were a far cry from the audience participation shows that developed later. It was principally through commercial local radio that the phone-in was pioneered, with the format slowly spreading to national media (McNair et al., 2003). In terms of political programming, public participation started in the late 1970s, when the BBC began the first regular public access show, *Question Time* – a show that continues today (McNair et al., 2003). Now there are a host of similar shows and they have become staple fare of political coverage, especially during election campaigns. A large number of political programmes have their own website, or pages on a website, where views can be left; they also advertise their email address and phone numbers whilst on air. Much of this political output encourages its viewers and listeners to phone, email or text their views, or to use the interactive facilities on their digital television, if they have one. One high-profile example in both countries was a political equivalent of the successful show *Pop Idol*, where viewers of *The American Candidate* in the US, and *Vote for Me* in the UK were given the opportunity to vote for a series of would-be politicians and their policies.

Encouraging audience comment is now almost a prerequisite for news bulletins. Network news shows bombard their viewers with requests to communicate their views, and not just the populist network news and current affairs programmes; serious news outlets do it as well. In the press, newspaper columnists supply their email addresses for readers to respond (see Gunter, 2003), and the tabloid papers regu-larly provide phone numbers for their readers to register their opinions on particular issues – indeed phone-polls are a regular feature of these papers (see chapter 5). In the US, a study of the websites of television news outlets found that 10 per cent of sites offered discussion forums, and 35 per cent offered feedback forms on site (Chan-Olmsted and Park 2000, cited in ibid.: 72). Nearly all leading US newspapers offer their readers the opportunity to respond to editorials online.

The public's poor experiences as patients, passengers and consumers often act as a powerful mobilizing force for the vocalizing of complaints and, as a result, watchdog bodies have emerged over the last 40 years to help facilitate and direct complaints, with the aim of improving these and other services. In the UK, the Rail Passenger Council and Postwatch are two of many that have been particularly adept at channelling complaints about the rail network and the postal service respectively – two of the most complained-about public services.

In sum, members of the public are inundated with requests from a variety of actors to register their support or opposition, satisfaction or dissatisfaction, to a range of issues or experiences. These actors and organizations have, in addition, sought to subsidize the cost of public attitude-expression through non-traditional individualistic means.

The communicating public?

While there are more opportunities for members of the public to register their opinions, and there is greater encouragement, are they actually taking advantage of these opportunities? The evidence available from a variety of sources produces a complex picture.

Protest action

In the UK, there are two national surveys tracking public political participation over time: the British Social Attitudes Survey (see Bromley et al., 2001) and the Democracy and Participation Programme (see Pattie et al., 2003a, 2003b). While the number of those voting has fallen (see chapter 6), the findings from both surveys show a growth of the number of people engaging in certain non-traditional individualistic political repertoires. Table 7.2 shows that the percentage of those who said they signed a petition increased from 34 per cent to 42 per cent between 1986 and 2000 and those saying they participated in a boycott of products increased from 4 per cent in 1984 to 31 per cent in 2000 (see also Inglehart, 1997b). The numbers engaging in traditional forms of attitude-expression have not risen substantially; the table shows that the percentage attending demonstrations in the UK between 1986 and 2000 increased slightly from 6 to 10 per cent over the same period (see also ibid.).

In the US, as is shown in table 7.3, the percentage claiming to have signed a petition rose from 58 per cent in 1974 to 68 per cent in 1981 and then 71 per cent in 1990. The percentage of those claiming to have joined a boycott, or considering joining one, rose from 58 per cent in 1974, falling back to 52 per cent in 1981 before rising 64 per cent in 1990. Table 7.3 also shows that the numbers engaging in demonstrations have grown by a small amount in the US. According to the table, the percentage of those claiming to have joined a demonstration rose from 10 per cent in 1974, to 12 per cent in the early 1980s, and to 15 per cent in the early 1990s.

Table 7.2 Those participating in three types of political action in the UK, 1984–2000			
Action/year	1984	1986	2000
Joining a boycott[a]	4%	–	31%
Signing a petition	–	34%	42%
Attending a demonstration	–	6%	10%

[a] Figures from Pattie et al., 2003b

Source: Compiled from Democracy and Participation Programme (Pattie et al., 2003b) and British Social Attitudes Survey (Bromley et al., 2001)

Table 7.3 Those participating in three types of political action in the US, 1974–90			
Action/year	1974	1981	1990
Signing a petition	58%	68%	71%
Joining a boycott	58%	52%	64%
Attending a demonstration	10%	12%	15%

Source: Compiled from World Values Survey (Inglehart, 1997b)

The findings in both countries fit well with evidence from comparative data that reveals that the numbers engaging in newer 'non-traditional' kinds of direct action of one kind or another has increased in a selection of advanced industrial democracies (Norris, 2002b: 197). For instance, the percentage of those admitting to signing a petition increased from 32 per cent in the mid-1970s to 60 per cent by the mid-1990s, and those engaged in a consumer boycott from 5 to 15 per cent. However, the numbers participating in more traditional forms of collective direct action have grown but not to the same extent. Those involved in demonstrations rose over the same period, from 9 to 17 per cent; those involved in unofficial strike action rose from 2 to 4 per cent; and those occupying buildings from 1 to 2 per cent (Norris, 2002b).

Making contact

Members of the public also seem more willing to contact their elected representatives. In the UK, a survey has found that around 17 per cent of the public claim to have contacted their MP in 2002, an increase from 11 per cent in 1986 (Curtice and Seyd, 2003). A survey in 1967 found that '45 per cent of MPs received fifty or more letters a week from constituents', but by 1986 another survey found that a large majority of 'MPs received between twenty to fifty letters a day' (Rush, 2001: 207). Research has also shown a growing number writing to the

Prime Minister. Between 1970 and 1974, Edward Heath received on average 300 letters a week; in 2000, Tony Blair was getting an estimated 10,000 a week, with a new unit in Downing Street being formed to cope with the flood of mail (Seymour-Ure, 2003).

The numbers contacting a government department have also increased, if only slightly. In the UK they rose from 3 per cent in 1986 to 4 per cent in 2000 (Bromley et al., 2001). The number of people complaining about the postal service also rose by a factor of four, from 35,995 in 2000/1 to 137,464 in 2003/4. In the US, the numbers contacting government have grown, in 2004, 54 per cent of citizens contacted the government directly (Pew Internet, 2004).

The public also seem more willing to approach the media to express their views. In the UK, Curtice and Seyd show that the numbers contacting a radio or TV programme or newspaper rose from 3 per cent of their sample in 1986 to 7 per cent in 2002 (2003: 102). Pattie et al.'s research shows a similar trend, with the numbers increasing from 4 to 9 per cent between 1984 and 2000; both figures confirm a more than doubling of those contacting the media (2003a: 631). In the US, Hart (2001) observes that there has been a steady rise in the number of people writing letters to newspapers, with an estimated 2 million letters written annually.

While the public utilize certain individualistic modes of expression, there are no national time series data about the extent to which members of the public use new technological versions of those repertoires to communicate their views, so the data used here are derived from a variety of sources. A survey of online political participation in the UK found that around 17 per cent – that is, about a fifth of all internet users – 'reported having participated in any one of the range of behaviours put forward', such as 'visiting a website, signing an online petition, sending an e-postcard, or participating in a chat room or email discussion board' (Ward et al., 2003: 664). In the US, the number of people joining political discussions and chat groups during election campaigns has grown from 2 million in 1996 to 6 million in 2004 (Pew Internet, 2005a). In 2004, 7 per cent also sent emails urging others to vote for a particular candidate (Pew Internet, 2005a).

Research also shows that the internet is being used by the public to contact the news media. In 1996, in the UK, *The Times* online received around 100 emails a day; by 1999, the same paper was receiving six times that figure (Gunter, 2003: 71). Responses to requests for comment by television shows run into the thousands, if not hundreds of thousands. Often the response is just to register an opinion for or against an issue; in the UK, for example, in 2005, 100,000 people texted *Radio Five Live* to vote on whether the press was right to publish cartoons of the prophet Mohammed (Shaw, 2006).

New communication technologies are also being used by the public to contact government and elected representatives: in 2001, 11 per cent of the UK public used government online facilities; in 2003, that figure had risen to 18 per cent (Taylor Nelson Sofres 2003, cited in Dunleavy et al., 2003). In 2000, the then Home Secretary, Jack Straw, received 70,000 emails urging him to 'extradite General Pinochet', who was under house arrest in Britain (Duffy, 2000). While those who complained about the national postal service by letter doubled over the period 2000–4, those complaining by email or phone rose slightly more than fourfold (Postwatch Annual Report 2004). In the US, in 2003, according to a Pew survey, of the 54 per cent of the public who contacted the government, 42 per cent used old technology such as the phone, 47 per cent used the internet and 22 per cent used both old and new technologies. While most of the contacts related to e-services, 19 per cent went online to register their opinions with government agencies on issues and policy questions (Pew Internet, 2004). In the US, the number of emails received by Congress increased dramatically, from 51 million in 1999 to 128 million in 2002 (Johnson, 2004), and in the UK the numbers emailing their MP also increased. The number of emails sent to the White House and Downing Street has also risen: in 1993 the White House received 800 email messages a day; this has increased dramatically, to thousands (Davis and Owen, 1998). Downing Street also receives large quantities of email on a daily basis.

A nation of activists?

While, with the exception of voting, members of the public are increasingly willing to engage in protest action and to contact the media and those in authority to express their views, survey data tend to suggest that the vast majority only get involved in a variety of activities occasionally. In the UK, for instance, 42 per cent of those sampled engaged in just one or two acts, while only 11 per cent engaged in three or more (Curtice and Seyd, 2003; see also the Electoral Commission, 2006b; Pattie et al. , 2003b). In the US, 40 per cent of those sampled by Survey2000 engaged in one or two types of political activity, while only 10 per cent engaged in four acts or more (Weber et al., 2003: 35; see also Verba et al., 1995).

In terms of online activity, the majority of the US public tend to participate in one or two acts. In the UK, members of the public, according to one piece of research, tend to be 'non-cumulative in their online participatory behaviour, engaging in only one or two activities' (Ward et al., 2003: 664); further, the kinds of repertoire engaged in most regularly are individualistic non-traditional acts. As mentioned, all are 'low cost', relatively quick and do not take up much time or involve much effort. As Bromley et al. observe, 'few have taken part in significant time consuming activity' (2001: 202), a point echoed by Pattie et al. (2003b). The most common form of activity online according to a UK survey was of the 'less active type' (Ward et al., 2003: 665). In the US, according to Weber et al., the most prevalent form of online activities are sending and receiving email (66 per cent), followed by taking part in mailing lists and accessing digital libraries, newspapers and magazines (2003: 35).

Although the number of those seeking to express themselves through traditional collective means has risen only slightly, there has been an increase in those seeking to articulate their opinions through different kinds of individualistic non-traditional means. However, this is certainly not an activist generation; the data show that a majority of the public are more likely to express themselves through a few activities a year, and only a minority could be considered to be regularly engaging in numerous types of activity.

The loudest and quietest voices

While there has been a growth in public expression through 'newer' individualistic 'low-cost' means, research also reveals that some are more willing than others to exploit the opportunities before them. The willingness to express political views seems intimately bound up with a number of socio-economic factors, such as income and education. The exercise of a political voice is indeed stratified, as Schlozman et al. (2004) and Pattie et al. (2003b) observe. In the US, when 'it comes to protest the well educated and well-heeled are more likely to take part' than the poor (Schlozman et al., 2004: 24); those earning over $75,000 are more likely to engage in political activity than those earning less then $15,000. In the UK, Pattie et al. show that those most likely to register their views through political action were employed professionals, earning more than £30,000 per annum, who have remained in education to at least the age of 19. Those least likely were the poor and very poor, earning under £10,000, with the fewest number of years of education (2003a: 627). This picture was affirmed by a MORI survey, which found that, of those participating in five or more acts (the most active), 80 per cent were from social categories A, B and C1, compared to 19 per cent from C2, D and E (Worcester, 2002).

These findings fit with the results from comparative survey data. Norris notes that in 15 advanced industrial democracies, 40 per cent with a 'high' level of education had engaged in at least one protest action, compared to only 24 per cent with 'low' levels of education. A similar gap exists by occupation; while 43 per cent of managerial-professional and 43 per cent of white-collar workers had engaged in at least one protest action, only 26 per cent of unskilled manual workers had (2002b: 202).

The limited evidence shows that the same groups that engage in various repertoires are more likely to seek to articulate their views on political matters through the media. In their qualitative study, McNair et al. observe that working-class interviewees felt excluded from the more 'established' participation shows. Many in their focus group saw 'access to and participation in political debate as a pastime of "them" rather than "us" – them being the educated middle classes; "us" the "ordinary folk"' (2003: 88). These findings are confirmed in part by Davis and Curtice, whose study of participation in a talk radio show, *Election Call*, showed that the successful callers were largely from a professional managerial background – 35 per cent of all callers, compared to 10 per cent manual and 8 per cent unemployed (2000: 68).

The relatively wealthy and well-educated members of society are also more likely to seek to articulate their views on political matters to their elected representatives. In the US, those earning over $75,000 are more likely to contact government than those earning less than $30,000 (Pew Internet, 2004). The most educated are also likely to be more active in contacting government than the least educated (Bimber, 1999). In the UK, 10 per cent of A, B and C1s 'recall presenting their views to an MP' in the last 2–3 years compared to 3 per cent of C2, D and Es (Electoral Commission, 2004c).

Ward et al.'s survey of those using the internet for political purposes showed that participation is dominated by the educated upper-middle classes: 'While professional classes made up 18 per cent of the sample overall, they comprised almost one third of online participators. Manual and semi-skilled workers, however, while they comprised 32 per cent of the sample formed only 16 per cent of the online participators' (2003: 665). In addition, '17 per cent of the most highly educated [accounted] for two-fifths of the online participators' (ibid.).

In the US, Pew Center data showed that, of their sample of those who regularly sent political emails (62 per cent) or who regularly engaged in political discussion online (59 per cent), 67 per cent were college-educated, or had some college education, and 67 per cent earned more than $30,000 (Davis and Owen, 1998: 156). Bimber found that the most educated were more likely to contact government via email than the least educated (1999).

The evidence points to a well-educated, relatively wealthy, politically motivated citizen elite keen to embrace newer forms of political action and participation. In the UK, Pattie et al. note that 'political voice is concentrated among those with the greatest resources, defined in terms of those with skills and income' (2003: 627). A similar point could be made in the US (see Schlozman et al., 2004).

Young people and political attitude-expression

Comparative research shows that young people's pattern of political activity has undergone a generational transformation (Norris, 2003). They attach less weight to traditional means of political action than have previous generations, embracing different forms of direct action. The young are far less likely to vote than their older colleagues; they see voting as just one more method of articulating their views (see chapter 6). Comparative research by Norris shows that 'compared with older age groups young people were 8 per cent more likely to have signed a petition, 7 per cent more likely to have bought a product for political reasons, and 6 per cent more likely to have demonstrated' (ibid.: 12). According to her data, young people 'are more likely than their parents and grandparents to engage in cause oriented political action' (ibid.). In the US, specifically, 23 per cent of those aged 18–24 have signed a petition compared to 21 per cent of those over 65, and 38 per cent have boycotted a good or company compared to 28 per cent of those over 65 (Pew Research Center, 2006a). In the UK, 35 per cent of those surveyed aged 11–21 have signed a petition and 23 per cent have boycotted a good or company (Nestlé Social Research Programme, 2005).

But is this true for other means of attitude-expression? The short answer is 'no'. For example, in the US, according to a 2006 survey, only 10 per cent of those aged 18–24 have contacted a newspaper or magazine to express an opinion and 7 per cent have contacted a TV or radio station; this compares to 12 per cent and 10 per cent of those aged 50–59 (Pew Research Center, 2006a). In the UK, 11 per cent of 15–24 year olds, considered active, had phoned a newspaper to raise an issue, compared to 19 per cent of those aged 45–54 (Worcester, 2002).

The young are more likely, though, to use new technologies to express their views. SMS text-messaging is now an integral part of most radio shows, with listeners being urged to send in their views and requests. Ownership of mobile phones is widespread and it is easy and quick for audience members to text in their views. Still mainly concentrated on the young, the Radio One breakfast show claims to receive, on average, 5,000 text messages per show; with 9.5 million listeners, that equates to one message per 1,900 listeners (John, 2004). According to the survey, the 16–24 age group in the UK, 'despite being one of the smallest age groups represented in the sample, formed the biggest group of internet-based participators. . . . 30 per cent of the youngest age groups reported that they had engaged in some form of online participation compared with only 11 per cent of [45–54 year olds]' (Gibson et al., 2005: 665). In the US, research by the Pew Center found that those who regularly sent political emails were under the age of 50 (83 per cent) – 28 per cent being under the age of 29. The Pew Survey also revealed that those who regularly engaged in political discussion online were under the age of 50 (85 per cent) – 49 per cent being under the age of 29 (Davis and Owen, 1998: 156).

While the young are active online, their activity is still interest-driven. As Henn et al. observe, whereas many 'eschew much of what could be characterised as formal or conventional politics, they are interested in a different type of politics that is more participative and which focuses on local, immediate (and some post-material) issues' (2002: 186). For example, an analysis of the UK election programme *Election Call* found that 6 per cent of callers were under 25, compared to 25 per cent over 65 (Coleman, 2002b: 250). In the US, research found that the young were less likely than their older counterparts to contact their elected representatives via email or phone (Bimber, 1999). The difference can perhaps be explained by the perceptions of conventional politics amongst the young (see chapter 6).

However, young people's reaction to the invasion of Iraq in 2003 illustrates their propensity to engage in direct forms of political attitude-expression. The start of hostilities in March 2003 led to a wave of protest in both countries. In the UK, on the day after the night of 'shock and awe', an estimated 8,000 teenagers left school and engaged in a series of anti-war protests, many defying their teachers in order to do so. Word of the action spread quickly via text messages and email. In large cities around the UK, there were meetings in school playgrounds, streets were blocked, MPs and media offices were occupied and, in London, students converged on Parliament Square chanting anti-war slogans, waving placards and blowing whistles (Brooks, 2003; Vidal, 2003). Research found that in the UK some 82 per cent of 10–14 year olds were against the invasion of Iraq and that 7 per cent of 11–21 year olds had taken part in demonstrations against it (Brooks, 2003; Nestlé Social Research Programme, 2005).

In general, the young may well be more ready to engage in particular forms of expression, but there are significant socio-economic divides between them. In the US, for example, Survey2000 shows that the most active young people online were educated young males (Weber et al., 2003: 36). In the UK, a MORI survey of engagement in political protest found that one of the strongest determining factors in whether a young person became actively involved was whether he or she was attending a sixth form college; this factor accounted for 20 per cent of all variation in attitudes (Nestlé Family Monitor, 2003; see also Nestlé Social Research Programme, 2005).

Conclusion

This chapter has tried to map the changing nature of public attitude-expression. Traditionally, the exercise of political voice has been limited to certain events, has required commitment and has not necessarily been convenient, in some instances requiring the co-presence of others. Over the last 40 or so years, and especially since the mid-1990s, public attitude-expression has been freed from these constraints, as the 'opportunity structures' for expression have expanded (see Scott and Street, 2001). Individuals, through the web or SMS options, can swiftly respond when asked. Technological advances also mean they can easily create and maintain an online presence with limited technical know-how (Ferguson and Howell, 2004). The public does not need to sacrifice any of its leisure or work time to express its views. There is no need to wait for actors to organize the opportunity. For instance, voting may be a 'low-cost' activity, but the timing of an election or referendum is not usually determined by the public.

Issue advocates, media hosts, celebrities, the government and political parties continually encourage attitude-expression and facilitate it through these newer repertoires and outlets. Quickly and conveniently, and at low personal cost, these actors organize opportunities to register views on a variety of issues: response to a question asked by a broadcast news show, a newspaper or a chat show host; a signature on a petition; the wearing of a t-shirt or coloured ribbon; the substitution of certain boycotted goods and services with others; the emailing of complaints or concerns; or the buying of a CD. Indeed, the limited evidence there is shows that the public responds to all the above appeals through a variety of non-traditional individualistic means.

These factors could be said to constitute a 'new' self-expressive political culture, one characterized by a plurality of voices talking across each other, promoting and responding to a myriad of agendas: against a ban on hunting with dogs; for increased rights for divorced fathers; in favour of animal rights; in opposition to the war in Iraq; in favour of tougher sentences for juvenile offenders; against stem cell research; against the placing of a mobile phone mast near a junior school; and so on. The majority of those expressing an opinion on these and other matters do so through non-traditional individualistic methods, often in direct response to appeals and a few times a year.

This is not to argue that there are not collective outbursts, expressions of outrage, dissent or revulsion, nor is it to argue that there are no spaces for deliberation in the public arena – indeed, the growth of blogging and Usenet groups shows that this is possible (Davis, 2005). This is not, though, a culture of greater political activism. Research shows that collective means of attitude-expression is no more used today than by previous generations, and that those engaged in deliberation are often a small core of strongly opinionated and like-minded individuals (Coleman, 2002b; Davis and Owen, 1998; Hill and Hughes, 1998; Margolis and Resnick, 2000).

This self-expressive culture is one where the public – at least perhaps the more educated and relatively wealthy – can and do move fleetingly from local issues to national and global issues, expressing opposition or support in a variety of ways, as and when they see fit, without having to move outside their immediate locale or be a member of an organization: a feat which previous generations would have found difficult, if not impossible.

Conclusion: Political Communication in an Uncertain, Divided and Unequal Age

THIS book has explored the impact of systemic trends on political communication systems in the US and the UK, and the knock-on effects of these forces on the activities of organizations and actors. The conclusion seeks to draw out some of the key themes of the book, as well as considering some of the consequences for democracy.

Responding to uncertainty

One of the key ways we can comprehend the activities of political communicators is to see them as the response of strategic actors who operate with particular goals in a rapidly changing socio-political environment. Political communicators act purposively and are reflexive, continually reviewing and analysing their environment, responding to problems that may adversely affect their chances of achieving their aims, monitoring and responding to the increasing uncertainties of the political communication system and 'devising and revising the means to realise their intentions' (Hay, 2002: 152). The increasing uncertainty of the environment in which they operate has prompted a wide variety of responses in order to ensure that particular goals can still be secured.

A key source of uncertainty for both office-seekers and the media in the second modernity has been the changes that have reordered their relations with citizen audiences. The process of partisan dealignment has forced political parties and candidates to reconsider their relationships with the citizen voters. Traditional partisan identity no longer acts as a mobilizing mechanism, with party membership falling and party support declining. As chapter 1 has shown, support for political parties is fickle and conditional. Parties and candidates have had to find new ways of reaching citizen audiences and building and maintaining their support. The outcome of this drive is that the individual has become the subject of intensive investigation. Citizens are increasingly treated as consumers on whom personal information needs be gathered and messages carefully targeted. The techniques of the campaign are continually used after the government is elected, as chapter 2 revealed, and governments find themselves locked into an almost permanent campaign in order to maintain support.

Office-seekers, in competition with each other, continually innovate new ways of reaching disloyal political consumers in a bid to gain competitive advantage. This has led political advocates to employ ever-more elaborate means of message dissemination – as chapters 1 and 2 revealed – and a growing army of specialists are now routinely employed by candidates and parties and by governments. These actors, attuned to the problems of communication, have routinized the use of certain techniques and skills and introduced new ones. In such an environment, ideas developed in campaign conditions become a permanent feature of communication efforts. However, this environment has also led office-seekers to 'go personal' – as we saw in chapter 3. Political appeals increasingly involve a certain amount of personal self-disclosure. Political leaders relations with their voters have never been more intimate.

Chapter 1 has shown that the cost of communication in this increasingly uncertain environment has risen dramatically. The wider use of data-driven campaigning, polling and marketing techniques and expensive advertising has led to an ever-greater need for money. Indeed, in the US presidential campaign, advertising is one of the major costs. Candidates for all major offices in the US have to raise ever-larger amounts of money to fund campaign activities. In total, the lead candidates for presidential office raised and spent in excess of $300 million in 2004. In the UK, the main two political parties spend tens of millions of pounds, a sum which has grown, despite constraints. As we saw in chapter 1, fundraising in both countries has become an essential and continuous activity.

With the end of spectrum scarcity and the multiplication of media outlets, audiences have fragmented. The reconfiguring of once-stable audience/media dynamics has hit the 'old' media hard, as chapter 4 has shown. The arrival of new national news challengers and cable and satellite outlets and the rise of non-traditional forms of political media, such as talk radio, mean that the news networks share of the national audience is falling. The networks in both countries have to compete ever-more aggressively for a shrinking slice of the audience cake. At the same time, the pressure to maintain profitability has increased. It is not only the networks that face these pressures; the same is true for newspapers, brought on by growing competition and a declining, ageing, readership. Further, less predictable media consumption habits are forcing media organizations to reconsider their relations with audiences. Like political parties, greater resources are devoted to market research. The audience are seen as consumers and, as 'media consumers', they are increasingly the subject of investigation.

The findings of market research are more and more influential in shaping the response of traditional news organizations. Political journalists no longer command the 'sheltered' position within news organizations that they once did and the once-dominant professional culture of responsible public service journalism has, according to some, yielded to market pressures (see for example, Swanson, 1997: 1269). There has been a widely documented decline in the 'sacerdotal' approach of journalists to political institutions and events, and an increasing importance of news values in determining political coverage. Chapter 4 revealed that in both countries, but especially the US, the main networks have reduced their coverage of public affairs. Falling ratings and circulation have also 'led to pressure to cover politics only in the ways and to the extent that it is good for business' (ibid.). Issues that scintillate and titillate, such as the coverage of the sexual peccadilloes of politicians, are now a major part of political communication. In addition, there has been a 'ghettoization' of conventional political coverage on special TV channels, online and in additional segments of newspapers, and, as chapter 4 has also shown, the news media have cut back on investment in news-gathering operations – 'downsizing', in Kimball's (1994) phrase.

Chapter 5 showed that certain media outlets seek to maintain audience share in other ways. In both countries, some media channels increasingly embrace populist politics, articulating and fermenting popular reaction to a variety of issues. These outlets, many of which are right-wing, play on their audience's anxieties and fears about their changing environment. They address them as members of a wider community whose values and ways of life are continually confronted by a variety of threats, but in a way designed to exploit anxieties and fears. The mobilization of audiences is a key tactic of populist media outlets; however, unlike traditional populist political movements they do not want audience votes, they want their custom.

The process of strategic adaptation produces a series of unintended consequences, which in turn have further series of consequences. Paradoxically, one outcome of the obsession with promotion, as chapter 2 has shown, has been that promotional strategies have themselves become the news story. Attempts by politicians and spin doctors to manage the media and the strategies they use have become a newsworthy issue. Political news is increasingly about 'backstage manoeuvres of campaign operatives to guide or influence journalists' (Esser et al., 2001: 19). So, instead of leading to the effective dissemination of the message, the message becomes one of media manipulation.

Another of the outcomes of the personalization of politics – of leading politicians 'going personal' – is the disappearance of the 'zone of privacy' which once surrounded leading political actors. Chapter 3 has shown that politicians' self-disclosure has acted in many cases as a green light for media intrusion and journalistic revelation. Such coverage in turn generates conflict between politicians and journalists about where the proper limits of privacy lie.

The need for competitors to raise ever greater amounts of money to finance communication efforts for a variety of offices has led to a string of fundraising scandals – see chapter 2. Such scandals in turn have gone a considerable way towards undermining the reputation of those who hold elected office.

This uncertain environment in which political communicators operate is also profoundly unequal and divided. The next section argues that such strategic goal-oriented activity by political communicators exacerbates exclusivity within both countries' political communication systems, reinforcing political divisions and patterns of citizen marginalization from the political process.

Exacerbating exclusion and division

With exceptions (see Bennett, 2003a; Gandy, 2001; Golding, 1990), there has been a tendency in political communication research to overlook the divided nature of many advanced industrial societies and the often profound inequalities that exist between different citizens, or to play down the importance of these inequalities. Income differentials between citizens have grown in recent years, as chapter 6 has shown. The US and the UK are now more unequal than at any other time during the post-Second World War period, with inequalities that cut across the ethnicity and age profiles of these democracies. The combination of these factors often reveals some of the starkest differences in democratic societies. The most economically deprived are often ethnic minority groups, the unemployed and the infirm.

In both countries, as chapter 6 has shown, these divisions underlie the different levels of citizen engagement with the media coverage of conventional politics. If the engaged citizen could be pictured, he or she would be relatively wealthy (broadly defined), with higher levels of education, and most would be middle-aged and white. These actors have remained politically active, and not only at key periods such as elections; they also increasingly embrace, as chapter 7 reveals, non-traditional individualistic forms of political attitude-expression. To argue that these 'self-motivated', citizens, are not served by a marketized media or are not provided with opportunities to express themselves is not accurate: they participate, are active and pursue a political life and engage in 'monitorial' and information-seeking pursuits as full citizens. Whether they could be better served by the media and government is indeed a question that can be debated.

However, other groups of citizens, variously described as disadvantaged, are becoming inactive. These groups are on the margins, not only economically but also politically. As chapter 6 shows, the US and UK have witnessed the emergence of public disengagement from the electoral process. There has been a decline of voter turnout in both countries, especially in deprived areas. These citizens seem less willing to turn out and vote at elections, especially second-order elections. There has been significant lack of interest in election coverage amongst the ethnic minority and economically deprived sectors of society. In both countries, members of ethnic minority groups are less likely to watch electoral programmes compared to members of the racial majority. For these marginalized communities, government is seen as out of touch with their lives, not concerned, or 'hopelessly corrupt' and 'oppressive' (Boggs, 2000: 37). Divisions are not only socio-economic: as chapter 6 highlights, the young are also less likely to be interested in the coverage of conventional politics than older cohorts, and the media are not encouraging them to gain such a viewing habit.

There are emerging ghettos of exclusion, where low levels of efficacy often mean that communities exclude themselves from political activity – ignoring messages, not participating in elections and avoiding any coverage. In sum, a communicative engagement gap is emerging between the wealthy and the less well-off, between the well educated and the less well educated, between majorities and ethnic minorities and between the young and older cohorts.

When politicians perform, they play to a specific audience: the citizen audience that votes, that is engaged. They have sought 'to cultivate support [of this group] through marketing strategies' (Swanson, 1997: 1267). This self-motivated but unpredictable electorate has become the target of information-gathering techniques such as surveys, opinion polls and focus groups. These are the groups that contestants seek to activate. Those who exclude themselves, or are excluded, do not attract the attention of office-seekers and the targeting of this group of actors makes little sense for parties and candidates with limited resources;

the most economically deprived groups, those who are, in general, less likely to participate or donate, are left out of the political process. The different levels of political engagement are therefore reinforced by strategies of the parties and candidates. The consequence is that cleavages between the included majority and the excluded minority are widening and hardening. As chapter 1 has shown, the rationality of targeted communication sees cleavages developing between those voters in marginal electoral jurisdictions whose votes may count toward the outcome, and those outside these areas. These cleavages are reinforced by the rationality and limited resources of strategic actors.

It is not just office-seekers: the commercially driven news industry is also interested in attracting the right demographic – the audience with a high disposable income that advertisers are interested in. The news media cater for specific taste sectors, segmenting markets and targeting profitable sections that sponsors want to access. Conventional political output, central for the nourishment of the civic self, is increasingly becoming a specialist consumer product. Election coverage, in particular, is seen as a niche concern to be accessed by those who are interested. The strategies of news organizations reinforce existing communicative engagement gaps. Moreover, as chapter 5 has shown, some newer media outlets have joined with existing partisan outlets in catering for audiences with specific political views. The strategies of these organizations exacerbate partisan and political divisions in society, reinforcing a potential 'Balkanization' of civic space: in the US, for example, Fox News has grown increasingly conservative and pro-Republican since 2000; at the same time the percentage of its viewers who are Republican grew from 24 per cent in 1998 to 41 per cent in 2004 and the percentage who describe themselves as conservative has grown from 40 per cent in 1998 to 52 per cent in 2004 (Pew Research Center, 2004b; see also National Annenberg Election Survey, 2004).

The political communication system not only perpetuates the winners and losers scenario, constructed by wider socio-economic and socio-political forces, but also reinforces divides between citizens where perhaps, in an age of spectrum scarcity, with the full-employment welfare state, smaller wealth discrepancies and a strong rights agenda, citizens might have been less likely to miss political messages and more likely to feel included. In a liberalized market economy, with spectrum plenty and widespread message targeting, the chance of being activated, for some, is slim and the incentives to engage are small; the activities of politicians become a spectacle not aimed at them and not worth viewing.

For the political and media elites their rationale is the most efficient allocation of scarce resources. They have little incentive to target such marginalized groups if it does not represent a good return on their investment. The gap between the engaged majority and a disengaged minority is widened by the strategic activities of media and political advocates. Such divides pose problems for conceptions of media 'burglar alarms' and 'monitorial citizens' (Zaller, 2003). There is little incentive for those who are marginalized to monitor the activities of political elites or heed media warning bells when they ring. The media coverage of conventional politics is hardly going to be monitored by the disinterested. At the same time, the partisan citizen may well only monitor some media alarms, ignoring others. However, citizens, especially the partisan but also the marginalized and the disengaged, may not necessarily be deaf to the appeals of extremist political advocates who seek to address their fears and concerns.

Instead of seeing citizens as homogeneously disadvantaged by marketization, or advantaged by the ability to access political resources or access new communication technology, we need to think about which citizens we are referring to. In the US and the UK there is a growing divide between those citizens who participate, who watch and read, who are regularly targeted and mobilized, who benefit from policy initiatives and generous tax cuts, and those citizens who do not and who are not activated, and who are marginalized from the political process. How the included respond to party messages or media coverage will be different from how the 'marginalized' do so.

This is not so much the traditional critique of media failure (Cappella and Jamieson, 1997), or politician manipulation (Barnett and Gaber, 2001; Johnson, 2001), but one that locates its criticism in wider structural inequalities and divisions. Democracy more than ever requires a healthy political communication system, but political communication systems face a central conundrum. Strategic political communicators are motivated by the aim of achieving particular objectives. The use of particular techniques in pursuit of specific outcomes which are beneficial to the individual actor have unintentional and detrimental impacts on the system as a whole, and there seem to be few incentives for the strategic political communicators to pay any heed to the health of the system.

The growing segmentation and fragmentation of society means a significant minority become marginalized from the political process, and from the rituals and mediated imagery and information that accompanies it. There are no incentives for strategic political communicators to address or activate these citizens. This surely poses serious problems for democracies like the US and the UK and could be considered critical for their future wellbeing.

Resources Appendix

This appendix brings together the main online primary and secondary data sources used in the book for the benefit of students and researchers. This is by no means an exhaustive list of sources, but highlights those websites that provide free access to data and research findings. The list of sources has been organized by theme, and, where appropriate, it indicates the national focus of the data.

Civic and political engagement

Center for the Study of Democracy (US, UK and other countries): <http://www.democ.uci.edu/>
The Electoral Commission (UK): <http://www.electoralcommission. gov.uk/>
Hansard Society (UK): <http://www.hansardsociety.org.uk/>
Power: An Independent Inquiry into Britain's Democracy (UK): <http://www.powerinquiry.org/>
Joseph Rowntree Foundation (UK): <http://www.jrf.org.uk/>
Nestlé Social Research Programme (UK): <http://www.spreckley.co.uk/ nestle/>
Survey2000 Data (US): <http://business.clemson.edu/socio/ s2kdata211.html>
World Values Survey (US, UK and other countries): <http://www. worldvalues-survey.org/>

Civic engagement and the internet

Institute for Politics, Democracy and the Internet (US): <http://www.ipdi.org/>
Hansard Society (UK): <http://www.hansardsociety.org.uk/>
Pew Internet and American Life Project (US): <http://www.pewinternet.org/>
Politics Online (US, UK and other countries): <http://www.politicsonline.com/>

Election campaign finance

Center for Responsive Politics (US): <http://www.opensecrets.org/>
The Electoral Commission (UK): <http://www.electoralcommission. gov.uk/>
Federal Election Commission (US): <http://www.fec.gov/>
Heyden Phillips Review of Party Funding (UK): <http://haydenphillipsreview. org.uk/>
Political Money Line (US): <http://www.fecinfo.com/>

Press and broadcasting

Campaign Media Analysis Group (US): <http://www.tnsmi-cmag. com/>
Center for Media and Democracy (US): <http://www.prwatch.org/>
Euromyths at the European Commission in the UK: <http://ec. europa.eu/unit-edkingdom/press/euromyths/index_en.htm>
Media Matters for America (US): <http://mediamatters.org/>
The Norman Lear Center (US): <http://www.learcenter.org/html/>
Office of Communications (UK): <http://www.ofcom.org.uk/>
Pew Research Center for People and the Press (US): <http://people-press.org/>
Project for Excellence in Journalism (US): <http://www.stateofthemedia.org/>
The Tyndall Report (US): <http://www.tyndallreport.com/>

Public opinion and approval ratings

IPSOS/MORI (UK) : <http://www.mori.com/>
Office for National Statistics (UK): <http://www.statistics.gov.uk/>
Pew Research Center for People and the Press (US): <http://people-press.org/>
Pollingreport.com (US): <http://www.pollingreport.com/>
The Roper Center for Public Opinion Research (US):
    <http://www. ropercenter.uconn.edu/>
UK polling report (UK): <http://www.ukpollingreport.co.uk>
US Official's Job Approval ratings (US): <http://www.unc.edu/~beyle/ jars.html>
United States Census Bureau (US): <http://www.census.gov/>
YouGov (UK): <http://www.yougov.com/>

Voting and voter turnout

American National Election Studies: Guide to Public Opinion and Electoral Behaviour (US): <http://www.umich.edu/~nes/nesguide/ gd-index.htm#6>
British Election Study (UK): <http://www.essex.ac.uk/bes/>
Election Assistance Commission (US): <http://www.eac.gov/>
Electoral Commission (UK): <http://www.electoralcommission. gov.uk/>
International Institute for Democracy and Electoral Assistance (US, UK and other countries): <http://www.idea.int/>
Lijphart Elections Archive (US, UK and other countries): <http://dodgson. ucsd.edu/lij/>
National Annenberg Election Survey (US): <http://www.annenbergpublicpolicy-center.org/naes/>
National Research Commission on Elections and Voting (US): <http://www.elec-tions.ssr.org/>
Pew Research Center for People and the Press (US): <http://people-press.org/>
The Vanishing Voter Project (US): <http://www.vanishingvoter.org/>
United States Census Bureau (US): <http://www.census.gov/>
United States Elections Project (US): <http://elections.gmu.edu/voter_ turnout.htm>

Notes

Preface and Acknowledgements

1 The project used data from: the British Election Study; the Electoral Commission; the Federal Election Commission; Media Matters Action Network; National Annenberg Election Study; the American National Election Studies; the Norman Lear Center; Ofcom; the Project for Excellence in Journalism; Pew Research Center for the People and the Press; Pew Internet and American Life Project; Political Money Line; the Tyndall Report. It should be noted that none of these bodies bears responsibility for any conclusions based on the data they provided.

Introduction

1 The era of spectrum scarcity refers to the period before the arrival of cable, satellite, digital terrestrial television and the internet, when there was limited frequency space over which radio and television could broadcast (for more information, see Crisell, 1997; Curran and Seaton, 2003).

Chapter 1   Data-Driven Electioneering and the Costs of Exclusive Campaign Communication

1 The Conservative party has witnessed the most dramatic fall in membership. In 1953 it had 2.8 million members; by 1964 membership stood at 2,150,000; by 1992 it was half a million. And it has continued to decline, falling below 400,000 in 1997; in 2004 it stood at 320,000 (Norris, 1997; Webb, 2000; Wintour and Hall, 2004). Membership of the other two main political parties has also fallen. Labour's 1952 membership level stood at 1,015,000; by 1964 it was 830,116, and it subsequently plummeted, reaching 279,530 in 1992 (Norris, 1997; Webb, 2000). Although there was a rise of membership in the three years leading up to the 1997 election, peaking at around 401,000, it has since continued to fall back, reaching 190,000 in 2004 (Seyd and Whitely, 2002; Wintour and Hall, 2004). The Liberal Democrats' membership levels over the same period fell from 278,690 to 100,000 in 1997, to around 80,000 in 2006 (Webb, 2000).

2 This term includes: political action committees (PACs), 501(c)s and 527s. PACs are groups that raise and spend money expressly to support a candidate, 527s and 501(c)s cannot fundraise under the law: 501(c)s are charitable social welfare organizations – named after the section of the US tax code which created them – that are not supposed to engage in political activity but can be involved in welfare-type activities such as voter registration; 527s are 'independent'

campaigning groups – named after the section of the US tax code which created them – and cannot expressly support or oppose a particular candidate (see Center for Responsive Politics for more details).

3 In 1987, the Conservatives spent £6,357,000, equivalent to 70 per cent of their budget on advertising; Labour spent £2,175,000, equivalent to 53 per cent of their budget. In 1997, the Conservatives spent £13,183,000, equivalent to 47 per cent of their budget; Labour spent £7,386,000, equivalent to 27 per cent of their budget (Butler and Kavanagh, 1997; Scammell, 1995).

4 While all donations to political parties have to be declared, loans, until recently, did not, and therefore have escaped public scrutiny. Revelations in 2006 that millions of pounds worth of loans were converted into donations after they had been spent during the 2005 election led to a public outcry and the closing of this loophole.

5 'Soft money' is money raised and spent by candidates on unregulated elements of campaigning like administrative costs, which finds its way back into campaigns (Gierzynski, 2000: 45).

6 Bush spent 17 per cent of his budget on Florida, 10 per cent in Ohio, 14 per cent in Pennsylvania, 9 per cent in Michigan and 14 per cent in California. Gore and the Democrats spent 20 per cent of their budget in Pennsylvania, 13 per cent in Ohio, 13 per cent in Michigan, 12 per cent in Florida and 7 per cent in Wisconsin (Campaign Media Analysis Group Report, 2001).

Chapter 2   Governing and the Push for Effective Promotion

1 For a more detailed discussion of the emergence of promotional culture in late modern societies, see Wernick, 1991.

2 Information subsidies in this context are background materials, press releases, press conferences etc., deployed by news sources to make the news-gathering process easier for journalists. This differs slightly from Gandy's original definition: see Gandy, 1982.

Chapter 4   The News Media, Their Audiences and Changing Organizational Roles

1 'The five Ws' – who, what, when, where and why – is a popular maxim in American and British journalism. It signifies what a journalist needs to establish when reporting an event.

2 First-order elections are elections for a national parliament or high office such as the presidency. They are contests that are considered of particular importance for a nation. Second-order elections, as the name implies, are elections that are considered of less importance, such as for state legislatures, regional or local parliaments and other offices.

Chapter 5   The Media and the Populist Political Impulse

1 As an aside, it should be noted, the largest-selling women's weekly magazine in Britain, *Take a Break*, has launched a political party, the Mum's Army, consisting of volunteer readers. In 2006, *Mum's Army* fielded 54 candidates in the local government elections across England and Wales, standing on a ticket of cracking down on anti-social behaviour.

Chapter 6   Turning On, Tuning Out?

1 The survey used the following definitions of social class:
   - Group A are described as 'professionals such as doctors . . . ; chartered people like architects; fully qualified people with a large degree of responsibility; senior civil servants, senior business executives and managers, and high ranking grades of the service';
   - Group B as 'people with very responsible jobs such as university lecturers, hospital matrons, heads of local government departments, middle management in business, qualified scientist, bank managers, police inspectors, and upper grades of the services';
   - Group C1 as 'all others doing non-manual jobs; nurses, technicians, pharmacists, salesmen, publicans, people in clerical positions, police sergeants/constables and middle ranks of the Services';
   - Group C2 as 'skilled manual workers/craftsmen who have served apprenticeships; foremen, manual workers with special qualifications such as long distance lorry drivers, security officers, and lower grade of Services';
   - Group D as 'semi-skilled and unskilled manual workers, including labourers and mates of occupations in the C2 grade and people serving apprenticeships; machine minders, farm labourers, bus and railway conductors, laboratory assistants, postmen, door-to-door and van salesmen';
   - Group E as 'those on lowest levels of subsistence, including some pensioners, casual workers and others with minimum levels of income'.

   Such classifications are of course not without their criticisms (see Moores, 1993: 125, for instance).
2 The data on communicative engagement in this chapter refer to watching television and going online. It should be noted that there were no databases containing all the necessary information, and evidence had to be gleaned from a variety of sources in both countries.
3 Defined as 'coverage of international affairs, political events in Washington, local government, and business and finance' (Pew Research Center, 2004b).

Chapter 7   The Rise of Self-Expressive Politics

1 Research by Pattie et al. (2003b) reveals three distinct types of activism – individualistic, contact and collective. Individualistic activism refers to relatively individual acts such as boycotting a product, making a donation, signing a petition, raising funds. Contact activism refers to the contacting of the media and those in authority. Collective activism refers to participation in group activity, such as demonstrations, or attending political meetings. Collective activism tends to be high-cost in terms of time and effort required, while the cost of individual and contact activism is less (p. 448). In borrowing these concepts I have included contact activism as an individualistic form of attitude-expression. There are of course further attempts to differentiate types of participation. Bucy and Gregson (2001), for instance, distinguish between media and non-media participation; for a discussion of attempts to differentiate types of participation, see Scheufele and Eveland, 2001.
2 Mcleod et al. (1999) distinguish between traditional and non-traditional forms of participation: 'Traditional forms were defined as institutionalised activities such as voting and donating money. Non-traditional participation was defined as participation in public deliberative forums' (cited in Scheufele and Eveland, 2001: 27). The distinction in this chapter is broader, namely between traditional

modes of expression that existed prior to the emergence of new social movements in the 1960s and non-traditional modes of expression which have emerged since. A note of caution should be sounded. Some forms of expression thought of as quintessentially non-traditional, like the consumer boycott, are, as Friedman reminds us in his study of consumer boycotts, something that started life in the nineteenth century as a response to labour issues and consumer price rises; today, they are a used in response to a much broader series of issues (1999: 216–17).

References

Abrahamson, J. B., Arterton, F. C. and Orren, G. R. 1990: *The Electronic Commonwealth: The Impact of New Media Technologies on Democratic Politics*. New York: Basic Books.

Addley, E. 2003: It's Just a lot of Suits and Faceless Men. *Guardian*, 25 November. <http://www.mediaguardian.co.uk> (accessed 11.12.04).

Aldridge, J. and Cole, S. 2001: Jon Snow Slams ITV's Crazy Cut in News Budget. *Observer*, 2 December. <http://www.mediaguardian.co.uk> (accessed 3.2.05).

Aldridge, M. 2003: The Ties that Divide: Regional Press Campaigns, Community and Populism. *Media, Culture and Society*, 25 (4): 491–509.

American National Election Studies, Center for Political Studies, University of Michigan. *The NES Guide to Public Opinion and Electoral Behavior*. Ann Arbor, MI: University of Michigan. <http://www.umich.edu/~nes/nesguide/nesguide. htm>.

Andersen, R. 2000: The Commercial Politics of the 1996 US Presidential Campaign. In Andersen, R. and Strate, L. (eds.), *Critical Studies in Media Commercialism*. New York: Oxford University Press.

Ansolabehere, S. D. and Iyengar, S. 1995: *Going Negative: How Political Advertisements Shrink and Polarise the Electorate*. New York: Free Press.

Attaway-Fink, B. 2004: Market-Driven Journalism: Creating Special Sections to Meet Reader Interests. *Journal of Communication Management*, 9 (2): 145–54.

Bara, J. and Budge, I. 2001: Party Policy and Ideology: Still New Labour? In Norris, P. (ed.), *Britain Votes 2001*. Oxford: Oxford University Press.

Barker, D. C. 1998: Rush to Action: Political Talk Radio and Health Care (un)Reform. *Political Communication*, 15 (1): 83–97.

Barnett, S. and Gaber, I. 2001: *Westminster Tales: The Twenty-First Century Crisis in Political Journalism*. London: Continuum.

Bartels, L. M. 2006: Is the Water Rising? Reflections on Inequality and American Democracy. *PS: Political Science and Politics* (January): 39–42.

Bartle, J. and Griffiths, D. 2002: Social-Psychological, Economic and Marketing Models of Voting Behaviour Compared. In O'Shaughnessy, N. J. and Henneberg S. C. (eds.), *The Idea of Political Marketing*. Westport, CT: Praeger.

BBC programme archive. <http://open.bbc.co.uk/catalogue/infax/>.

Beam, R. A. 2001: Does It Pay to be a Market Oriented Newspaper? *Journalism and Mass Communication Quarterly*, 78 (3): 466–84.

Beck, U. 1997: *The Reinvention of Politics: Rethinking Modernity in the Global Social Order*. Cambridge, UK: Polity.

Beck, U. 2002: Interview with Ulrich Beck. In Beck, U. and Beck-Gernsheim, E. *Individualization: Institutionalised Individualism and Its Social and Political Consequences*. London: Sage.

Beck, U. 2003: Interview with Ulrich Beck. In Beck, U. and Willms, J. *Conversations with Ulrich Beck*. Cambridge, UK: Polity.

Beck, U. and Beck-Gernsheim, E. 2002: *Individualization: Institutionalised Individualism and Its Social and Political Consequences*. London: Sage.

Bennett, S. E. 1998: Young Americans' Indifference to Media Coverage of Public Affairs. *PS: Political Science and Politics* (September). <http://www.apsanet.org/PS/sept98/bennett.cfm> (accessed 12.9.03).

Bennett, W. L. 1998: The Uncivic Culture: Communication, Identity, and the Rise of Lifestyle Politics. *PS: Political Science and Politics* (December). <http://www.apsanet.org/PS/dec98/lbennett.cfm> (accessed 27.03.02).

Bennett, W. L. 2001: Mediated Politics: An Introduction. In Bennett, W. L. and Entman, R. M. (eds.), *Mediated Politics: Communication in the Future of Democracy*. Cambridge, UK: Cambridge University Press.

Bennett, W. L. 2003a: Lifestyle Politics and Citizen-Consumers: Identity, Communication and Political Action in Late Modern Societies. In Corner, J. and Pels, D. (eds.), *Media and the Restyling of Politics*. London and Thousand Oaks, CA: Sage.

Bennett, W. L. 2003b: Communicating Global Activism. *Information, Communication and Society*, 6 (2): 143–68.

Bennett, W. L. and Entman, R. M. 2001: (eds.), *Mediated Politics: Communication in the Future of Democracy*. Cambridge, UK: Cambridge University Press.

Bennett, W. L. and Manheim, J. B. 2001: The Big Spin: Strategic Communication and the Transformation of Pluralist Democracy. In Bennett, W. L. and Entman, R. M. (eds.), *Mediated Politics: Communication in the Future of Democracy*. Cambridge, UK: Cambridge University Press.

Betz, H. G. 1998: Introduction. In Betz, H. G. and Immerfall, S. (ed.), *The New Politics of the Right*. Basingstoke: Macmillan.

Bimber, B. 1999: The Internet and Citizen Communication with Government: Does the Medium Matter? *Political Communication*, 16 (3): 409–28.

Blumler, J. G. 1990: Elections, the Media and the Modern Publicity Process. In Ferguson, M. (ed.), *Public Communication: The New Imperatives*. London: Sage.

Blumler, J. G. 1997: Origins of the Crisis of Communication for Citizenship. *Political Communication*, 14 (3): 395–404.

Blumler, J. G. 1999: Political Communication Systems: All Change. *European Journal of Communication*, 14 (2): 241–9.

Blumler, J. G. and Gurevitch, M. 1995: *The Crisis of Public Communication*. London: Routledge.

Blumler, J. G. and Gurevitch, M. 2000: Rethinking the Study of Political Communication. In Curran, J. and Gurevitch, M. (eds.), *Mass Media and Society*, 3rd edn. London: Arnold.

Blumler, J. G. and Gurevitch, M. 2001: Americanization Reconsidered: UK–US Campaign Communications Across Time. In Bennett, W. L. and Entman, R. M. (eds.), *Mediated Politics: Communication in the Future of Democracy*. Cambridge, UK: Cambridge University Press.

Blumler, J. G. and Kavanagh, D. 1999: The Third Age of Political Communication: Influences and Features. *Political Communication* 16 (3): 209–30.

Blumler, J. G., McLeod, J. M. and Rosengren, K. E. 1992: An Introduction to Comparative Communication Research. In Blumler, J. G., McLeod, J. M. and Rosengren, K. E. (eds.), *Comparatively Speaking: Communication and Culture Across Space and Time*. London and Newbury Park, CA: Sage.

Boggs, C. 2000: *The End of Politics: Corporate Power and the Decline of the Public Sphere*. New York: The Guilford Press.

Bolce, L., De Maio, G. and Muzzio, D. 1996: Dial-In Democracy: Talk Radio and the 1994 Election. *Political Science Quarterly* 111 (3): 457–81.

Bowman, K. (2000) Polling to Campaign and to Govern. In Ornstein, N. and Mann, T. (eds.), *The Permanent Campaign and its Future*. Washington, DC: American Enterprise Institute.

Boyd-Barrett, O. 2005: Journalism, Media Conglomerates and the Federal Communications Commission. In Allan, S. (ed.), *Journalism: Critical Issues*. Buckingham: Open University Press.

Brandoleni, A. and Smeeding, T. M. 2006: Patterns of Economic Inequality in Western Democracies: Some Facts on Levels and Trends. *PS: Political Science and Politics*, (January): 21–6

Brants, K. 1998: Who's Afraid of Infotainment. *European Journal of Communication*, 13 (3): 315–35.

Brants, K. and van Kempen, H. 2002: The Ambivalent Watchdog: The Changing Culture of Political Journalism and its Effects. In Kuhn, R. and Neveu, E. (eds.), *Political Journalism: New Challenges, New Practices*. London: Routledge.

Bromley, C. and Curtice, J. 2002: Where Have All the Voters Gone? In Park, A., Curtice, J., Thomson, K., Jarvis, L. and Bromley, C. (eds.), *British Social Attitudes: The 19th Report*. London: Sage.

Bromley, C., Curtice, J. and Seyd, B. 2001: Political Engagement, Trust and Constitutional Reform. In Park, A., Curtice, J., Thomson, K., Jarvis, L. and Bromley, C. (eds.), *British Social Attitudes: The 18th Report*. London: Sage.

Bromley, M. 1998: The Tabloiding of Britain: Quality Newspapers in the 1990s. In Bromley, M. and Stephenson, H. (eds.), *Sex Lies and Democracy: The Press and the Public*. Harlow: Longman.

Brookings Institution, 1997: *The Hess Report on Campaign Coverage in Nightly Network News*. <http://www.brook.edu/dybdocroot/ge/projects/hessreport/hd_quantity.htm> (accessed 4.2.03).

Brooks, L. 2003: Kid Power. *Guardian Magazine*, 26 April. <http://www.guardian.co.uk/> (accessed 5.08.04).

Brown, M. 2006: Breaking News: Sky Blunders. *Media Guardian*, 12 June, p. 6.

Bryson, A and Gomez, R. 2002: Marching on Together? Recent Trends in Union Membership. In Park, A., Curtice, J., Thomson, K., Jarvis, L. and Bromley, C. (eds.), *British Social Attitudes: The 19th Report*. London: Sage.

Buckingham, D. 2000: *The Making of Citizens: Young People, News and Citizenship*. London: Routledge.

Bucy, E. P. and Gregson, K. S. 2001: Media Participation: A Legitimizing Mechanism of Mass Democracy. *New Media and Society*, 3 (3): 357–80.

Budge, I. and Farlie, D. J. 1983: *Explaining and Predicting Elections*. London: Allen and Unwin.

Burkeman, O. 2002: There Goes the News. *Media Guardian*, 11 March, p. 4.

Butler, D. and Kavanagh, D. 1997: *The British General Election of 1997*. Basingstoke: Macmillan.

Butler, D. and Kavanagh, D. 2001: *The British General Election of 2001*. Basingstoke: Palgrave Macmillan.

Butler, D. and Westlake, M. 2000: *British Politics and European Elections 1999*. Basingstoke: Palgrave Macmillan.

Calabrese, A. 2000: Political Space and the Trade in Television News. In Sparks, C. and Tulloch, J. (eds.), *Tabloid Tales: Global Debates Over Media Standards*. Lanham, MD: Rowman and Littlefield.

Campaign Media Analysis Group Report, 2001: *$188 million spent on 261,000 Ads in Pursuit of the Presidency*. <http://www.cmagreports.com> (accessed 4.02.03).

Campaign Media Analysis Group Report, 2004: *Findings Memo: Election '04 Edition: Issues in Political Advertising*. <http://www.cmagreports.com> (accessed 4.12.04).

Campaign Media Analysis Group Report, 2005: *Election Year Ends; Issue Advertising Begins*. <http://www.cmagreports.com> (accessed 14.06.06).

Campbell, D. 2004: Florida Caught in Political Crosswinds Again. *Guardian*, 14 August, p. 12.

Cappella, J. N. and Jamieson, Hall K. 1997: *Spiral of Cynicism: The Press and the Public Good*, 2nd edn. Oxford: Oxford University Press.

Cappella, J. N., Turow, J. and Jamieson, Hall K. 1996: *Call-In Talk Radio: Background, Content, Audiences' Portrayal in Mainstream Media*. Annenberg Public Policy Center, University of Pennsylvania.

Carper, A. 1997: Marketing News. In Norris, P. (ed.), *Politics and the Press: The News Media and Their Influences*. Boulder, CO: Lynne Rienner.

Castells, M. 2000: *The Information Age: Economy, Society and Culture. Vol. 3. The End of the Millennium*, 2nd edn. Oxford: Blackwell Publishing.

Castells, M. 2004: *The Information Age: Economy, Society and Culture. Vol. 2. The Power of Identity*, 2nd edn. Oxford: Blackwell Publishing.

Center for Responsive Politics. Available at <http://www.opensecrets.org/>.

Chadwick, A. 2006: *Internet Politics: States, Citizens and New Communication Technology*. New York: Oxford University Press.

Charter, D. and Simon, M. 2006: The Most Important Man in Washington You've Never Heard Of. *Times Magazine*, 25 February: 25–9.

Clarke, T. N. 2002: The Presidency and the New Political Culture. *American Behavioral Scientist*, 46 (4): 535–52.

Clawson, D., Neustadt, A. and Weller M. 1998: *Dollars and Votes: How Business Campaign Contributions Subvert Democracy*. Philadelphia: Temple University Press.

Cloud, J. 2004: How the Wedge Issues Cut. *Time Magazine*, 25 October: 28–31.

Cockerell, M. 1988: *Live From Number Ten*. London: Faber and Faber.

Cohen, S. 1973: *Folk Devils and Moral Panics*. St Albans: Paladin.

Cole, P. 2001: Going Bananas Over Fate of the Metric Martyr. *Guardian*, 14 April.

Coleman, S. 2001: *2001: Cyber Space Odyssey, the Internet in the UK Election*. The Hansard Society. <http://www.hansard-society.org.uk/cyberodyssey.htm.> (accessed 10.10.01).

Coleman, S. 2002a: The People's Voice? In Bartle, J., Atkinson, S. and Mortimore, R. (eds.), *Political Communications: The General Election Campaign of 2001*. London: Frank Cass.

Coleman, S. 2002b: Election Call 2001: How Politicians and the Public Interacted. *Parliamentary Affairs*, 55 (4): 731–42.

Coleman, S. 2004: Blogs as Listening Posts Rather than Soapboxes. Afterword in

Ferguson, R. and Howell, M. 2004: *Political Blogs: Craze or Convention?* London: Hansard Society. <http://www.hansardsociety.org.uk> (accessed 7.9.04).

Conboy, M. 2002: *The Press and Popular Culture*. London: Sage

Conboy, M. 2006: *Tabloid Britain: Constructing a Community Through Language*. London: Routledge.

Conlan, T. 2005: ITV News Channel Axed. *Media Guardian*, 14 December. <http://media.guardian.co.uk> (accessed 15.12.05).

Cook, C. 2002: The Contemporary Presidency: The Permanence of the Permanent Campaign: George W Bush's Public Presidency. *Presidential Studies Quarterly*, 32 (4): 753–65.

Cook, T. E. 1998: *Governing With the News: The News Media as a Political Institution*. Chicago, IL: University of Chicago Press.

Corner, J. 2003: Mediated Persona and Political Culture. In Corner, J. and Pels, D. (eds.), *Media and the Restyling of Politics*. London: Sage.

Cornfield, M., Carson, J., Kalis, A. and Simon, E. 2005: *Buzz, Blogs and Beyond: The Internet and the National Discourse in the Fall of 2004*. <http://www.pewinternet.org/ppt/buzz_blogs__beyond_Final05-16-05.pdf> (accessed 05.06.05).

Corrigan, M. 2000: The Transformation of Going Public: President Clinton, the First Lady, and Health Care Reform. *Political Communication*, 17 (2): 149–68.

Cozens, C. 2004: Government Ad Spend Rockets. *Media Guardian*, 26 February. <http://media.guardian.co.uk> (accessed 15. 8. 04).

Crewe, I. and Thomson, K. 1999: Party Loyalties: Dealignment or Realignment? In Evans, G. and Norris, P. (eds.), *Critical Elections: British Parties and Voters in Long-Term Perspective*. London and Thousand Oaks, CA: Sage.

Crigler, A. N. and Jensen, K. Bruhn. 1991: Discourses on Politics: Talking about Public Issues in the United States and Denmark. In Dahlgren, P. and Sparks, C. (eds.), *Communication and Citizenship*. London: Routledge.

Crisell, A. 1997: *An Introductory History of British Broadcasting*. London: Routledge.

Critcher, C. 2005: Mighty Dread: Journalism and Moral Panics. In Allan, S. (ed.), *Journalism: Critical Issues*. Buckingham: Open University Press.

Cross, S. 2005: Paedophiles in the Community: Inter-agency Conflict, News Leaks and the Local Press. *Crime, Media, Culture*, 1 (3): 284–300.

Crouse, T. 1972: *The Boys on the Bus: Riding with the Campaign Press Corps*. New York: Random House.

Curran, J. 2000: Rethinking the Media and Democracy. In Curran, J. and Gurevitch, M. (eds.), *Mass Media and Society*, 3rd edn. London: Arnold.

Curran, J. and Seaton, J. (2003) *Power Without Responsibility*, 6th edn. London: Routledge.

Curtice, J. 2005: Turnout: Electors Stay Home – Again. In Norris, P. and Wlezien, C. (eds.), *Britain Votes 2005*. Oxford: Oxford University Press.

Curtice, J. and Seyd, B. 2003: Is There a Crisis of Political Participation? In Park, A., Curtice, J., Thomson, K., Jarvis, L. and Bromley, C. (eds.). *British Social Attitudes: The 20th Report*. London: Sage.

Curtice, J. and Steed, M. 2002: An Analysis of the Results. In Butler, D. and Kavanagh, D. (eds.), *The British General Election of 2001*. Basingstoke: Palgrave.

Dahlgren, P. 1991: Introduction. In Dahlgren, P. and Sparks, C. (eds.), *Communication and Citizenship: Journalism and the Public Sphere*. London: Routledge.

Dahlgren, P. 2004: Theory, Boundaries and Political Communication: The Uses of Disparity. *European Journal of Communication*, 19 (1): 7–18.

Dahlgren, P. and Gurevitch, M. 2005: Political Communication in a Changing

World. In Curran, J. and Gurevitch, M. (eds.), *Mass Media and Society*, 4th edn. London: Hodder Arnold.

Dalton, R. J. 1999: Political Support in Advanced Industrial Democracies. In Norris, P. (ed.), *Critical Citizens: Global Support for Democratic Governance*. Oxford: Oxford University Press.

Dalton, R. J. 2000: The Decline of Party Identifications. In Dalton, R. J. and Wattenberg, M. P. (eds.), *Parties Without Partisans: Political Change in Advanced Industrial Democracies*. Oxford: Oxford University Press.

Dalton, R. J. 2002: Political Cleavages, Issues, and Electoral Change. In LeDuc, L., Niemi, R. G., and Norris, P. (eds.), *Comparing Democracies 2: New Challenges in the Study of Elections and Voting*. London and Thousand Oaks, CA: Sage.

Dalton, R. J. and Wattenberg, M. P. 2000: Unthinkable Democracy. In Dalton, R. J. and Wattenberg, M. P. (eds.), *Parties Without Partisans: Political Change in Advanced Industrial Democracies*. Oxford: Oxford University Press.

Dalton, R. J., McAllister, I. and Wattenberg, M. P. 2000: The Consequences of Partisan Dealignment. In Dalton, R. J. and Wattenberg, M. P. (eds.), *Parties Without Partisans: Political Change in Advanced Industrial Democracies*. Oxford: Oxford University Press.

Dalton, R. J., Scarrow, S. E. and Cain, B. E. 2003: Democracy Transformed? Expanding Political Opportunities in Advanced Industrial Democracies. Paper 0304, Center for the Study of Democracy eScholarship Repository, University of California. <http://repositories.cdlib/cds/03–04> (accessed 03.04.05).

Davies, P. J. 1999: *US Elections Today*. Manchester: Manchester University Press.

Davis, A. 2002: *Public Relations Democracy: Public Relations, Politics and the Mass Media in Britain*. Manchester: Manchester University Press.

Davis, R. 1997: Understanding Broadcast Political Talk. *Political Communication*, 14 (4): 323–32.

Davis, R. 2005: *Politics Online: Blogs, Chat Rooms and Discussion Groups in American Democracy*. London: Routledge.

Davis, R. and Curtice, J. 2000: Speaking for the Public: Representation and Audience Participation During the 1997 British General Election Campaign. *Harvard International Journal of Press/Politics*, 5 (1): 62–77.

Davis, R. and Owen, D. 1998: *New Media and American Politics*. Oxford: Oxford University Press.

Davis, S. 2005: Presidential Campaigns Fine Tune Online Strategies. *Journalism Studies*, 6 (2): 241–4.

Deacon, D. 2004: Politicians, Privacy and Media Intrusion in Britain. *Parliamentary Affairs*, 57 (1): 9–23.

Deacon, D. and Wring, D. 2002: Partisan De-alignment and the British Press. In Bartle, J., Atkinson, S. and Mortimore, R. (eds.), *Political Communications: The General Election Campaign of 2001*. London: Frank Cass.

Deacon, D., Golding, P. and Billig, M. 2001: Press and Broadcasting: 'Real Issues' and Real Coverage. In Norris, P. (ed.), *Britain Votes 2001*. Oxford: Oxford University Press.

Deacon, D., Wring, D., Billig, M., Downey, J., Golding, P. and Davidson, S. 2005: *Reporting the 2005 UK General Election*. Unpublished report. Communication Research Centre, Loughborough University.

Dean, J. 1999: Making (It) Public. *Constellations*, 6 (2): 157–66.

Deans, J. 2001: ITN Staff Air Grave Concerns Over Quality. *Media Guardian*, 4 December. <http://www.mediaguardian.co.uk> (accessed 3.10.03).

Deans, J. 2002: ABC Current Affairs Show Hangs in the Balance. *Media Guardian*, 13 March. <http://www.mediaguardian.co.uk> (accessed 4.5.03).

Deans, J. 2004: The Threat to TV's Old Guard. *Media Guardian*, 5 January. <http://www.mediaguardian.co.uk> (accessed 25.6.04).

Deans, J. 2006: ITN Offers Mobile TV News Channel. *Media Guardian*, 13 April. <http://www.mediaguardian.co.uk> (accessed 13.4.06).

Delli Carpini, M. X. 2000: Gen.com: Youth, Civic Engagement and the New Information Environment. *Political Communication*, 17 (3): 341–9.

Delli Carpini, M. X. and Williams, B. A. 2001: Let Us Infotain You: Politics in the New Media Environment. In Bennett, W. L. and Entman, R. M. (eds.), *Mediated Politics: Communication in the Future of Democracy*. Cambridge, UK: Cambridge University Press.

Denton, R. E. and Woodward, G. C. 1998: *Political Communication in America*, 3rd edn. Westport, CT: Praeger.

Denver, D., Hands, G. and MacAllister, I. 2004: The Electoral Impact of Constituency Campaigning in Britain, 1992–2001. *Political Studies*, 52 (2): 289–306.

Denver, D., Hands, G., Fisher, J. and MacAllister, I. 2002: Constituency Campaigning in 2001: The Effectiveness of Targeting. In Bartle, J., Atkinson, S. and Mortimore, R. (eds.), *Political Communications: The General Election Campaign of 2001*. London: Frank Cass.

Diamond, E. and Silverman, R. A. 1997 [1995]: *White House to Your House: Media and Politics in Virtual America*. Cambridge, MA: MIT Press.

Dionne, E. J. 1992: *Why Americans Hate Politics*. New York: Touchstone.

Diplock, S. 2001: *None of the Above: Non-voters and the 2001 Election*. London: The Hansard Society.

Domke, D. 2004: *God Willing? Political Fundamentalism in the White House, the War on Terror and the Echoing Press*. Ann Arbor, MI: Pluto Press.

Doppelt, J. C., and Shearer, E. 1999: *Nonvoters*. London and Thousand Oaks, CA: Sage.

Dougal, J. 2003: Living with Press Eurotrash. *British Journalism Review*, 14 (2): 29–34.

Drezner, D. W. and Farrell, H. 2004: The Power and Politics of Blogs. Paper presented to the APSA annual conference, September. <http://www.utsc.utoronto.ca/~farrell/blogpaperfinal.pdf> (accessed 14.10.04).

Dudley, D. 2005: The Nays Have It. *New Media Age*, 24 June: 22–3.

Duffy, J. 2000: You've Got Mail, Minister. *BBC News Online*, 7 March. <http://www.news.bbc.co.uk> (accessed 25.4.01).

Dunleavy, P., Margetts, H., Bastow, S. and Tinkler, J. 2003: E-Government and Policy Innovation in Several Liberal Democracies. Paper presented to the Political Studies Association Annual Conference, University of Leicester, 11–13 April.

Electoral Commission, 2002: *Election 2001: Campaign Spending*. <http://www.electoralcommission.gov.uk> (accessed 22.02.06).

Electoral Commission, 2003: *Attitudes Towards Voting and the Political Process*. <http://www.electoralcommission.gov.uk> (accessed 3.08.04).

Electoral Commission, 2004a: *The June 2004 Elections – The Public's Perspective* <http://www.electoralcommission.gov.uk> (accessed 3.10.04).

Electoral Commission, 2004b: *Political Engagement Among Young People: An Update*. <http://www.electoralcommission.gov.uk> (accessed 3.08.04).

Electoral Commission, 2004c: *An Audit of Political Engagement*. <http://www.electoralcommission.gov.uk> (accessed 3.06.04).

Electoral Commission, 2005a: *Understanding Electoral Registration: The Extent and*

Nature of Non-registration in Britain. <http://www.electoralcommission.gov.uk> (accessed 20.09.05).

Electoral Commission, 2005b: *Social Exclusion and Political Engagement.* <http://www.electoralcommission.gov.uk> (accessed 2.03.06).

Electoral Commission, 2005c: *The 2004 European Parliamentary Elections in the United Kingdom: Campaign Expenditure.* <http://www.electoralcommission.gov.uk> (accessed 2.03.06).

Electoral Commission, 2005d: *An Audit of Political Engagement 2.* <http://www.electoralcommission.gov.uk> (accessed 2.03.05).

Electoral Commission, 2005e: *Election 2005: Turnout: The Reasons.* <http://www.electoralcommission.gov.uk> (accessed 13.02.06).

Electoral Commission, 2006a: *Election 2005: Engaging the Public in Great Britain.* <http://www.electoralcommission.gov.uk> (accessed 3.03.06).

Electoral Commission, 2006b: *Election 2005: Campaign Spending.* <http://www.electoralcommission.gov.uk> (accessed 3.05.06).

Eliasoph, N. 1998: *Avoiding Politics: How Americans Produce Apathy in Everyday Life.* Cambridge, UK: Cambridge University Press.

Entman, R. M. 1989: *Democracy Without Citizens.* Oxford: Oxford University Press.

Esser, F. and Pfetsch, B. 2004: Meeting the Challenges of Global Communication and Political Integration: The Significance of Comparative Research in a Changing World. In Esser, F. and Pfetsch, B. (eds.), *Comparing Political Communication: Theories, Cases and Challenges.* Cambridge, UK: Cambridge University Press.

Esser, F., Reinemann, C. and Fan, D. 2001: Spin Doctors in the United States, Great Britain, and Germany: Metacommunication about Media Manipulation. *Harvard International Journal of Press/Politics*, 6 (1): 16–45.

European Commission in the UK: *Press Euromyths* <http://ec.europa.eu/united-kingdom/press/euromyths/index_en.htm> (accessed 13.3.05).

Evans, J. 2005: Celebrity, Media and History. In Evans, J. and Hesmondhalgh, D. (eds.), *Understanding Media: Inside Celebrity.* Maidenhead: Open University Press.

Federal Election Commission, 2005a: *2004 Presidential Campaign Financial Activity Summarized.* <http://www. fec.gov> (accessed 14.6.05).

Federal Election Commission, 2005b: *Congressional Candidates Spend $1.16 Billion During 2003–2004.* <http://www. fec.gov> (accessed 14.12.05).

Ferguson, R. and Howell, M. 2004: *Political Blogs: Craze or Convention?* London: Hansard Society. <http://www.hansardsociety.org.uk/> (accessed 7.9.04).

Finlayson, A. 2006: For the Sake of Argument: Re-Imagining Political Communication. *Soundings*, 33, July: 34–43.

Firmstone, J. 2003: Britain in the Euro? British Newspaper Editorial Coverage of the Introduction of the Euro. European Political Communication Working Paper Series 5.03, Centre for European Political Communication. <http://ics.leeds.ac.uk/eurpolcom/exhibits/paper5.pdf>.

Fletcher, K. 2006: The Web Trail. *Media Guardian*, 12 June, p. 7.

Foley, M. 2000: *The British Presidency.* Manchester: Manchester University Press.

Franklin, B. 1997: *Newszak and News Media.* London: Arnold.

Franklin, B. 2001: The Hand of History: New Labour News Management and Governance. In Ludlam, S. and Smith M. J. (eds.), *New Labour in Government.* Basingstoke: Macmillan.

Franklin, B. 2003: A Damascene Conversion? New Labour and Media Relations.

In Ludlam, S. and Smith M. J. (eds.), *New Labour in Government: Power, Politics, Policy*. Basingstoke: Palgrave.

Franklin, C. H. 2005: Presidential Approach in Perspective. <http://ploisci.wisc.edu/users/franklin/Content/perspectives.pdf.> (accessed 7.2.06).

Franklin, M. N. 2002: The Dynamics of Electoral Participation. In LeDuc, l., Niemi, R. G. and Norris, P. (eds.), *Comparing Democracies 2: New Challenges in the Study of Elections and Voting*. London and Thousand Oaks, CA: Sage.

Franklin, M, N. 2004: *Voter Turnout and the Dynamics of Electoral Competition in Established Democracies Since 1945*. Cambridge, UK: Cambridge University Press.

Freedman, A, L. 2000: *Political Participation and Ethnic Minorities: Chinese Overseas in Malaysia, Indonesia and United States*. London: Routledge.

Friedman, M. 1999: *Consumer Boycotts: Effecting Change Through the Market Place and the Media*. New York: Routledge.

Fritz, B., Keefer, B. and Hyhan, B. 2004: *All the President's Spin: George W. Bush, the Media and the Truth*. New York: Touchstone.

Gamson, W. A. 1992: *Talking Politics*. Cambridge, UK: Cambridge University Press.

Gandy, O. H. 1982: *Beyond Agenda Setting: Information Subsidies and Public Policy*. Norwood, NJ: Ablex Publishing.

Gandy, O. H. 2001: Dividing Practices: Segmentation and Targeting in the Emerging Public Sphere. In Bennett, W. L. and Entman, R. M. (eds.), *Mediated Politics: Communication in the Future of Democracy*, Cambridge, UK: Cambridge University Press.

Gans, C. 2005: Low Voter Turnout and the Decline of American Civic Participation. In McKinney, M. S., Kaid, L. L., Bystrom, D. G. and Carlin, D. B. (eds.), *Communicating Politics: Engaging the Public in Democratic Life*. New York: Peter Lang.

Gardner, J. and Oswald, A. 2001: Internet Use: The Digital Divide. In Park, A., Curtice, J., Thomson, K., Jarvis, L. and Bromley, C. (eds.), *British Social Attitudes: The 18th Report*. London: Sage.

Gibson, O. 2004: BARB to Offer Viewer Profiles. *Media Guardian*, 3 September. <http://www.mediaguardian.co.uk> (accessed 8.6.06).

Gibson, R. K., Lusoli, W. and Ward, S. 2005: Online Participation in the UK: Testing a 'Contextualised' Model of Internet Effects. *British Journal of Politics and International Relations*, 7 (3): 561–83.

Giddens, A. 1991: *The Consequences of Modernity*. Stanford, CA: Stanford University Press.

Giddens, A. 1999: *Runaway World: How Globalisation is Reshaping Our Lives*. London: Profile Books.

Gierzynski, A. 2000: *Money Rules: Financing Elections in America*. Boulder, CO: Westview Press.

Gitlin, T. 1991: Bites and Blips: Chunk News Savvy Talk and the Bifurcation of American Politics. In Dahlgren, P. and Sparks, C. (eds.), *Communication and Citizenship: Journalism and the Public Sphere*. London: Routledge.

Glassman, R. M. 1997: *The New Middle Class and Democracy in Global Perspective*. New York: St Martin's.

Goddard, P., Scammell, M. and Semetko, H. 1998: Too Much of a Good Thing? Television in the 1997 Election Campaign. In Crewe, I., Gosschalk, B. and Bartle, J. (eds.), *Political Communications: Why Labour Won the General Election of 1997*. London: Frank Cass.

Golding, P. 1990: Political Communication and Citizenship: The Media and

Democracy in an Inegalitarian Social Order. In Ferguson, M. (ed.), *Public Communication: The New Imperatives*. London: Sage.

Golding, P. and Deacon, D. 2001: An Election that Many Watched but Few Enjoyed. *Guardian*, 12 June, p. 5.

Golding, P. and Murdock, G. 2000: Culture, Communications and Political Economy. In Curran, J. and Gurevitch, M. (eds.), *Mass Media and Society*, 3rd edn. London: Arnold.

Gould, P. 1998a: *The Unfinished Revolution*. London: Abacus.

Gould, P. 1998b: Why Labour Won. In Crewe, I., Gosschalk, B. and Bartle, J. (eds.), *Political Communications: Why Labour Won the General Election Campaign of 1997*. London: Frank Cass.

Gould, P. 2002: Labour Party Strategy. In Bartle, J., Atkinson, S. and Mortimore, R. (eds.), *Political Communications: The General Election Campaign of 2001*. London: Frank Cass.

Grant, R. 2005: Digital Politicking Will Put the Snap into the 2005 Election. *Revolution Magazine*, April. <http://revolutionmagazine.com> (accessed 13.04.05).

Gronbeck, B. E. and Wiese, D. R. 2005: The Representation of Presidential Campaigning in 2004. *American Behavorial Scientist*, 49 (4): 520–34.

Grossman, M. B. and Kumar, M. J. 1981: *Portraying the President: The White House and the News Media*. Baltimore, MD: John Hopkins University Press.

Gunter, B. 2003: *News and the Net*. Mahwah, NJ: Lawrence Erlbaum Associates.

Gurak, L. J. and Logie, J. 2003: Internet Protests, from Texts to Web. In McCaughey, M. and Ayers, M. D. (eds.), *Cyberactivism: Online Activism in Theory and Practice*. London: Routledge.

Gurevitch, M. and Blumler, J. G. 1990: Political Communication Systems and Democratic Values. In Litchtenberg, J. (ed.), *Democracy and the Mass Media*. Cambridge, UK: Cambridge University Press.

Hall, S. and Watt, N. 2001: Number Ten Took Clinton Guru's Advice. *Guardian*, 23 January, p. 2.

Hallin, D. C. 1992a: Soundbite News: Television Coverage of Elections, *Journal of Communication*, 42 (2): 5–24.

Hallin, D. C. 1992b: The Passing of High Modernism of American Journalism. *Journal of Communication*, 42 (3): 14–25.

Hallin, D. C. 2000: Commercialism and Professionalism in the American News Media. In Curran, J. and Gurevitch, M. (eds.), *Mass Media and Society*, 3rd edn. London: Arnold.

Hallin, D. C. 2006: The Passing of the 'High Modernism' of American Journalism Revisited. *Political Communication Report*, 16 (1). <http://www.mtsu.edu/~pcr/1601_2005_winter/commentary-hallin.htm> (accessed 6.2.06).

Hallin, D. C. and Mancini, P. 2004: Americanization, Globalization and Secularization: Understanding the Convergence of Media Systems and Political Communication. In Esser, F. and Pfetsch, B. (eds.), *Comparing Political Communication: Theories, Cases and Challenges*. Cambridge, UK: Cambridge University Press.

Han, L. Cox. 2001: *Governing From Center Stage: White House Communication Strategies During the Television Age of Politics*. Cresskill, NJ: Hampton Press.

Hargreaves, I. and Thomas, J. 2002: *New News, Old News*, London: ITC and BSC Research Publication.

Harris, J. 2006: The Vision Thing. *Media Guardian*, 11 October. <http://www.mediaguardian.co.uk> (accessed 11.10.06).

Harrison, J. 2000: *Terrestrial TV News in Britain: The Culture of Production.* Manchester: Manchester University Press.

Hart, R. P. 2001: Citizen Discourse and Political Participation: A Survey. In Bennett, W. Lance and Entman, R. M. (eds.), *Mediated Politics: Communication in the Future of Democracy.* Cambridge, UK: Cambridge University Press.

Hay, C. 2002: *Political Analysis.* Basingstoke: Palgrave.

Hayden, J. 2002: *Covering Clinton: The President and the Press in the 1990s.* Westport, CT: Praeger.

Heclo, H. 1996: Growing Income Inequalities in America? A Review Essay. *Political Science Quarterly*, 111 (3): 523–7.

Heffernan, R. 2004: Managing the News Agenda: How the Media Can Empower the British Prime Minister. Paper presented to the ECPR Joint Sessions, April, University of Uppsala.

Heffernan, R. and Stanyer, J. 1998: The British Prime Minister and the Labour Government: Political Communications Strategies and the Formation of the News Media Agenda. Paper presented at the ECPR Joint Sessions, April, University of Warwick.

Heith, D. J. 2004: *Polling to Govern: Public Opinion and Presidential Leadership.* Palo Alto, CA: Stanford University Press.

Helmore, E. 2000: News Going Nowhere? *Observer Business*, 20 August, p. 7.

Hencke, D. 2006: Government Creates Post to Stem Flow from Whitehall. *Guardian*, 21 March, p. 4.

Henn, M., Weinstein, M. and Wring, D. 2002: A Generation Apart? Youth and Political Participation in Britain. *The British Journal of Politics and International Relations*, 4 (2): 167–92.

Henning, J. 2004: *The Blogging Iceberg: Of 4.12 Million Hosted Web Logs, Most Little Seen and Quickly Abandoned.* Perseus Development Corp. <http://www. perseus.com/ blogsuvey/the blogginginceberg.html> (accessed 21.3.05).

Herbst, S. 1996: Public Expressions Outside the Mainstream. *Annals of the American Academy of Political and Social Science*, 546 (July): 120–51.

Herrnson, P. S. 2000: *Congressional Elections: Campaigning at Home and in Washington*, 3rd edn. Washington, DC: Congressional Quarterly Press.

Hess, S. 2000: The Washington Reporter Redux, 1978–1998. In Tumber, H. (ed.), *Media Power, Professionals and Policies.* London: Routledge.

Hewlet, S. 2005: Anyone Remember Panorama? *Media Guardian*, 12 December, p. 3.

Hill, K. A. and Hughes, J. E. 1998: *Cyberpolitics: Citizen Activism in the Age of the Internet.* Lanham, MD: Rowman and Littlefield Publishers.

Hill, S. 2002: *Fixing Elections: The Failure of America's Winner Take All Politics.* New York: Routledge.

Hodgson, J. 2001: CBS Makes Surprise Cutbacks at 60 Minutes. *Media Guardian*, 12 November. <http://www.mediaguardian.co.uk> (accessed 3.5.02).

Hodgson, J. 2001a: Election-weary Viewers Switch Off News. *Media Guardian*, 29 May. <http://www.mediaguardian.co.uk> (accessed 21.2.03).

Holbert, R. L. 2005: A Typology for the Study of Entertain Television and Politics. *American Behavioral Scientist*, 49 (3): 436–53.

Holmes, M. 2000: When is the Personal Political? The President's Penis and Other Stories. *Sociology*, 34 (2): 305–21.

Holmwood, L. 2006: BBC News Seeks Younger Viewers. *Media Guardian*, 29 May. <http://www.mediaguardian.co.uk> (accessed 21.2.03).

Hunter, J. D. 2000 [1990]: Cultural Conflict in America. In Crothers M. L.

and Lockhart, C. (eds.), *Culture and Politics: A Reader*. New York: St Martin's Press.

Huntington, S. P. 1981: *American Politics: the Promise of Disharmony*. Cambridge, MA: Harvard University Press.

Inglehart, R. 1997a: Post-materialist Values and the Erosion of Institutional Authority. In Nye J. S., Zelikow, P. D. and King D. C. (eds.), *Why People Don't Trust Government*. Cambridge, MA: Harvard University Press.

Inglehart, R. 1997b: *Modernization and Postmoderization: Cultural Economic and Political Change in 43 Societies*. Princeton, NJ: Princeton University Press.

Jackson, N. 2004: Political Parties and Their E-Newsletters and Subscribers: One Night Stand or Marriage Made in Heaven. Paper presented to the Political Studies Association Annual Conference, University of Lincoln, April.

Jacobs, L. R. and Skocpol, T. 2006: Restoring the Tradition of Rigor and Relevance to Political Science. *PS: Political Science and Politics*, January: 27–31.

Jacobs, L. R., Barber, B., Bartels, L., Dawson, M., Fiorina, M., Hacker, J., Hero R., Heclo, H., Kim C. J., Mettler, S., Page, B., Pinderhughes, D., Scholzman, K. L., Skocpol, T. and Verba, S. 2004: *American Democracy in an Age of Rising Inequality*. Report of the American Political Science Association Task Force on Inequality and American Democracy.

John, B. 2004: Text if You're Tuned In. *Media Guardian*, 26 April, p. 46.

Johnson, B. 2005: Surfers Sign Up to Web Pledges. *Media Guardian*, 13 June. <http://mediaguardian.co.uk> (accessed 14.06.05).

Johnson, D. W. 2001: *No Place for Amateurs: How Political Consultants are Reshaping American Democracy*. London: Routledge.

Johnson, D. W. 2004: *Congress Online: Bridging the Gap Between Citizens and Their Representatives*. London: Routledge.

Jones, N. 1995: *Soundbites and Spin Doctors*. London: Cassell.

Jones, N. 1997: *Campaign 1997*. London: Indigo

Jones, N. 1999: *Sultans of Spin: The Media and the New Labour Government*. London: Orion.

Jones, N. 2001: *Campaign 2001*. London: Politicos.

Jones. S. 2005: Viewers Find Election A Turn-Off. *Media Guardian*, 28 April. <http://media.guardian.co.uk> (accessed 29.04.05).

Justice, G. and Rutenberg, J. 2004: Advocacy Groups and Campaigns: An Uneasy Shuttle. *New York Times*, 8 September. <http://www.nytimes.com/> (accessed 13.9.04).

Justice, G. 2004: Despite New Financing Rules, Parties Collect Record $1 Billion. *New York Times*, 26 October. <http://www.nytimes.com/> (accessed 26.10.04).

Kaid, L. L. and Dimitrova, D. V. 2005: The Television Advertising Battleground in the 2004 Presidential Election. *Journalism Studies*, 6 (2): 165–75.

Kaid, L. L., Gerstle, J. and Sanders, K. (eds.) 1991: *Mediated Politics in Two Cultures: Presidential Campaigning in the United States and France*. Westport, CT: Praeger

Kaplan, M. and Hale, M. 2001: Local Television Coverage of the 2000 General Election. Norman Lear Center, Campaign Media Monitoring Project, USC Annenberg School for Communication. Unpublished paper.

Katz, E. 1996: And Deliver US from Segmentation. *Annals of the American Academy of Political and Social Science*, 546 (July): 22–33.

Kavanagh, T. 2002: Don't Be Fooled by This Death, *British Journalism Review*, 13 (2): 14–18.

Kazin, M. 1998: *The Populist Persuasion: An American History*, Ithaca, NY: Cornell University Press.

Kellner, D. 2002: September 11, the Media and War Fever. *Television and New Media*, 3 (2): 143–51.

Kendall, K. E. and Paine, S. C. 1995: Political Images and Voting Decisions. In Hacker, K. L. (ed.), *Candidate Images in Presidential Elections*. Westport, CT: Praeger.

Kenski, K. and Stroud, N. J. 2005: Who Watches Presidential Debates: A Comparative Analysis of Presidential Debate Viewing in 2000 and 2004. *American Behavioral Scientist*, 49 (2): 213–28.

Kerbel, M. R. 1999: *Remote and Controlled: Media Politics in an Cynical Age*, 2nd edn. Boulder, CO: Westview Press.

Kernell, S. 1997: *Going Public: New Strategies of Presidential Leadership*, 3rd edn. Washington, DC: Congressional Quarterly Press.

Kettle, M. 2000a: Parties about to Top $1bn on TV Ads. *Guardian*, 28 October, p. 17.

Kettle, M. 2000b: Bush Breaks $100m Barrier. *Guardian*, 16 August, p. 2.

Kimball, P. 1994: *Downsizing the News: Network Cutbacks in the Nation's Capital*. Baltimore, MD: John Hopkins University Press

King, A. 2002: Do Leaders' Personalities Really Matter? In King, A. (ed.), *Leaders' Personalities and the Outcomes of Democratic Elections*. Oxford: Oxford University Press.

Klam, M. 2004: Fear and Laptops on the Campaign Trail, *New York Times*. <http://www.nytimes.com> (accessed 27.9.04).

Kronig, J. 2004: A Crisis in the Fourth Estate. *Media Guardian*, 16 August, p. 2.

Kuhn, R. 2002: The First Blair Government and Political Journalism. In Kuhn, R. and Neveu, E. (eds.), *Political Journalism: New Challenges, New Practices*. London: Routledge.

Kumar, M. Joynt. 2000: The Office of the Press Secretary. *The White House 2001 Project, Report Number 31*. <http://whitehouse2001.org/files/press/Press-OD.PDF> (accessed 25.5.05).

Kumar, M. Joynt. 2001a: Presidential Publicity in the Clinton Era: The White House Communications Quartet. <http://www.towson.edu/polisci/whc/readings/WhiteHouseCommunicationsQuartet.pdf> (accessed 3.3.05).

Kumar, M. Joynt. 2001b: The Office of the Press Secretary. *Presidential Studies Quarterly*, 31 (2): 296–322.

Kurtz, H. 1998: *Spin Cycle: Inside the Clinton Propaganda Machine*. London: Pan Books.

Kurtz, H. 2002: Troubled Times for the Evening News: Once-sacrosanct Broadcasts Vulnerable to Corporate Owners. *Washington Post*, 13 March. <http://www.msnbc.com/> (accessed 13.7.03).

Lambert, D. 2002: *Independent Review of BBC News 24*. Department of Media, Culture, and Sport. London: The Stationery Office.

Le Texier, E. 2004: *El Barrio: Exclusion and Participation in a US Urban Enclave*. Rencontre du CEDEM, 3 March. <http://www.ulg.ac.be/cedem/downloads/ELWP.PDF> (accessed 11.10.04).

Liebovich L. W. 2001: *The Press and the Modern Presidency: Myths and Mindsets from Kennedy to Election 2000*. Westport, CT: Praeger.

Lister, R. 1993: *The Exclusive Society: Citizenship and the Poor*. London: Calvert's Press.

Livingstone, S: 2003: On the Challenges of Cross-National Comparative Media Research. *European Journal of Communication*, 18 (4): 477–500

Lusoli, W. and Ward, S. (2005), Logging On or Switching Off? In Coleman, S. and Ward, S. (eds.), *Spinning on the Web: Online Campaigning in the 2005 General Election Campaign*. Hansard Society, London.

MacArthur, B. 1999: The Euro is Still Off-Message. *The Times*, 12 February, p. 40.

Macedo, S. and Karpowitz, C. F. 2006: The Local Roots of American Inequality. *PS: Political Science and Politics*, (January): 59–64.

Macedo, S., Alex-Assensoh, Y., Berry, J. M., Brintnall, M., Campbell, D. E., Fraga, L. R., Fung, A., Galston, W. A., Karpowitz, C. F., Levi, M., Levinson, M., Lipsitz, K., Niemi, R. G., Putnam, R. D., Rahn, W. M., Reich, R., Rodgers, R. R., Swantrom, T. and Walsh, K. C. 2005: *Democracy at Risk: How Political Choices Undermine Citizen Participation, and What We Can Do About it*. Washington, DC: Brookings Institution Press.

Mair, P. and van Biezen, I. 2001: Party Membership in Twenty European Democracies, 1980–2000. *Party Politics*, 7 (1): 5–21.

Maltese, J. A. 2000: The Media: The New Media and the Lure of the Clinton Scandal. In Rozell, M. J. and Wilcox, C. (eds.) *The Clinton Scandal and the Future of American Government*. Washington, DC: Georgetown University Press.

Maltese, J. A. 2003: The Presidency and the News Media. In Rozell, M. J. (ed.), *Media Power, Media Politics*. Lanham, MD: Rowman and Littlefield.

Mancini, P. and Swanson, D. L. 1996: Politics, Media, and Modern Democracy: Introduction. In Swanson, D. L. and Mancini, P. (eds.), *Politics, Media and Modern Democracy*. Westport, CT: Praeger.

Manin, B. 1997: *The Principles of Representative Government*. Cambridge, UK. Cambridge University Press.

Manza, J., Brooks, C. and Uggen, C. 2004: Public Attitudes to Felon Disenfranchisement in the US. *Public Opinion Quarterly*, 68 (2): 275–86.

Margolis, M, and Resnick, D. 2000: *Politics As Usual: The Cyberspace Revolution*. Thousand Oaks, CA and London: Sage.

Marriner, C. 2006: Publishers and Politicians Want a Word in Your Ear. *Media Guardian*, 1 February. <http://media.guardian.co.uk> (accessed 16.05.06).

Mazzoleni, G. 2003: The Media and the Growth of Neo-Populism in Contemporary Democracies. In Mazzoleni, G., Stewart, J. and Horsfield, B. (eds.), *The Media and Neo-Populism: a Contemporary Analysis*. Westport, CT: Praeger.

Mazzoleni, G. and Schulz, W. 1999: Mediatization of Politics: A Challenge for Democracy. *Political Communication*, 16 (2): 247–61.

McChesney, R. W. 1999: *Rich Media, Poor Democracy: Communication Politics in Dubious Times*. New York: The New Press.

McGuigan, J. 1992: *Cultural Populism*. London: Routledge.

McKinney, M. S., Kaid, L. L. and Bystrom, D. G. 2005: The Role of Communication in Civic Engagement. In McKinney, M. S., Kaid, L. L., Bystrom, D. G. and Carlin, D. B. (eds.), *Communicating Politics: Engaging the Public in Democratic Life*. New York: Peter Lang.

McLachlan, S. and Golding, P. 2000: Tabloidization in the British Press: A Quantitative Investigation into Changes in British Newspapers, 1952–1997. In Sparks, C. and Tulloch, J. (eds.), *Tabloid Tales: Global Debates Over Media Standards*. Lanham, MD: Rowman and Littlefield.

McLeod, J. M., Scheufele, D. A. and Moy, P. 1999: Community, Communication and Participation: The Role of the Mass Media and Interpersonal Discussion in Local Political Participation. *Political Communication*, 16 (3): 315–36.

McManus, J. 1994: *Market Driven Journalism: Let the Citizen Beware?* Thousand Oaks, CA: Sage.

McNair, B. 2000: *Journalism and Democracy: an Evaluation of the Political Public Sphere.* London: Routledge.

McNair, B. 2001: Public Relations and Broadcast News: an Evolutionary Approach. In Bromley, M. (ed.), *No News is Bad News: Radio, Television and the Public.* Harlow: Longman.

McNair, B. 2002: Journalism and Democracy in Contemporary Britain. In Kuhn, R. and Neveu, E. (eds.), *Political Journalism: New Challenges, New Practices.* London: Routledge.

McNair, B. 2003: What a Difference a Decade Makes. *British Journalism Review*, 14 (1): 42–8.

McNair, B. 2006: *Cultural Chaos: Journalism, News and Power in a Globalised World.* London: Routledge.

McNair, B., Hibberd, M. and Schlesinger, P. 2003: *Mediated Access: Broadcasting and Democratic Participation in the Age of Mediated Politics.* Luton: University of Luton Press.

McSmith, A. 2000: Spin Doctors Peddle New Twists to Soap Opera Plots. *Observer*, 30 January, p. 4.

McWilliam, R. 1998: *Popular Politics in Nineteenth Century England.* London: Routledge.

Media Matters Action Network, 2004: Meet the New Rush, Same as the Old Rush. <http://mediamatters.org/items/200405020008> (accessed 11.04.06).

Milano, D. 2005: Freeview Expected to Overtake BSkyB as Britain's Leading Digital Television service. *Guardian*, 16 September, p. 26.

Miller, D. 2004: The Propaganda Machine. In Miller, D. (ed.), *Tell Me Lies: Propaganda and Media Distortion in the Attack on Iraq.* London: Pluto.

Moog, S. 2001: American Political Communication in the Information Age: The Mixed Promise of the New Media and Public Journalism. In Splichal, S. (ed.), *Public Opinion and Democracy: Vox Populi – Vox Dei.* Cresskill, NJ: Hampton Press.

Moores, S. 1993: *Interpreting Audiences: The Ethnography of Media Consumption.* Thousand Oaks, CA and London: Sage.

Morley, D. 1980: *The Nationwide Audience.* London: BFI.

Mountfield, R. 1997: *Report of the Working Group on the Government Information Service.* London: HMSO.

Muir, H. 2003: Shock Jocks Against the Mayor. *Media Guardian*, 11 August, p. 2.

Munck, R. 2005: *Globalization and Social Exclusion: A Transformationalist Perspective.* Bloomfield, CT: Kumarian Press

Murdock, G. 2000: Digital Futures: European Television in the Age of Convergence. In Wieten, J., Murdock, G. and Dahlgren, P. (eds.), *Television Across Europe: A Comparative Introduction.* London and Thousand Oaks, CA: Sage.

Nahra, C. 2001: British and American Television Documentaries. In Bromley, M. (ed.), *No News is Bad News: Radio, Television and the Public.* Harlow: Longman.

National Annenberg Election Survey, 2004: *Fahrenheit 9/11 Viewers and Limbaugh Listeners About Equal in Size Even though They Perceive Two different Nations.* Annenberg Public Policy Center, University of Pennsylvania, <http://www.naes04.org> (accessed 03.04.06).

Needham, C. 2005: Clinton, Blair and the Permanent Campaign. *Political Studies*, 53 (2): 343–61.

Negrine, R. 1996: *The Communication of Politics*. London and Thousand Oaks, CA: Sage.

Negrine, R. and Lilleker, D. G. 2002: The Professionalisation of Political Communication: Continuities and Change in Media Practice. *European Journal of Communication*, 17 (3): 305–23.

Nelson, J. 2002: *US Government Secrecy and the Current Crackdown on Leaks*. Joan Shorenstein Center on the Press, Politics and Public Policy Working Paper Series.

Nestlé Family Monitor. 2003: *Young People's Attitudes Towards Politics*. Number 16, July. <http://www.nestlefamilymonitor.co.uk>.

Nestlé Social Research Programme. 2005: *My Voice, My Vote, My Community: A Study of Young Peoples Civic Action*. <http://www.spreckley.co.uk/nestle/>.

Neveu, E. 2002: Four Generations of Political Journalism. In Kuhn, R. and Neveu, E. (eds.), *Political Journalism: New Challenges, New Practices*. London: Routledge.

Newman, B. I. 1999: *The Mass Marketing of Politics: Democracy in an Age of Manufactured Images*. Thousand Oaks, CA: Sage.

Newman, B. 2002: Bill Clinton's Approval Ratings: The More Things Change, the More They Stay the Same. *Political Research Quarterly*, 55 (4): 781–804.

Nie, N. H., Junn, J. and Stehlik-Barry, K. 1996: *Education and Democratic Citizenship in America*. Chicago, IL: University of Chicago Press.

Nimmo, D, 1999: The Permanent Campaign: Marketing as a Governing Tool. In Newman, B. I. (ed.), *Handbook of Political Marketing*. London and Thousand Oaks, CA: Sage.

Norris, P. 1997: *Electoral Change Since 1945*. Oxford: Blackwell Publishers.

Norris, P. 1999: Introduction: The Growth of Critical Citizens? In Norris, P. (ed.), *Critical Citizens: Global Support for Democratic Governance*. Oxford: Oxford University Press.

Norris, P. 2000: *A Virtuous Circle: Political Communication in Post-industrial Societies*. Cambridge, UK: Cambridge University Press.

Norris, P. 2001a: Apathetic Landslide: The 2001 British General Election. In Norris, P. (ed.), *Britain Votes 2001*. Oxford: Oxford University Press.

Norris, P. 2001b: A Failing Grade? The News Media and Campaign 2000. *Harvard International Journal of Press/Politics*, 6 (2): 3–9.

Norris, P. 2002a: Campaign Communications. In LeDuc, L., Niemi, R. G., and Norris, P. (eds.), *Comparing Democracies 2: New Challenges in the Study of Elections and Voting*. London and Thousand Oaks, CA: Sage.

Norris, P. 2002b: *Democratic Phoenix*. Cambridge, UK: Cambridge University Press.

Norris, P. 2003: *Young People and Political Activism: From Loyalties to the Politics of Choice?* Report for the Council of Europe Symposium, Strasbourg, 27–28 November.

Ofcom. 2005: *Viewers and Voters: Attitudes to Television Coverage of the 2005 General Election*. <http://www.ofcom.org.uk/> (accessed 3.12.05).

Office for National Statistics. 2006: *Internet Access: Households and Individuals*, 18 September. <http://www.statistics.gov.uk> (accessed 20.9.06).

Office of the E-envoy, 2002: *In the Service of Democracy: A Consultation Paper on a Policy for Electronic Democracy*. <http://www.edemocracy.gov.uk/downloads/eDemocracy.pdf> (accessed 8.10.04).

Orren, G. R. 1997: Fall From Grace: The Public's Loss of Faith in Government. In

Nye J. S., Zelikow, P. D. and King D. C. (eds.), *Why People Don't Trust Government*. Cambridge, MA: Harvard University Press.

Owen, D. 2000: Popular Politics and the Clinton/Lewinsky Affair: Implications for Leadership. *Political Psychology*, 21 (1): 161–77.

Palmer, J. 2000: *Spinning into Control: News Values and Source Strategies*. London: Leicester University Press.

Parry-Giles, S. and Parry-Giles, T. 2002: *Constructing Clinton*. New York: Peter Lang Publishing.

Patterson, B. H. 2000: *The White House Staff: Inside the West Wing and Beyond*. Washington DC: The Brookings Institution Press.

Patterson, T. E. 1993: *Out of Order*. New York: Alfred A. Knopf

Patterson, T. E. 2000: The United States: News in a Free Market Society. In Gunther, R. and Mughan, A. (eds.), *Democracy and the Media: A Comparative Perspective*. Cambridge, UK: Cambridge University Press.

Patterson, T. E. 2002: *The Vanishing Voter*. New York: Alfred A. Knopf

Patterson, T. E. 2003: *Diminishing Returns: A Comparison of the 1968 and 2000 Election Night Broadcasts*. Report for Joan Shorenstein Center on the Press, Politics and Public Policy, Harvard University.

Patterson, T. E. 2004: *Young Voters and the 2004 Election*. Report for Joan Shorenstein Center on the Press, Politics and Public Policy, Harvard University.

Pattie, C. and Johnston, R. J. 2003: Hanging on the Telephone? Doorstep and Telephone Canvassing at the British General Election of 1997. *British Journal of Political Science*, 33 (3): 303–22.

Pattie, C., Seyd, P. and Whiteley, P. 2003a: Civic Attitudes and Engagement in Modern Britain. *Parliamentary Affairs*, 56 (4): 616–33.

Pattie, C., Seyd, P. and Whiteley, P. 2003b: Citizenship and Civic Engagement: Attitudes and Behaviour in Britain. *Political Studies*, 51 (3): 443–68.

Pattie, C., Seyd, P. and Whiteley, P. 2004: *Citizenship in Britain: Values, Participation and Democracy*. Cambridge, UK: Cambridge University Press.

Peters, B. G. 1998: *Comparative Politics: Theory and Methods*. Basingstoke: Palgrave.

Petrocik, J. R. 1995: Reporting Campaigns: Reforming the Press. In Thurber, J. A. and Nelson, C. J. (eds.), *Campaigns and Elections American Style*. Boulder, CO: Westview Press.

Petrocik, J. R. 1997: Campaigning and the Press: The Influence of Candidates. In Iyengar, S. and Reeves, R. (eds.), *Do the Media Govern?* London and Thousand Oaks, CA: Sage.

Pew Internet and American Life Project 2004: *How Americans Get in Touch with Government*. <http://pewinternet.org/> (accessed 11.08.04).

Pew Internet and American Life Project 2005a: *The Internet and the Campaign 2004*. <http://pewinternet.org/> (accessed 06.06.05).

Pew Internet and American Life Project 2005b: *Fahrenheit 9–11 Had Broad Political Reach*. <http://pewinternet.org/> (accessed 07.06.05).

Pew Internet and American Life Project 2006: *There's a Robot on the Line for You*. <http://pewinternet.org/> (accessed 21.12.06).

Pew Research Center for the People and the Press 1996: *TV News Viewership Declines*. <http://people-press.org/> (accessed 2.10.05).

Pew Research Center for the People and the Press 2000a: *Internet Sapping Broadcast News Audiences*. <http://people-press.org/> (accessed 14.08.02).

Pew Research Center for the People and the Press 2000b: *Turnout May Slip Again*. <http://people-press.org/> (accessed 21.07.04).

Pew Research Center for the People and the Press 2002: *Public's News Habits Little Changed by September 11*. <http://people-press.org/> (accessed 16.08.03).

Pew Research Center for the People and the Press 2003a: *The 2004 Political Landscape*. <http://people-press.org/> (accessed 21.07.04).

Pew Research Center for the People and the Press 2003b: *Bottom Line Pressures Now Hurting Coverage Say Journalists*. <http://people-press.org/> (accessed 11.10.04).

Pew Research Center for the People and the Press 2003c: *Political Sites Gain, But Major News Sites Still Dominant*. <http://people-press.org/> (accessed 23.7.04).

Pew Research Center for the People and the Press 2004a: *Voters More Engaged but Campaign Gets Lukewarm Ratings*. <http://people-press.org/> (accessed 11.08.04).

Pew Research Center for the People and the Press 2004b: *News Audiences Increasingly Politicized*. <http://people-press.org/> (accessed 11.06.04).

Pew Research Center for the People and the Press 2004c: *Cable and Internet Loom Large in Fragmented Political News Universe*. <http://people-press.org/> (accessed 6.02.04).

Pew Research Center for the People and the Press 2004d: *Voters liked Campaign 2004, But Too Much Mud-Slinging*. <http://people-press.org/> (accessed 11.11.04).

Pew Research Center for the People and the Press 2004e: *Public Opinion Little Changed by Presidential Election*. <http://people-press.org/> (accessed 11.1.05).

Pew Research Center for the People and the Press 2004f: *The CSpan Audience* <http://people-press.org/> (accessed 11.1.05).

Pew Research Center for the People and the Press 2006a: *Politics and the 'DotNet' Generation*. <http://people-press.org/> (accessed 08.6.06).

Pew Research Center for the People and the Press 2006b: *Online Papers Modestly Boost Newspaper Readership*. <http://people-press.org/> (accessed 10.9.06.

Pew Research Center for the People and the Press 2006c: *Regular Voters, Intermittent Voters, and Those That Don't*. <http://people-press.org/> (accessed 28.10.06).

Pickering, M. 2001: *Stereotyping: The Politics of Representation*. Basingstoke: Palgrave.

Plasser, F., Scheucher, C. and Senft, C. 1999: Is There a European Style of Political Marketing? In Newman, B. I. (ed.), *Handbook of Political Marketing*. London and Thousand Oaks, CA: Sage

Plasser, F., with Plasser, G. 2002: *Global Political Campaigning: A Worldwide Analysis of Campaign Professionals and their Practices*. Westport, CT: Praeger.

Plunkett, J. 2005: BBC Staff Face Compulsory Exit. *Media Guardian*, 15 December. <http://media.guardian.co.uk> (accessed 15.12.05).

Political Money Line, 2004: *Money in Politics Databases*. <http://www.tray.com/cgi-win/irs_ef_527.exe?DoFn+&sYR=2004> (accessed 26.10.04).

Ponder, S. 1999: *Managing the Press: Origins of the Media Presidency, 1897–1933*. Basingstoke: Palgrave

Popkin, S. L. 2006: Changing Media, Changing Politics. *Perspectives on Politics*, 4 (2): 327–41.

Post Watch Annual Report 2004: <http://www.postwatch.co.uk> (accessed 10.11.04).

Pratchett, L. 1999: New Fashions in Public Participation: Towards Greater Democracy? *Parliamentary Affairs*, 52 (4): 616–33.

Prescott, M. 2000: No More Mr Nice Guy. *Sunday Times, New Review*, 26 November. <http://www.sundaytimes.co.uk/> (accessed 17.12.03).

Project for Excellence in Journalism, 2006: *The State of the News Media: An Annual Report on American Journalism*. <http://www.stateofthenewsmedia.com> (accessed 8.6.06).

Putnam, R. 2000: *Bowling Alone: The Collapse and Revival of American Community*, New York: Touchstone.

Rallings, C. and Thrasher, M. 2000: Personality Politics and Protest Voting: The First Elections to the Greater London Authority. *Parliamentary Affairs*, 53 (4): 753–64.

Rampton, S. and Stauber, J. 2003: *Weapons of Mass Deception: The Uses of Propaganda in Bush's War on Iraq*. London: Robinson.

Ranney, A. 1983: *Channels of Power: The Impact of Television on American Politics*. New York: Basic Books.

Rogers, B. 2005: Turnout is Really about Class. *Guardian*, 14 May. <http://www.guardian.co.uk/> (accessed 5.08.05).

Rooney, D. 2000: Thirty Years of Competition in the British Tabloid Press: The Mirror and The Sun, 1968–1998. In Sparks, C. and Tulloch, J. (eds.), *Tabloid Tales: Global Debates Over Media Standards*. Lanham, MD: Rowman and Littlefield.

Rose, R. 2001: *The Prime Minister in a Shrinking World*. Cambridge, UK: Polity.

Rosenbaum, M. 1997: *From Soap Box to Soundbite: Party Political Campaigning in Britain Since 1945*. Basingstoke: Macmillan.

Ruddock, A. 2006: Invisible Centres: Boris Johnson, Authenticity, Cultural Citizenship and a Centrifugal Model of Media Power. *Social Semiotics*, 16 (2): 263–81.

Rudenstine, D. 1998: *The Day the Press Stopped: A History of the Pentagon Papers Case*. Berkeley, CA: University of California Press.

Rush, M. 2001: *The Role of Members of Parliament Since 1868: From Gentlemen to Players*. Oxford: Oxford University Press.

Rutherford, D. 2004: *Weapons of Mass Persuasion: Marketing the War Against Iraq*. Toronto: University of Toronto Press.

Sabato, L. J. 1991: *Feeding Frenzy: How Attack Journalism has Transformed American Politics*. New York: The Free Press.

Sabato, L. J., Stencel, M. and Lichter, S. R. 2000: *Peepshow: Media and Politics in an Age of Scandal*. Lanham, MD: Rowman and Littlefield.

Sambrook, R. 2004: Tragedy in the Fog of War. *British Journalism Review*, 15 (3): 7–13.

Sancho, J. 2001: *Election 2001: Viewers Response to the Television Coverage*. London: ITC

Sanders, D., Clarke, H., Stewart, M. and Whiteley, P. 2005: *The 2005 General Election Campaign in Great Britain*. Report for the Election Commission.

Savigny, H. 2005: Labour, Political Marketing and the 2005 Election: A Campaign of Two Halves. *Journal of Marketing Management*, 21 (9–10): 925–42.

Scammell, M. 1995: *Designer Politics: How Elections are Won*. Basingstoke: Macmillan.

Scheufele, D. A. and Eveland, W. P. 2001: Perceptions of Public Opinion and Public Opinion Expression. *International Journal of Public Opinion Research*, 13 (1): 25–44.

Schickel, R. 2000: *Intimate Strangers: The Culture of Celebrity in America*. Chicago, IL: Ivan R. Dee.

Schier, S. E. 2000: *By Invitation Only: The Rise of Exclusive Politics in the United States*. Pittsburgh, PA: University of Pittsburgh Press.

Schifferes, S. 2006: 'Downloading Democracy: Election News on the Internet'. Unpublished manuscript.

Schlesinger, P. 2006: Is There a Crisis in British Journalism? *Media, Culture and Society*, 28 (2): 299–307.

Schlozman, K. L., Page B. I., Verba, S. and Fiorina, M. 2004: *Inequalities of Political Voice*. Report for the Task for Inequality and American Democracy, American Political Science Association. <http://www.apsanet.org/section_256.cfm> (accessed 13.10.05).

Schroeder, A. 2004: *Celebrity-in-Chief: How Show Business took over the White House*. Boulder, CO: Westview Press.

Schudson, M. 1978: *Discovering the News: A Social History of American Newspapers*. New York: Basic Books.

Schudson, M. 1995: *The Power of News*. Cambridge, MA: Harvard University Press.

Schudson, M. 2004: Notes on Scandal and the Watergate Legacy. *American Behavioral Scientist*, 47 (9): 1231–8.

Schulz, W. 2001: Changes in Mass Media and the Public Sphere. In Splichal, S. (ed.), *Public Opinion and Democracy: Vox Populi – Vox Dei*. Cresskill, NJ: Hampton Press.

Scott, A. and Street, J. 2001: From Media Politics to E-Protest. In Webster, F. (ed.), *Culture and Politics in the Information Age*. London: Routledge.

Seaton, J. 2003: Public, Private and the Media. *Political Quarterly*, 74 (2): 174–83.

Seawright, D. 2005: On a Low Road: The 2005 Conservative Campaign. *Journal of Marketing Management*, 21 (9–10): 943–58.

Segura, G. M., Pachon, H. and Woods, N. D. 2001: Hispanics, Social Capital, and Civic Engagement. *National Civic Review*, 90 (1): 85–96.

Select Committee on Public Administration, Sixth Report, 1998: *The Government Information and Communication Service*. London: The Stationery Office.

Semetko, H., Blumler, J. G., Gurevitch, M. and Weaver, D. 1991: *The Formation of Campaign Agendas: A Comparative Analysis of Party and Media Roles in Recent American and British Elections*. Hillsdale, NJ: Lawrence Erlbaum.

Seyd, P. and Whiteley, P. 2002: *New Labour's Grass Roots*, Basingstoke: Palgrave.

Seymour-Ure, C. 1991: *The British Press and Broadcasting Since 1945*. Oxford: Blackwell Publishing.

Seymour-Ure, C. 2003: *Prime Ministers and the Media: Issues of Power and Control*. Oxford: Blackwell Publishing.

Shaw, C. 2003: TV News: Why More is Less. *British Journalism Review*, 14 (2): 58–64.

Shaw, C. 2006: By Public Demand . . . *Media Guardian*, 9 February. <http://www.mediaguardian.co.uk> (accessed 08.06.06).

Shogan, C. J. 2006: The Contemporary Presidency: the Sixth Year Curse. *Presidential Studies Quarterly*, 36 (1): 98–101.

Silver, J. 2005: The Truth About Lies. *Media Guardian*, 27 June. <http://www.mediaguardian.co.uk> (accessed 29.06.05).

Sinderbrand, R. 2003: What Do We Want . . .? A Scholar Looks at the Future of the Anti-War Movement. *Newsweek*, 28 March. <http://www.keepmedia. com> (accessed 20.10.04).

Smucker, P. 2004: US Talk Show Rhetoric Sounds a Rwandan Echo. *Mediachannel. org*. <http://www.mediachannel.org/views/dissector/ affalert202.shtml> (accessed 11.04.06).

Southwell, P. L. and Everest, M. J. 1998: The Electoral Consequences of Alienation:

Non-Voting and Protest Voting in the 1992 Presidential Race. *Social Science Journal*, 35 (1): 43–51.

Sparks, C. 1992: Popular Journalism: Theories and Practice. In Dahlgren, P. and Sparks, C. (eds.), *Journalism and Popular Culture*, London and Newbury Park, CA: Sage.

Sparks, C. 2000: Introduction: The Panic Over Tabloid News. In Sparks, C. and Tulloch, J. (eds.), *Tabloid Tales: Global Debates Over Media Standards*. Lanham, MD: Rowman and Littlefield.

Sparrow, N. and Turner, J. 2001: The Permanent Campaign: The Integration of Market Research Techniques in Developing Strategies in a More Uncertain Political Climate. *European Journal of Marketing*, 35 (9/10): 984–1002.

Stanyer, J. 2002: Politics and the Media: A Loss of Political Appetite. *Parliamentary Affairs*, 55 (2): 377–88.

Stanyer, J. 2003: Politics and the Media: A Breakdown in Relations for New Labour. *Parliamentary Affairs*, 56 (2): 309–21.

Stanyer, J. 2004: Politics and the Media: A Crisis of Trust? *Parliamentary Affairs*, 57 (2): 420–34.

Stephanopoulos, G. 1997: White House Confidential. *Newsweek*, 5 May, p. 34.

Stepp, C. S. 2000: Reader Friendly: Their Futures Uncertain, Newspapers are Undergoing a Profound Change in the Way They Carry Out Their Missions. *American Journalism Review* (July/August). <http://www.ajr.org> (accessed 2.11.05).

Stevenson, N. 2003: *Cultural Citizenship: Cosmopolitan Questions*. Buckingham: Open University Press.

Stonecash, J. M. 2003: *Political Polling: Strategic Information in Campaigns*. Lanham, MD: Rowman and Littlefield.

Stonecash, J. M. 2006: The Income Gap. *PS: Political Science and Politics* (July): 461–465

Stothard. P. 2003: *Thirty Days: A Month at the Heart of Blair's War*. London: Harper Collins.

Straw, J. 1993: Parliament on the Spike. *British Journalism Review*, 4 (4): 45–54.

Street, J. 1997: *Politics and Popular Culture*. Cambridge, UK: Polity.

Street, J. 2003: The Celebrity Politician: Political Style and Popular Culture. In Corner, J. and Pels, D. (eds.), *Media and the Restyling of Politics: Consumerism, Celebrity and Cynicism*. London and Thousand Oaks, CA: Sage.

Street, J. 2004: Celebrity Politicians: Popular Culture and Political Representation. *The British Journal of Politics and International Relations*, 6 (4): 435–52.

Sullivan, A. 2000: Whose Soaps Are They Anyway? *Sunday Times, News Review*, 13 February, p. 11.

Summers, J. H. 2000: What Happened to Sex Scandals? Politics and Peccadilloes, Jefferson to Kennedy. *Journal of American History*, 87 (3): 825–54.

Sunstein, C. 2001: *Republic.com*. Princeton, NJ: Princeton University Press.

Sussman, G. 2005: *Global Electioneering*. Lanham, MD: Rowman and Littlefield.

Swanson, D. L. 1992: Managing Theoretical Diversity in Cross-National Studies of Political Communication. In Blumler, J. G., McLeod, J. M. and Rosengren, K. E. (eds.), *Comparatively Speaking: Communication and Culture Across Space and Time*. London and Newbury Park, CA: Sage.

Swanson, D. L. 1997: The Political-Media Complex at 50: Putting the 1996 Presidential Campaign in Context. *American Behavioral Scientist*, 40 (8): 1264–82.

Swanson, D. L. 2004: Transnational Trends in Political Communication: Conventional Views, New Realities. In Esser, F. and Pfetsch, B. (eds.), *Comparing Political Communication: Theories, Cases and Challenges*. Cambridge, UK: Cambridge University Press.

Swanson, D. L. and Mancini, P. 1996: Patterns of Modern Election Campaigning and their Consequences. In Swanson, D. L. and Mancini, P. (eds.), *Politics, Media and Modern Democracy*. Westport, CT: Praeger.

Taggart, P. 2000: *Populism*. Buckingham: Open University Press.

Tant, A. P. 1995: Leaks and the Nature of British Government. *Political Quarterly*, 66 (2): 197–208

Taylor, A. 1997: The Conservative Party, Electoral Strategy and Public Opinion, 1945–64. In Pattie, C., Denver, D., Fisher, J. and Ludlam. S. (eds.), *British Elections and Parties Review Volume 7*. London: Frank Cass.

Taylor, P. 2000: TV's Political Profits. <http://www.motherjones.com/mother_jones/MJ00/profits.html> (accessed 31.01.03).

Tebbel, J. and Watts S. M. 1985: *The Press and the Presidency: From George Washington to Ronald Reagan*. New York: Oxford University Press.

Tenpas, K. D. 2000: The American Presidency: Surviving and Thriving Amidst the Permanent Campaign. In Ornstein, N. and Mann, T. (eds.), *The Permanent Campaign and its Future*. Washington, DC: American Enterprise Institute.

Tenpas, K. D. 2003: *Presidents as Candidates: Inside the White House for the Presidential Campaign*. New York: Routledge.

Thompson, J. B. 1995: *The Media and Modernity*. Cambridge, UK: Polity.

Thompson, J. B. 2000: *Political Scandal: Power and Visibility in the Media Age*. Cambridge, UK: Polity.

Tomlinson, J. 1999: *Globalization and Culture*. Cambridge, UK: Polity.

Towler, R. 2002: *The Public's View 2002*. London: ITC/BSC Research Publication.

Tryhorn, C. 2004: Kelner Defends Independent Splashes. *Media Guardian*, 9 November. <http://media.guardian.co.uk> (accessed 9.11.04).

Tryhorn, C. 2005: BBC News Ratings Up Despite Strike. *Media Guardian*, 24 May. <http://media.guardian.co.uk> (accessed 16.12.05).

Tulloch, J. 1993: Policing the Public Sphere: The British Machinery of News Management. *Media, Culture and Society*, 15 (3): 363–84.

Tulloch, J. 1998: Managing the Press in a Medium Sized European Power. In Stephenson, H. and Bromley, M. (eds.), *Sex, Lies and Democracy: The Press and the Public*. Harlow: Longman.

Tumber, H. 2004: Scandal and Media in the United Kingdom. *American Behavioral Scientist*, 47 (8): 1122–37.

Tunstall, J. 1996: *Newspaper Power: The New National Press in Britain*. Oxford: Oxford University Press.

Tunstall, J. 2002: Trends in News Media and Political Journalism. In Kuhn, R. and Neveu, E. (eds.), *Political Journalism: New Challenges, New Practices*. London: Routledge.

Turner, G. 2004: *Understanding Celebrity*. London and Thousand Oaks, CA: Sage.

Tyndall Report <http://www.tyndallreport.com/>.

Underwood, D. 1998: Market Research and the Audience for Political News. In Graber, D., McQuail, D. and Norris, P. (eds.), *The Politics of News, the News of Politics*. Washington, DC: CQ Press.

US Census Bureau, 2005: *US Voter Turnout in 2004*. <http://www.census.gov/> (accessed 13.10.06).

Verba, S., Scholzman, K. L. and Brady, H. E. 1995: *Voice and Equality: Civic Voluntarism in American Politics*. Cambridge, MA: Harvard University Press.

Vidal, J. 2003: School Children in Countrywide Protests. *Guardian*, 20 March. <http://education.guardian.co.uk/> (accessed 5.08.04).

Wahl-Jorgensen, K. 2001: Letters to the Editor as a Forum for Public Deliberation: Modes of Publicity and Democratic Debate. *Critical Studies in Media Communication*, 18 (3): 303–20.

Walsh, K. C. 2004: *Talking About Politics: Informal Groups and Social Identity in American Life*. Chicago: University of Chicago Press.

Ward, S., Gibson, R. and Lusoli, W. 2003: Online Participation and Mobilisation in Britain: Hype, Hope and Reality. *Parliamentary Affairs*, 56 (4): 652–68.

Wattenberg, M. P. 1996: *The Decline of American Political Parties 1952–1994*. Cambridge, MA: Harvard University Press.

Wattenberg, M. P. 2000: The Decline of Party Mobilization. In Dalton, R. J. and Wattenberg, M. P. (eds.), *Parties Without Partisans: Political Change in Advanced Industrial Democracies*. Oxford: Oxford University Press.

Wattenberg, M. P. 2002: *Where Have All the Voters Gone?* Cambridge, MA: Harvard University Press.

Wattenberg, M. P. 2004: The Changing Presidential Media Environment. *Presidential Studies Quarterly*, 34 (3): 557–72.

Wayne, S. J. 2000: Presidential Personality: The Clinton Legacy. In Rozell, M. J. and Wilcox, C. (eds.), *The Clinton Scandal*. Washington, DC: Georgetown University Press.

Webb, P. 2000: *The Modern British Party System*. London and Thousand Oaks, CA: Sage.

Weber, L. M., Loumakis, A. and Bergman, J. (2003) Who Participates and Why? An Analysis of Citizens on the Internet and the Mass Public. *Social Science Computer Review*, 21 (1): 26–42.

Wernick, A. 1991: *Promotional Culture: Advertising, Ideology and Symbolic Expression*. London: Sage.

West, D. M. 2000: *Checkbook Democracy: How Money Corrupts Political Campaigns*. Boston, MA: Northeastern University Press.

West, D. M. and Orman, J. 2003: *Celebrity Politics*. Upper Saddle River, NJ: Prentice Hall.

Wheeler, M. 2004: Spinning Out of Control? The Labour Government and the Government Information Communication Service. Paper presented to the Political Studies Association, Media and Politics Group Special Conference, Oxford, 19–20 November.

White, M. 2004: Number 10 'Worked with Sun to Manage News'. *Guardian*, 24 May, p. 8.

Whiteley, P. 2003: The State of Participation in Britain. *Parliamentary Affairs*, 56 (4): 610–15.

Whiteley, P. and Seyd, P. 2003: Party Election Campaigning in Britain: The Labour Party. *Party Politics*, 9 (5): 637–52

Whiteley, P., Clarke, H., Sanders, D. and Stewart, M. 2001: Turnout. In Norris, P. (ed.), *Britain Votes 2001*. Oxford: Oxford University Press.

Wilkes, G. and Wring, D. 1998: The British Press and European Integration. In Baker, D. and Seawright, D.(eds.), *Britain For and Against Europe? British Politics and the Question of European Integration*. Oxford: Clarendon Press.

Williams, B. A. and Delli Carpini, M. X. 2000: Unchained Reaction: The Collapse of Media Gatekeeping and the Clinton-Lewinsky Scandal. *Journalism*, 1 (1): 61–85.

Williams, B. A. and Delli Carpini, M. X. 2004: Monica and Bill All the Time and Everywhere. *American Behavioral Scientist*, 47 (9): 1208–30.

Williams, M. 1991: Scandal the Culture of Mistrust in American Politics. *Washington Monthly Book Reviews*. <http://findarticles.com> (accessed 18.10.06).

Winfield, B. H. 1997: The Making of an Image: Hillary Rodham Clinton and American Journalists. *Political Communication*, 14 (3): 241–53.

Wintour, P. and Hall, S. 2004: Labour Membership Halved. *Guardian*. 3 August, p. 4.

Witcover, J. 2001: *No Way to Pick a President: How Money and Hired Guns Have Debased American Elections*. New York: Routledge.

Worcester, R. 2002: *Consumer Activism in Great Britain*. Study conducted for the National Consumer Council. <http://www.mori.co.uk/> (accessed 15.07.04).

Worcester, R. and Mortimore, R. 2002: The Most Boring Election Ever? In Bartle, J., Atkinson, S. and Mortimore, R. (eds.), *Political Communications: The General Election Campaign of 2001*. London: Frank Cass.

Wring, D. 2003: Focus Group Follies? Qualitative Research and Labour Party Strategy. Paper presented to the Political Studies Association Annual Conference, University of Leicester, UK, 11–13 April.

Wring, D. 2004: The Passing of the Iron Law? The New Labour Project, Marketing and Democratic Politics in Modern Britain. Paper presented to the Internationalisation of Political Marketing, IAMCR Workshop, Paris, 30 June – 2 July.

Wring, D. 2005: The Labour Campaign. In Norris, P. and Wlezien, C. (eds.), *Britain Votes 2005*. Oxford: Oxford University Press.

Wring, D. and Horrocks, I. 2001: Virtual Hype? The Transformation of Political Parties. In Axford, B. and Huggins, R. (eds.), *New Media and Politics*. London: Sage.

Zaller, J. 1999: Market Competition and News Quality. Paper presented to the American Political Science Association Annual Conference, Atlanta, GA.

Zaller, J. 2003: A New Standard of News Quality: Burglar Alarms for the Monitorial Citizen. *Political Communication*, 20 (2): 109–30.

Zoonen, L. van 1998: The Ethics of Making Private Life Public. In Brants, K. Hermes, J. and Zoonen, L. van (eds.), *The Media in Question: Popular Cultures and Public Interests*. London: Sage.

Zoonen, L. van 1998b: 'Finally, I have My Mother Back': Politicians and their Families in Popular Culture. *Harvard International Journal of Press/Politics* 3 (1): 48–64.

Index